Religion Evolving

Advances in the Cognitive Science of Religion

Series Editors
Armin W. Geertz Aarhus University
Jesper Sørensen Aarhus University
Valerie van Mulukom Coventry University

This series seeks to publish empirical, experimental and theoretical studies in the cognitive science of religion. Cognition is here broadly conceived as consisting of both internal and bottom-up processes on the one hand and external, extended, materialized and top-down processes on the other. This series is committed to a conception of human beings as highly social, embodied, embrained and encultured organisms. Therefore, studies that emphasize any or several of these aspects are welcomed.

This series incorporates the series Religion, Cognition and Culture, formerly published by Routledge, and is associated with the *Journal for the Cognitive Science of Religion*, the official journal of the International Association for the Cognitive and Evolutionary Sciences of Religion.

Religion Evolving

Cultural, Cognitive, and Ecological Dynamics

Benjamin Grant Purzycki
and
Richard Sosis

equinox

SHEFFIELD UK   BRISTOL CT

Published by Equinox Publishing Ltd.

UK: Office 415, The Workstation, 15 Paternoster Row, Sheffield, South Yorkshire S1 2BX

USA: ISD, 70 Enterprise Drive, Bristol, CT 06010

www.equinoxpub.com

First published 2022

ISBN-13 978 1 80050 051 8 (hardback)
         978 1 80050 052 5 (paperback)
         978 1 80050 053 2 (ePDF)
         978 1 80050 054 9 (ePub)

British Library Cataloguing-in-Publication Data

A catalogue record for this book is available from the British Library.

Library of Congress Cataloging-in-Publication Data
Names: Purzycki, Benjamin Grant, author. | Sosis, Richard, author.
Title: Religion evolving : cultural, cognitive, and ecological dynamics /
    Benjamin Grant Purzycki and Richard Sosis.
Description: Bristol, CT : Equinox Publishing Ltd, 2022. | Series: Advances in the
    cognitive science of religion | Includes bibliographical references and index. |
    Summary: "Based in the evolutionary, cognitive, and anthropological sciences,
    Religion Evolving offers a holistic approach that attends to the complex, interacting
    features of religious systems"—Provided by publisher.
Identifiers: LCCN 2021046015 (print) | LCCN 2021046016 (ebook) | ISBN 9781800500518
    (hardback) | ISBN 9781800500525 (paperback) | ISBN 9781800500532 (epdf) | ISBN
    9781800500549 (epub)
Subjects: LCSH: Religion.
Classification: LCC BL48 .P87 2022 (print) | LCC BL48 (ebook) | DDC
    306.6—dc23/eng/20211123
LC record available at https://lccn.loc.gov/2021046015
LC ebook record available at https://lccn.loc.gov/2021046016

Typeset by JS Typesetting Ltd, Porthcawl, Mid Glamorgan

B.G.P. dedicates this work to Al and Paula. I still appreciate it.

R.S. dedicates this work to Dennison Nash, who turned his entire life's savings into an endowment for anthropological humanism, but was too humble to name the endowment after himself.

Contents

Figures

Acknowledgements

Most of the chapters in this book are based on previous publications. Many of our colleagues read and/or provided critical feedback during these papers' original development. Once again, we thank the following for their help: Candace Alcorta, Joseph Bulbulia, Adam Cohen, Lee Cronk, Helen de Cruz, Agustín Fuentes, Dominic Johnson, Chris Kavanagh, Jordan Kiper, Hillary Lenfesty, Leon Loveridge, Jessica McCutcheon, Michael Price, Gene Rogers, Jeffrey Schloss, John Shaver, John Smart, Paul Swartwout, Brian Wood, Connor Wood, John Vandergugten, and Aku Visala. We are particularly grateful to Connor Wood for his detailed comments on the entire book. We express our thanks to Theiss Bendixen for his feedback and discussions as well as to Cecilie Sandfeld for helping with the references and indexing.

We also thank Armin Geertz, Jesper Sørensen, and Valerie van Mulukom for their management, feedback, and encouragement of this volume. Thanks also go to two of our co-authors—Omar Haque and Azim Shariff—who gave their blessings to reproduce and update the works that they contributed to, the publishers of the original, and the respective editors of the volumes of which they were a part. The sources for the original versions of the chapters contained herein are as follows:

Chapter 1: 2013. "The Extended Religious Phenotype and the Adaptive Coupling of Ritual and Belief." *Israel Journal of Ecology and Evolution* 59(2): 99–108.

Chapter 2: with Azim F. Shariff. 2014. "Religions as Cultural Solutions to Social Living." In *Culture Reexamined: Broadening Our Understanding of Social and Evolutionary Influences*, edited by A. B. Cohen, 217–238. Washington, DC: American Psychological Association.

Chapter 3: 2021. "Resistance, Subversion, and the Absence of Religion in Traditional Societies." *The Cambridge History of Atheism*, edited by Stephen Bullivant and Michael Ruse, 982–1004. Cambridge: Cambridge University Press.

Chapter 4: 2011. "Our Gods: Variation in Supernatural Minds." In *Essential Building Blocks of Human Nature*, edited by U. J. Frey, C. Störmer, and K. P. Willführ, 77–93. New York: Springer-Verlag.

Chapter 5: 2019. "What Do Omniscient Agents Know?" In *The Cognitive Science of Religion: A Methodological Introduction to Key Empirical Studies*, edited by D. Jason Slone and W. McCorkle, 23–32. London: Bloomsbury.

Chapter 6: 2010. "Religious Concepts as Necessary Components of the Adaptive Religious System." In *The Nature of God: Evolution and Religion*, edited by Ulrich Frey, 37–59. Marburg: Tectum Verlag.

Chapter 7: 2009. "The Religious System as Adaptive: Cognitive Flexibility, Public Displays, and Acceptance." In *The Biological Evolution of Religious Mind and Behavior*, edited by Eckart Voland and Wulf Schiefenhövel, 243–256. New York: Springer-Verlag.

Chapter 8: with Omar S. Haque. 2014. "Extending Evolutionary Accounts of Religion beyond the Mind: Religions as Adaptive Systems." In *Evolution, Religion, and Cognitive Science: Critical and Constructive Essays*, edited by F. Watts and L. P. Turner, 74–91. Oxford: Oxford University Press.

Chapter 9: 2019. "The Building Blocks of Religious Systems: Approaching Religion as a Complex Adaptive System." In *Evolution, Development and Complexity: Multiscale Models of Complex Adaptive Systems*, edited by G. Y. Georgiev, J. M. Smart, C. L. Flores Martinez, and M. Price, 421–449. New York: Springer.

Over the course of writing these works, we were supported by various grants both directly and indirectly. B.G.P. was supported by the SSHRC- and John Templeton Foundation-funded Cultural Evolution of Religion Research Consortium (CERC); the Max Planck Institute for Evolutionary Anthropology, an Understanding Unbelief Project grant that was managed by the University of Kent (JTF grant ID# 60624), a Consequences of Formal Education for Science and Religion project grant, and the Aarhus University Research Foundation. R.S. was supported by a CTI Fellowship (Evolution and Human Nature), an ESRC Large Grant (REF RES-060-25-0085) entitled "Ritual, Community, and Conflict," the U.S.-Israel Binational Science Foundation, the James Barnett Endowment, and the Russell Sage Foundation. We were both supported by Oxford University's Cognition, Religion, and Theology Project, the John Templeton Foundation, and the University of Connecticut. Chapter 10 directly benefitted from a workshop B.G.P. organized at the Max Planck Institute, which R.S. attended. We thank Richard McElreath, Julia Cissewski, and Claudia Bavero for their help and support with that event.

Lastly, we thank our parents, spouses, and children. Their collective support and tolerance enrich our lives every day. They make efforts such as this book worthwhile.

Introduction

The idea for this book emerged out of more than a decade of collaboration. While we have been frequent contributors to the biocultural science of religion, a broad enterprise that incorporates evolutionary, ecological, cognitive, neuroscientific, and cultural approaches to the study of religion, we have just as frequently found ourselves at odds with the main currents of this emerging field. Our research efforts often seemed like whack-a-mole scholarship, haphazardly challenging entrenched ideas and correcting what we viewed as misunderstandings of biocultural approaches to religion. However, on closer reflection and the advantage of a post hoc belvedere, it became obvious that our scholarly engagements had been laying the groundwork, almost methodically, for a novel approach to religion.

This volume presents a selection, updated and revised, of some of our co-authored writings and the approach to religion that ultimately emerged from our collaborative research. We wrote the earliest of these chapters when the dominant view in the cognitive and evolutionary sciences of religion was that religious beliefs and behaviors were merely byproducts of pan-human cognitive faculties. According to this view, by virtue of the way our minds have evolved, religion is virtually inevitable but does not amount to much in the way of providing benefits that contribute to human survival and reproduction. Apparently, the tide has turned and this byproduct view no longer appears to be the default position (or is at least wrapped in other packaging), and it is certainly no longer central (at least explicitly) to many of the conversations that enliven the field today.

Many of the chapters herein were direct responses to the byproduct view and most of them have elements that address this issue. Our work has been explicitly motivated by our shared hopes of somehow reconciling evolutionarily themed cognitive and behavioral approaches to religion, which led us to develop an alternative evolutionary framework that views

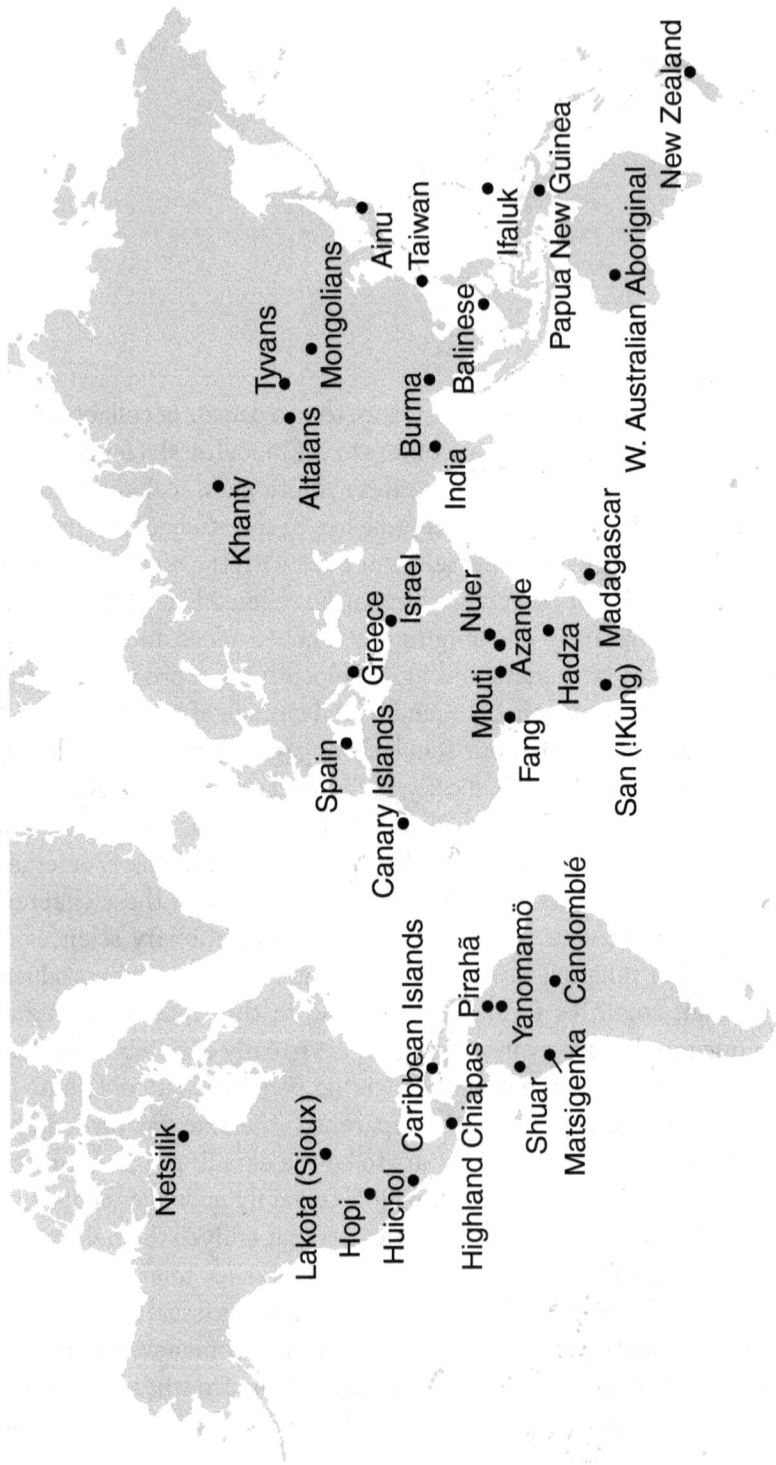

Figure 0.1 Populations mentioned herein. In some cases, region names are included instead of group names due to space constraints.

religions as complex systems. Our training is in behavioral ecology and cognitive science, but our home discipline is anthropology, or more specifically, evolutionary anthropology. It is likely that anthropology's inclination for holism and evolutionary biology's conceptual appreciation of ecosystems played formative roles in our turn toward a systemic analysis of religion. This book not only introduces our understanding of religions as complex, adaptive, and evolving systems, but it also shows how and why we arrived at this approach. In other words, it explains the limitations we found in other biocultural understandings of religion and the promise we see in a systemic approach. The systemic models we develop in this book integrate culture, cognition, and ecology and demonstrate how behavioral and cognitive approaches to religion, once viewed as intrinsically in conflict, are ultimately compatible and complementary.

Anthropology is inherently transdisciplinary and throughout this book we support our arguments with studies in cognitive science, behavioral economics, social psychology, demography, linguistics, behavioral ecology, analytic philosophy, cultural evolution, neuroscience, social history, and many other fields. But as anthropologists, we instinctively drew upon the ethnographic record to provide examples. The map above plots most of the peoples and places we refer to in the following chapters.

Volume Outline

We have organized this volume in terms of scope rather than chronology. Chapters 1–3 address the question of what religion is from a host of perspectives and provide an overview and glimpses of some of the topics covered in the subsequent chapters. Chapters 4 and 5 closely examine the mechanics of cognition and the production of religious beliefs. While these two chapters focus on the workings of individual minds, Chapters 6 and 7 shift the scope and explore how religions function *across* individual minds. They examine themes of sharedness, behavior, interpersonal relationships, the mechanics of social life, and institutions. In Chapters 8 and 9, we broaden the scope still further to set the recurring clusters of religious features surveyed thus far in context. Chapter 8 discusses how these clusters are conceptually and often physically embedded in the socioecological landscape. Chapter 9 more precisely frames the idea of religions as complex adaptive systems. Chapter 10, the final chapter before our Conclusion, illustrates how we can begin to apply this view to field research. Having briefly outlined the thematic progression, we now turn to a more detailed description of the subsequent chapters.

Chapter 1 considers the idea that religion is a transsomatic adaptation. We argue that at the genic level, the religious system manifests as an extended phenotype that has been fashioned by natural selection to overcome socioecological challenges to cooperation and coordination inherent in human sociality. At the collective level, the religious system manifests as a cognitive-cultural niche into which people are born. This chapter details the complex connections between genes, cognitive faculties, and their expression in religious contexts. We also discuss how the "sacred coupling" of supernatural agency and religious ritual functions to maintain relative social order. We conclude by exploring the relevance of niche construction theory for understanding the adaptive nature of religious systems.

When evolutionarily minded social scientists investigate fitness payoffs and the aforementioned "functional logic" of religion, they risk being dismissed as naive functionalists. As we embrace a form of evolutionary functionalism throughout the volume, Chapter 2 introduces this view and entertains the arguments that scholars have leveled against cultural functionalism. We show how contemporary evolutionary functionalist approaches avoid the pitfalls these scholars identify. In this chapter we also examine some of the socioecological problems that particular communities face and how religions overcome those challenges, thus bringing our analysis of beliefs, practices, and religious communication to bear on a variety of problems that religions address. This frames the discussion throughout the remainder of the volume.

While Chapters 1 and 2 offer initial conceptions of religion's flexibility, functionality, and universality, Chapter 3 addresses more concrete questions about the *absence* of religion around the world, such as: *How prevalent is religious doubt among the traditional, small-scale populations typically studied by anthropologists? Do traditional peoples resist religious mores? If so, how?* We first consider the claim that some small-scale populations lack religion, or certain forms of religion, by examining ethnographic material from the Hadza and Pirahã, two prominent examples of populations that allegedly lack religion. Our review of these materials demonstrates that these populations do indeed possess what most would define as religion. We then discuss cases where populations incorporate subversion into religious traditions, positing that while religion is universal, doubt is also a ubiquitous feature of our species.

The next two chapters (Chapters 4–5) focus on beliefs and cognition. Chapter 4 examines variation in the contents of supernatural minds across cultures and the social correlates of this variation. We first provide a sketch of how humans are capable of representing supernatural minds and emphasize the significance of the types of knowledge attributed to supernatural agents. We then argue that the contents of supernatural minds as represented cross-culturally will primarily rest on or between two poles: knowledge of people's moral behavior and knowledge of people's ritualized costly behavior. Communities that endorse omniscient supernatural agents that are highly concerned with moral behavior will emphasize the importance of shared beliefs (cultural consensus), whereas communities whose supernatural agents possess limited social knowledge and are concerned with ritual actions will emphasize shared behavioral patterns (social consensus). We conclude with a brief discussion about the contexts in which these patterns occur.

Chapter 5 describes a series of experiments we designed to determine whether or not people could rapidly process certain classes of information about God's and other agents' knowledge. Assessing predictions related to themes expressed in Chapter 4, it addresses the question: *Is there a cognitive link between moral information and thinking about other knowledgeable minds?* If so, it should be evident in how quickly and easily we respond to questions about the moral knowledge that others possess, including the moral knowledge of omniscient or effectively omniscient supernatural agents. If our reasoning about supernatural agents' minds taps into moral cognition, it should be easier to cognitively process information that explicitly links these two, which is precisely what we found in our experiments.

The next section (Chapters 6–7) explores religious behavior and practices as forms of communication. Chapter 6 broadens the discussion to examine how religious beliefs and cognition are dynamically bound together with practices and ritual expressions. We wager that concepts worthy of religious devotion are intriguing, emotion-triggering, and framed in such a way that makes them relevant to one's wellbeing. As such, these concepts are more likely to be transmitted and therefore recognized as shared. It is this sharedness—the perception of commonality—as well as the effects of entertaining supernatural agent concepts in particular, that motivate individuals to participate in costly rituals. These rituals indicate shared mental models and their costs signal devotion to the community. Ritual behaviors that are rationalized with unverifiable transcendent concepts have been shown to sustain cooperative relationships; we therefore argue that such concepts are a necessary component of the adaptive religious system.

Chapter 7 emphasizes cases where religions facilitate adaptive behaviors in the diverse environments that humans inhabit. Here we examine how religious systems, which are composed of a number of interacting components, generate these adaptive response patterns. We contend that religious systems accomplish this by: (1) employing highly flexible cognitive mechanisms, (2) evoking emotional responses that provide reliable information concerning individual physical and psychological states, (3) supporting specialists who introduce religious ideas that endorse and sustain the social order, and (4) encouraging collective acceptance of these ideas with public displays, typically in the form of rituals, badges, and taboos. These interacting components of religious systems ultimately promote prosocial behavior under diverse conditions.

Drawing upon the dynamism highlighted in previous chapters, Chapters 8–10 present a more holistic and multivariate perspective than those typically offered in the evolutionary and cognitive sciences of religion. It is here where the volume examines how the coupling of beliefs and behaviors links to features of human environments. We argue that an evolutionary approach to religion that isolates particular features of religion for analysis without understanding their influence on the full religious system can be misleading and generate trivial results. In this section we uncover the functional logic of religious systems and explain how they solve adaptive problems.

Chapter 8 contrasts byproduct and adaptationist accounts of religion and engages with some of the studies that have sought to evaluate these accounts. We expand on our discussion of signaling within religious communities and show its importance in understanding the adaptive benefits of religion. We also advance our analysis of religion as a system, arguing that by conceiving of religion as a system we can avoid the unproductive debates about whether religion is an adaptation or byproduct.

By drawing more directly from the complex adaptive systems literature, Chapter 9 offers a general schematic model of religion and focuses on religion's reach beyond beliefs and practices. It also emphasizes the energetic feedback that contributes to the evolution of religious traditions. This chapter shows how religious systems internally function, with ritual at its core, as well as how religious systems change over time, typically through a pattern of growth, decline, and revitalization.

Chapter 10 offers one way to attend to the feedback, drawing upon the ethnographic record to model religions as responses to social dilemmas and conflicts. We focus specifically on cases studies from the Tyva Republic, Bali, and Australia. We forge one possible path forward for the ethnographic sciences of religion, but we also stress the importance of maintaining the theoretical and methodological pluralism that currently flourishes within the evolutionary study of religion.

Our Conclusion summarizes the arguments of the volume and articulates the value of the systemic approach for scholars of religion. We also see the systemic approach as indispensable for those whose leadership roles call for a clear understanding of religion, particularly the dynamic relationship between religious systems and people's beliefs and behaviors.

Versions of Chapters 1–9 were originally published in various edited volumes and journals (see Acknowledgements), although each of these chapters has been revised considerably. To provide some of our most current thinking and important research advances since these chapters were originally published, we integrated new material throughout the text and updated our references. When we wanted to highlight some new material, or we couldn't quite settle on where or how to best integrate the new material we wanted to discuss, we inserted brief text boxes. We have also eliminated some redundancy across chapters, but some redundancies remain where we deemed the material critical for the development of an argument in a particular chapter. In addition to this Introduction, Chapter 10 and the Conclusion were written specifically for this volume and have not been previously published. Code and data for all materials used herein can be found at https://github.com/bgpurzycki/Religion-Evolving.

Chapter 1

The Extended Religious Phenotype

Religion as a Transsomatic Adaptation

In *The Extended Phenotype* (1982), Richard Dawkins asks us to consider the case of a beaver in relation to its environment. He persuasively makes the case that "its environment" is more a part of the beaver than we might typically think:

> By building a dam across the stream the beaver creates a large shoreline which is available for safe and easy foraging without the beaver having to make long and difficult journeys overland. If this interpretation is right, the lake may be regarded as a huge extended phenotype, extending the foraging range of the beaver in a way which is somewhat analogous to the web of a spider. As in the case of the spider web, nobody has done a genetic study of beaver dams, but we really do not need to in order to convince ourselves of the rightness of regarding the dam, and the lake, as part of the phenotypic expression of beaver genes. It is enough that we accept that beaver dams must have evolved by Darwinian natural selection: this can only have come about if dams have varied under the control of genes.
>
> (Dawkins 1982: 200)

Compare this to Leslie White's (1952) famous definition of culture as "an extrasomatic mechanism employed by a particular animal species in order to make its life secure and continuous" (8). Or consider Lewis Binford's (1962) revision of White's definition of culture as humanity's "extra-somatic means of adaptation ... to its total environment both physical and social" (218).

Several questions that arise from these perspectives warrant serious consideration. Like the beaver's lake, can we consider human manifestations of culture such as tools, jewelry, and residences as extended phenotypes of human genes (see Dawkins 2004)? Does selection favor such extrasomatic features in humans? If so, what types of selective forces might design such features—cultural selection or genic selection, or some combination of both? In Dawkins's terms, there need not be genes exclusively *for* lake construction, just as there need not be genes exclusively *for* projectile or necklace production. Rather, such phenotypes are "product[s] of the interaction of many genes whose influence impinges from both inside and outside the organism" (Dawkins 1982: 239).

Religions, on average, yield fitness benefits for individuals who are situated within them (e.g., Reynolds and Tanner 1995). However, religions are not simply a behavioral adaptation, such as a foraging strategy, or a cognitive adaptation, such as our ability to detect cheaters (Cosmides and Tooby 1992). Rather, religions—something often considered prototypically cultural—may be understood as an extended phenotype in Dawkins's sense (cf. Laland 2004). While lakes and dams are made of water and wood respectively, religions are made of concepts, propositions, rules, narratives, artifacts, and behaviors. Moreover, *sharedness* is a central feature of the adaptive religious system (Chapters 4 and 5); that is, the constituent components of religious systems exist within individuals, extend between individuals, and reach beyond human communities (Chapters 7–9). Therefore, we think it best to consider religion a *transsomatic* adaptation. In this chapter, we discuss how theoretical advances in the evolutionary and cognitive sciences have improved our understanding of the features that constitute religious systems, and we illustrate how religion is an essential—but neither exclusively *internal* nor *external*—feature of the human experience that has been fashioned by natural selection.

An increasing number of scholars have explicitly explored why religion evolved in the human lineage (Bulbulia et al. 2008; Feierman 2009; Shaver, Purzycki, and Sosis 2016; Turner et al. 2017; Voland and Schiefenhövel 2009). Their work has raised many vexing questions. For example, why do humans believe in unseen forces and agents with supernatural abilities? Why do humans engage in taxing collective rituals, and why do they appeal to supernatural agents when engaging in such activities? How does the relationship between rituals and supernatural agents vary across populations? What explains the variation in religious systems across cultures? There are various ways to address these questions from an evolutionary perspective (Kundt 2017; Shaver, Purzycki, and Sosis 2016) and researchers have undertaken careful and rigorous investigations into these concerns. One approach is to understand the evolutionary foundations of the religious mind by focusing on what kind of biological faculties make religious behavior possible. This was the standard approach in the "cognitive science of religion," largely a branch of evolutionary psychology (e.g., Atran 2002; Boyer 2001), though there have been dramatic changes in recent years (see Barrett 2021 and Geertz 2020 for reviews). Another approach, grounded in behavioral ecology, employs optimization and evolutionarily stable strategy models in order to identify the selective pressures that have shaped religious behaviors (Sosis and Bulbulia 2011). A third approach, termed gene-culture coevolutionary theory or dual inheritance theory, analyzes the social learning mechanisms involved in the transmission and spread of religious beliefs and practices (Richerson and Boyd 2005), and has paid particular attention to the role of religion in explaining human social complexity (Norenzayan 2013). Here, we illustrate an alternative approach that offers a more encompassing evolutionary view: religion is an adaptation that exists within, between, and beyond individuals.

One major debate resulting from the naturalistic study of religion revolves around whether religion is an adaptation or merely a byproduct of other evolved capacities (see Bulbulia et al. 2008; Pyysiäinen and Hauser 2010; Sosis 2009a; Chapters 2 and 8). Some researchers even characterize religion as inherently maladaptive. Dawkins (2006: 200–208), for instance, has likened religion to a moth engaging in "self-immolation behavior" by flying into a candle flame; the moth's perceptual algorithms, which normally serve well for navigational purposes, instruct it to do so. Because moths evolved such an apparatus, false positives under new conditions may entail an individual's demise (or at least nightly devotional practices toward porch lights). Similarly, evolved cognitive algorithms cause humans to be mistakenly attracted to stories about and worship of gods. The analogy, however, suffers from a gross oversimplification of what religion is. Moreover, like the other accounts we describe below, it ignores the remarkably consistent logic of religious systems' constituent parts (i.e., their design features), and the benefits that people can often reap through participation (i.e., their fitness effects). Additionally, it ignores the fact that around the world, the features of religious systems often converge under similar conditions.[1] We address these points below.

---

1. Dawkins's hostility toward religion is well known, but his characterization of religion as a maladaptive byproduct is notably odd in light of his other work. Of course, he knows the

Instinct, Habit, and Culture: Conceptualizing the Religious Mind

When trying to understand social systems, appealing to evolutionary processes and biological models has gained significant traction and attention again over the past few decades. Having largely transcended deterministic, unilinear, and Social Darwinian endorsement of the development of *cultures*, anthropologists, economists, psychologists, political scientists, and others are now bringing these questions into focus using insights drawn from their respective fields, equipped with a more sophisticated view of Darwinian evolution by natural selection. Particularly among scientifically oriented anthropologists, making sense of the relationships between evolution, cognition, and culture has become a primary focus of research, and in recent decades, explaining religion as a product of our evolved cognition has garnered considerable attention (Atran 2002; Barrett 2004; Bering 2011; Boyer 1994a, 2001; Guthrie 1993; Martin and Wiebe 2017; McCauley 2011). Here, we briefly detail the intellectual history of how some have come to conceive of this nexus between evolved cognition, individual (i.e., ontogenetic) histories, and shared (i.e., phylogenetic) histories.

In *The Descent of Man*, Darwin commented on the use of natural selection to make sense of the cognitive faculties of living organisms, particularly those of humans:

---

distinctions between "adaptive," "good," and "accurate." He also understands how flimsy "byproduct" arguments can be:

> A geneticist colleague has argued that there are virtually no behaviour-genetic traits, because all those so-far discovered have turned out to be "byproducts" of more fundamental morphological or physiological effects. But what on earth does he think *any* genetic trait is, morphological, physiological or behavioural, if not a "byproduct" of something more fundamental? If we think the matter through we find that all genetic effects are 'byproducts' except protein molecules.

(Dawkins 1982: 197)

Perhaps Dawkins's anti-religious sentiments primarily lie with religions in contemporary state-level societies rather than smaller, traditional societies. It is perfectly conceivable that under contemporary conditions, religion may be maladaptive. However, research suggests that religious people are doing remarkably well on the reproductive front (Blume 2009, 2010; Frejka and Westoff 2008; Kaufmann 2010; Shaver 2017).

we may easily underrate the mental powers of the higher animals, and especially of man, when we compare their actions founded on the memory of past events, on foresight, reason, and imagination, with exactly similar actions instinctively performed by the lower animals; in this latter case the capacity of performing such actions has been gained, step by step, through the variability of the mental organs and natural selection, without any conscious intelligence on the part of the animal during each successive generation.

(Darwin 2004 [1879]: 89)

This passage, remarkably, presaged the current field of evolutionary psychology. There is indeed "variability of the mental organs" that undergoes change through time by way of natural selection, and thus natural selection forges the content of human instincts. Note here, however, that Darwin suggests that some faculties are distinct from instinct, and confusing the two results in "underrat[ing] the mental powers" of humans and other "higher animals." Of course, humans learn things, but teasing apart genetically endowed instincts from instincts otherwise acquired from external sources has been difficult, especially for the cognitive science of religion (Purzycki and Willard 2016).

Like others (e.g., Dewey 1932: 87; cf. Vygotsky 1994: 57–72), Darwin characterizes the essential difference between *instinct* and *habit* with reference to their sources:

If we suppose any habitual action to become inherited—and it can be shown that this does sometimes happen—then the resemblance between what originally was a habit and an instinct becomes so close as not to be distinguished ... [However,] it would be a serious error to suppose that the greater number of instincts have been acquired by habit in one generation, and then transmitted by inheritance to succeeding generations.

(Darwin 2004 [1859]: 321)

Here Darwin indirectly argues against Lamarckian evolution, the idea that nonheritable traits can be passed down to future generations. Moreover, he observes that the learned information humans gather from their social and natural environments builds on previously acquired habits, is organized somehow, and operates as though it is instinctive:

An action, which we ourselves require experience to enable us to perform, when performed by an animal, more especially by a very young one, without experience, and when performed by many individuals in the same way, without their knowing for what purpose it is performed, is usually said to be instinctive. But I could show that none of these characters are universal.

(Darwin 2004 [1859]: 320)

John Dewey wrote that "Habits may be profitably compared to physiological functions, like breathing, digesting. The latter are, to be sure, involuntary, while habits are acquired. But important as is this difference for many purposes, it should not conceal the fact that habits are like functions in many respects, and especially in acquiring the cooperation of organism and environment" (Gouinlock 1994: 83–84). This is an important point; habits can operate identically to instincts insofar as they allow organisms to "cooperate" with their environment without constant reflection. If this "cooperation" results in fitness gains/loss avoidance for the organism, then the behavior can be said to be adaptive. Dewey argues that behaviors "are means only when they enter into organization with things which independently accomplish definite results. These organizations are habits" (ibid.: 86). In other words, habits function to achieve particular ends automatically and in a somatically cost-effective manner. They operate exactly as instincts, however, insofar as they are not conscious, deliberate processes and require the appropriate stimuli.

Some contemporary thinkers blur the distinction even more between "habit" and "instinct," claiming that we have specialized cognitive systems that function to organize, compute, and stabilize specific domains of information extracted from our social and natural environments (Hirschfeld and Gelman 1994). Noam Chomsky is often heralded as formalizing the study of what psychologist Steven Pinker (1994) calls the "language instinct" in this fashion. In his *Rules and Representations* (1980), Chomsky introduces how the modular conception of the human mind—that is, one composed of "mental organs"—relates to the biology of language, often considered the hallmark of human culture:

> We may usefully think of the language faculty, the number faculty, and others, as "mental organs," analogous to the heart or the visual system or the system of motor coordination and planning. There appears to be no clear demarcation line between physical organs, perceptual and motor systems, and cognitive faculties in the respects in question. In short, there seems little reason to insist that the brain is unique in the biological world in that it is unstructured and undifferentiated, developing on the basis

of uniform principles of growth or learning—say those of some learning
theory, or of some yet-to-be conceived general multipurpose learning
strategy—that are common to all domains.

(Chomsky 1980: 39)

Since the dawn of this newer phase of cognitive science, a considerable
amount of human thought and culture has been explained with appeals to
innate cognitive architecture.

The field of the "cognitive science of religion" developed in this context
(Barrett 2007a, 2021; cf. Geertz 2020). Just as major branches of linguistics search for abstract human universals of language processing, central
themes in the cognitive sciences of religion endorse—at least tacitly—cognitive universalism: all humans share cognitive mechanisms that evolved
for various purposes, and religious cognition often exploits, triggers, or
violates such devices. Many researchers endorse the notion that, similar
to language, there is a "belief instinct" (see Barrett 2012; Bering 2011).
Below, we critically examine several lines of research that aim to explain
essential aspects of religion by appealing to universal human cognitive
faculties and build upon this by reincorporating habit into the discussion.

Religious Thought and Storage

People readily and rapidly attribute agency to a wide variety of entities
in our world: people, animals, cars, institutions, ideas, and populations,
among other things. This ability to mentally represent others' mental
states is made possible by a complex suite of evolved mechanisms generally considered to be part of the "theory of mind" complex (Baron-Cohen
1995; Premack and Woodruff 1978). Agency detection, attribution, and
related forms of anthropomorphism are often considered to be essential features of religious thought. Indeed, central to all religious traditions are the mental representation of and commitment to gods, spirits,
and other supernatural agentive forces. These common features of our
species may therefore indicate the operation of pan-human cognitive
systems (Barrett 2004; Barrett and Keil 1996). For example, we are pro-
miscuous agency-detectors and religious concepts may hinge on this
ability (Guthrie 1980, 1993). Cognitive psychologists Barrett (2004) and
Keil (Barrett and Keil 1996) argue that we have a "hyperactive agency
detection device" (HADD), a cognitive mechanism designed to attribute
mental states. HADD is "hyperactive"—or, as subsequent work (Andersen

2019) suggests, "hypersensitive"—as it attributes agency even to agentless events and things such as rustling bushes, moving dots on a computer screen, surprising events, gods, and spirits.

Furthermore, religious discourse often converges around what gods know and care about (Chapter 5; Boyer 2001: 144). Some researchers have argued that humans commit to supernatural agents because these agents have access to important otherwise unknown social information (Atran 2002; Barrett 2008b; Boyer 2001, 2002; Purzycki et al. 2012). Their access to "socially strategic knowledge" makes supernatural agents particularly salient, and a growing evolutionary literature demonstrates that concepts of supernatural punishment actually minimize antisocial behavior and often promote prosocial behavior (Bering and Johnson 2005; D. Johnson 2005, 2016; Lang et al. 2019; McKay et al. 2011; Norenzayan and Shariff 2008; Purzycki et al. 2016a, 2016b; Schloss and Murray 2011; Shariff and Norenzayan 2007). So, while representing minds and morality appears to be a central process in religious cognition, the specific contents of those minds—what gods know and care about—are cross-culturally variable (Chapter 4; Purzycki 2011b). In other words, what exactly counts as "socially strategic" may also vary across contexts. This issue requires further investigation, however, and we return to it below.

Processing and generating religious concepts are crucial for religious cognition, but storage is important as well, particularly for habituating ideas and practices in their appropriate contexts. With respect to human memory stores, Graf and Schachter (1985) revealed that while much of what we remember is conscious, we also possess unconscious working memory. They note that "[i]mplicit memory is revealed when performance on a task is facilitated in the absence of conscious recollection [and] explicit memory is revealed when performance on a task requires conscious recollection of previous experiences" (ibid.: 501). In other words, while we can be aware of what we remember, there are memory processes that operate without awareness. Explicit memory can be broken into two categories as well: short-term or working memory and long-term memory. Atkinson and Shiffrin (1968: 90) define the "short-term store" as "the subject's working memory; it receives selected inputs from the sensory register and also from the long-term store." The "long-term store," on the other hand, "is a fairly permanent repository for information" (ibid.: 91). Specifically, long-term memory (also known as "autobiographical" or "episodic" memory) is the "mental representations of specific events that have been personally experienced and are remembered as distinct episodes" (Laidlaw 2004: 3), whereas "semantic memory" is the stored mental representations of general information (Gathercole 1997).[2]

The research foci we have been discussing strive to map the universal cognitive foundations of the central features of all religious thought and behavior. Supernatural agents are understood as an extension of agency detection systems, and their cultural transmission, supported by religious ritual, corresponds to human memory systems. Human religious thought in general, and the diffusion of particular religious ideas across generations and populations, are both partly explainable as predictable byproducts of evolved cognitive systems. However, as cultural evolutionary researchers emphasize, a host of learning biases and environmental variables may better account for why *some* ideas and concepts are transmitted with more frequency than others. In other words, while cognitive processes and memory stores play an important role in the evolution of religious systems, processes of social transmission partly account for the routes by which computed information arrives.

One strategy to study the transmission of religious concepts entails "biologizing" cultural phenomena. For example, cultural units can be treated like genes, *à la* Dawkins's notion of cultural "memes." According to Dawkins:

> Examples of memes are tunes, ideas, catch-phrases, clothes fashions, and ways of making pots or of building arches. Just as genes propagate themselves in the gene pool by leaping from body to body via sperms or eggs, so memes propagate themselves in the meme pool by leaping from brain to brain via a process which, in the broad sense, can be called imitation.
> (Dawkins 1989 [1976]: 192)

---

2. Anthropologist Harvey Whitehouse (2000, 2004) articulates a theory of religion that corresponds to these types of memory, identifying two "modes of religiosity" to incorporate cognitive systems with organized social behavior. In the doctrinal mode "ritual action tends to be highly routinized, facilitating the storage of elaborate and conceptually complex religious teachings in semantic memory, but also activating implicit memory in the performance of most ritual procedures" (Whitehouse 2004: 65–66). The imagistic mode, on the other hand, "relies on episodic [i.e. long-term store concerned with particular points in time] memory, is more emotional and personal, and ideas are conveyed nonverbally to a much greater degree" (Laidlaw 2004: 4). The two modes of religious activity thus correspond to the two general types of memory. Interestingly, however, Xygalatas et al. (2013) found that Spanish firewalkers' memories of arousal are actually *suppressed* during peak levels of actual arousal during rituals. The authors suggest that this gap in memory requires "filling in" with a culturally specific rationale.

Although the field of memetics failed to gain an academic foothold, it impacted several successful research paradigms. These included gene-culture coevolution, which applies population genetics models to cultural information.

Specifically, work in the field of gene-culture coevolution (also known as dual inheritance theory), has posited a number of transmission biases that maximize the "cultural fitness" of social traits (Boyd 2018; Boyd and Richerson 1985: 132–171; Henrich 2016; Henrich and Gil-White 2001; Kendal et al. 2018; Richerson and Boyd 2005: 58–98). The *prestige bias*, for instance, is marked by our species's collective tendency to replicate behaviors as expressed by successful individuals. Our tendency to follow what others are doing, known as the *conformist bias*, is arguably often a matter of survival, because most of the time the majority will converge on an adaptive strategy (for example, for how to hunt in the local savannah), so failing to copy others leads to wasted efforts and poor outcomes (Henrich and McElreath 2003: 129–131). At the risk of falsely dichotomizing the two approaches, cultural evolutionary modelers often focus on such *context* biases relating to external, often culturally specific phenomena (e.g., ideas from influential leaders; see Gervais and Henrich 2010; Sosis 2020a), while cognitive scientists of religion often focus on *content* biases and appeal to internal, evolved cognitive structures (e.g., emotive content). However, enculturation is an ontogenetic process; we *grow* our individual patterns of thought and behavior longitudinally in a complex interaction between evolved cognition and learned behavior. Much of what we might call culture is deeply embedded in our memory stores and inaccessible to our recollection, functioning much like instincts. Such habituated optimizations make "what to do and think" in particular contexts efficient and effortless. Yet, the *collective* habituation of religious beliefs and behaviors conform to local contexts with particular features, and explaining this aspect of religion is not reducible to evolved psychology and social learning. We rejoin this point below.

To summarize, some of the aforementioned researchers focus on the universal features of religious thought and behavior, including how cognitive structures constrain and make possible religious concepts and behavior. Other researchers focus on the routes by which religious thought and behavior are sustained and how learning biases constrain these routes. Unsurprisingly, given these foci, many of these researchers argue that religion is a byproduct of human biology with no significant returns for fitness. However, upon widening the scope of inquiry by looking at what religion *does* rather than merely how it is acquired and the contexts in which religious systems exist, we gain a far better sense of how religious systems are extended phenotypes that exist not only within us, but between us as well. Religion's dynamic quality, naturalistic design, and fitness effects suggest that it may be characterized as transsomatic adaptation. If this characterization of religion is accurate, religion must be collectively shared across individuals. We now turn to how such sharing is achieved, in part, through ritualized communications.

Ritual Behavior and the Forging of Human Bonds

From an outsider's perspective, religions appear to be curiously taxing for individuals, even remarkably wasteful. The pageantry, time and resource expenditures, bodily mutilations (e.g., circumcision, subincision, scarification, piercing, etc.), activism, organization, and so forth all demand considerable investment on the parts of those who engage in them. While traditions vary in terms of emphasizing religious belief and practice, we often say someone is "really religious" when they devote a lot of resources (time, thought, money, etc.) to the tradition. Individual variation in religious commitment can be measured in terms of such investments. Some evolutionary approaches to religious ritual consider individuals' religious investments as signals to other people (Bulbulia 2004a; Cronk 1994; Irons 2001; Sosis 2003). So, while religious rites may appear to be a squandering of resources, the tradeoff for paying the costs of these investments can be prolonged cooperative behavior.

The animal kingdom is rife with communicative signals (Hauser 1996; Searcy and Nowicki 2005). These are "behavioral, physiological, or morphological characteristics fashioned or maintained by natural selection because they convey information to other organisms" (Otte 1974: 385). Obviously, all one needs to do to appreciate the extent of animal signaling is take a step outside and observe the bright coloration of a butterfly, a complex birdsong, a barking squirrel, and so forth; these are all streams of ongoing communication between animals. One inherent challenge that organisms face is ascertaining the reliability of communicated information, and this challenge becomes particularly acute when an individuals' reproductive fitness is at stake. Amotz Zahavi's (Zahavi and Zahavi 1997) "handicap principle" explains that selection favors organisms when they pay high costs to produce signals that reliably indicate their own quality.

For example, the peacock's tail requires a significant energy investment to produce, and it certainly increases the risk of predation. However, the tail serves as a reliable indicator to peahens of the male's quality; males of lower quality are unable to pay the costs to produce an extravagant tail. Note the dynamic nature of this process; not only do genes, regulatory systems, and ontogenetic factors influence the growth of the tail, but the ability of signal receivers (peahens) to equate variation in tail quality with variation in mate quality has been forged by natural selection just as much as the tail has.

In terms of religious beliefs, anthropologist Lee Cronk (2005: 608) suggests that even a "willingness to suspend reason and to embrace beliefs that appear ridiculous to nonbelievers is itself a hard-to-fake sign of commitment to the religion and a defining feature of the boundary dividing believers from nonbelievers." Consider the social repercussions of "appearing ridiculous to nonbelievers" by engaging in unusual behaviors or simply rejecting a behavior that is common practice. Just like the somatic displays of other animals, the costs of religious rituals vary within and across individuals. Costly signaling theory, which anthropologists have found remarkably useful for explaining a vast array of behaviors (for reviews see Barker et al. 2019; Bliege Bird and Smith 2005), anticipates an optimal tradeoff between ritual costs and the stakes or risk involved in cooperative ventures. What costly rituals do for humans is reliably convey commitment to one's in-group. Human groups are difficult to maintain and human bonds are potentially tenuous, but religious rituals impose costs that convey important social information that may help to mitigate these challenges.

First, paying religious costs conveys commitment to the group to which one belongs. This overcomes problems of cooperation insofar as receivers intuit that one wouldn't engage in high-cost rituals if one weren't committed to the group. By indicating one's commitment to the group, then, costly religious rituals serve as an effective signal that one is a worthwhile partner for prolonged cooperative interaction (see Axelrod 1984; Dawkins and Krebs 1979). Secondly, as such, religious rituals also communicate to outsiders who might be considering participation. Specifically, costly requirements serve as a gatekeeper preventing potential low-commitment defectors from joining the group. Third, collective rituals convey messages to out-group members who can then gauge the level of solidarity between individuals in the observed group.

The evidence supporting the costly signaling theory of religious ritual has considerable cross-cultural breadth. For example, in economic game experiments, Israeli religious kibbutz members who attended synagogue regularly contributed more to the common pool than their non-synagogue attending religious co-residents, as well as secular kibbutz members (Ruffle and Sosis 2007; Sosis and Ruffle 2003, 2004). And Afro-Brazilian Candomblé members who were more engaged with their religious communities were more generous than those who were less engaged (Soler 2012). In South India, villagers who participate more often in ritual practices are perceived as having more prosocial traits in general (Power 2017a). Also, religious communes with costlier obligations outlive those with fewer requirements (Sosis and Bressler 2003).

The effects of religion on cooperation are not limited to resource production. For example, in a cross-cultural study Sosis et al. (2007) found that higher rates of warfare were correlated with costlier ritual obligations. In contexts such as war, where the challenges of organization and mobilization are especially acute, the individual incentives for defecting are particularly high because one's life, and the lives of one's kin, are at stake (e.g., Heider 1970; Meggitt 1977). In such conditions costlier rites may serve to strengthen social bonds and minimize the likelihood of defection. One index of such a bond is perceived trustworthiness. Religiosity has been found to predict trustworthiness in a host of studies from diverse populations (Purzycki and Arakchaa 2013; Ruffle and Sosis 2020; Tan and Vogel 2008). This approach to the communicative aspects of ritual participation addresses how costly rituals facilitate and maintain cooperation, which can increase individual fitness. Religion in this view can be seen as a transsomatic adaptation insofar as it exploits evolved predispositions and employs shared concepts and culturally specific rationalizations for costly behavior.

Anthropologists have long appreciated that socioecological factors affect patterns of religious expression (e.g., Rappaport 1984 [1968]). More recent theoretical and empirical work has focused on the inherent ecological problems that religious systems resolve and the adaptive response patterns of these systems under diverse environmental contexts. We now turn to these approaches, arguing that religions are contexts into which individuals habituate to become holders and transmitters of these traditions. These contexts predictably evolve according to local constraints and challenges.

Niche Construction, Collective Habits, and Evolving Religious Systems

Many of the approaches detailed above tend to focus on the evolution of psychological mechanisms in order to explain how we *produce, retain*, and *habituate* religious concepts and behavioral scripts for ritual protocol. They also suggest the importance of researching receiver psychology and how variation in religious signals and concepts affects behavior (Alcorta and Sosis 2005; Power 2017a; Soler et al. 2014). However, individuals operate *within* and are born *into* extant religious communities and institutions, and they must navigate such contexts by way of shared and habituated expectations, behavioral protocols, and the parameters of acceptable behavior. How can we account for the persistence of these contexts and their features? This concern has perplexed anthropologists since the field's inception and there are hints that disparate researchers are appealing to similar features of social life.

For example, loosely drawing from generative grammar (see Chomsky 1965), Pierre Bourdieu (1977: 26–29) suggests that, like human language, social practices indicate deeper structures; just as the word order and lexical shifts found in mundane statements indicate the existence of deeper, unconscious syntactical processes, mundane behaviors and beliefs indicate deeper, habitual, and ultimately unconscious structures of both mind (i.e., internal structures) and society as a whole (i.e., external structures). Each individual may not consciously represent or perform every aspect of a religious or linguistic system, but how they participate contributes to the replication and maintenance of the system. Bourdieu's insights are consistent with evolutionary accounts of religion as a form of niche construction (e.g., Fuentes 2020).

Laland et al. (2000: 132–133) define niche construction as "the activities, choices, and metabolic processes of organisms, through which they define, choose, modify, and partly create their own niches." Niche construction theorist Odling-Smee (1996: 196) details how "[o]rganisms change selection pressures by choosing or perturbing their local habitats, or by constructing artefacts." An anthill, for instance, is a perfect example of how a colony of organisms alters its natural environment and so introduces new selection pressures even in the act of overcoming extant ones. Ants are genetically predisposed to alter their environments and presumably have cognitive systems that influence what they use to build their colonies.

Humans of course are masters of niche construction, as we create tools, environments, and other artifacts that change how we can interact with the environment. However, we also create social realities in the form of institutions which, as already discussed, create particular—and often cross-cutting—avenues that we must navigate. Evolutionary psychologists refer to these avenues as a "cognitive niche," which is the "dramatic increase in the use of contingent information for the regulation of improvised behavior that is successfully tailored to local conditions" (Cosmides and Tooby 2000: 53; Tooby and DeVore 1987). Our social environments operate as natural environments insofar as individuals must acclimate to them or behave in such a way as not to violate the boundaries our institutions delimit (for discussion of the cumulative cultural evolution of "cultural niches," see Creanza et al. 2012; Yeh et al. 2019).

Here is where the relationships between individuals' habituation to their social and natural environments become clearer with respect to religion. The notion of "cognitive niche" is comparable to Bourdieu's (1977: 78) notion of *habitus*, which is "the durably installed generative principle of regulated improvisations." The *habitus*, comprised of "cognitive and motivating structures," constrains and informs "improvisations" that in turn adjust in accordance with "the demands inscribed as objective potentialities in the situation" (ibid.: 78, 82). *Habitus* is a product of individual (i.e., ontogenetic) and historical (i.e., phylogenetic) processes, that is, it is "history turned into nature" (ibid.: 78). In other words, the *habitus* is collectively held habits and the range in which their corresponding cognitive models and behavioral expressions safely deviate from the modally represented content of those habits. In sum, together, individuals' mental faculties, their representational content, and behavioral corollaries comprise habit-saturated niches that delimit the possible (and locally instituted as acceptable) range of behavior and thought. In the case of religion, this process is fundamentally about how individuals *ought* to comport themselves.

Indeed, religions are *moral communities* in the sense that they contain explicit and encoded expectations and forms of appropriate and inappropriate conduct (Kiper and Sosis 2014; McKay and Whitehouse 2015). Moreover, people navigate this social niche by engaging in rituals which, as discussed above, communicate sharedness and commitment *to* the niche and its constituents. What, then, explains the formation of religious niches' content? Viewing religions as niches into which people are born and subsequently become part of is a helpful view, but it does not address how these niches emerge in the first place and subsequently evolve.

Another helpful but seldom-explored way of conceiving of religious systems is analogous to the way biologists have come to appreciate complexity at various scales of abstraction. For example, skin is a deceptively homogeneous and relatively concrete object. However, skin is composed of interacting layers of smaller discrete cellular units and these cells are also composed of smaller and smaller units still. Skin is what some would call an "emergent property" of these interacting units insofar as it is an object identifiable at a particular scale which is not satisfactorily reducible to its constituent parts (Cronk and Leech 2013: 151–168; Holland 1995; Holland and Miller 1991; Miller and Page 2007; O'Connor 1994; Chapter 9).

If it is the case that under particular external conditions, religious systems perform optimally for individual agents (and their aggregations) when their constituent parts, both internal and external to the individual, converge in a particular way, then the question of whether or not natural selection also "operates" at an emergent level is an important one (see Sosis 2009a; Chapter 9). So, while groups may not actually be units of selection, and genes are the foundational replicators of the evolutionary process, it may be that emergent properties of human social systems provide benefits for individuals that would otherwise be unobtainable. But the benefits are only reaped when this convergence of units consists of a particular logic and that logic must exist within a compatible socioecological context. In other words, selection may favor the expression of specific kinds of religious systems, a possibility that lies beyond the scope of strictly cognitive approaches to religion (see Malley 1995, 1997; Sørensen 2004; Chapter 8).

One persistent problem for all humans is our reliance on the cooperative relationships that have served our species for millennia. Who are reliable cooperative partners? How can we negotiate access to limited resources? As detailed above, religious traditions regularly appear to address these particular problems. Costly rites keep potential defectors out of cooperative pools and reliably convey trustworthiness (Iannaccone 1992, 1995). And omniscient, moralistic gods often curb our self-interest, whereas other gods are often concerned with resource use and markers of in-group coalitions. Yet, scholars are just beginning to address the question of whether or not, under certain conditions, selection favors particular configurations and contents of the religious system.

Specific modes of subsistence create locally specific, persistent cooperation and coordination problems. Religious systems systematically correspond to these problems. Examples abound. In various cross-cultural studies, state-level social organization predicts the presence of moralistic high gods (Johnson 2005; Lahti 2009; Sanderson 2008b; Skoggard et al. 2020; Stark 2001; Swanson 1960; Wallace 1966), particularly in societies with high levels of out-group conflict (Roes and Raymond 2003). Such gods may have emerged, however, in pastoralist societies, where warfare and the challenges of coordination are particularly acute (Peoples and Marlowe 2012). It has also been found that the greater the population density, the higher the rate of religious ritual performance (Atkinson and Whitehouse 2011). Religious diversification has been linked to pathogen stress (Fincher and Thornhill 2012) and the development of revitalization cults predictably corresponds to resistance to colonialism around the world (Wallace 1956). Traditional communities with a strong sense of territory often sacralize boundaries and demand corresponding ritual piety from outsiders upon entry (Purzycki 2012: 341–360; Chapter 10). These facts all suggest that certain contexts will be especially likely to elicit religious appeals and trigger the kinds of psychological and social learning processes we have discussed. They also suggest that critical aspects of religious traditions—collective complexes of beliefs and practices—will evolve in specific ways in order to overcome local socioecological challenges. In other words, the beliefs and practices that recruit evolved psychology, learned habits, and explicit cultural information, mechanically operate and evolve together in ways that mediate the distribution of energy in a given social system. For the remainder of this volume, we examine these possibilities in more detail.

Conclusion

As traditionally conceived, phenotypes are limited to features of an organism's morphology, physiology, and behavior. Dawkins's notion of the extended phenotype expands our conception of phenotypes to include extrasomatic and often transsomatic adaptations. The extended phenotype helpfully characterizes religion or any cultural trait that is expressed across minds and confers advantages to its bearers. As we discussed throughout this chapter, genetic capacities "for" religious expression have a greater chance of replication when the contents and forms of religious systems are responsive to locally specific socioecological challenges. Successful religious systems not only have mechanisms that enable adaptive responses to local conditions, but they employ structural elements, such as ritual costs and counterintuitive concepts, that safeguard against exploitation of such a system. In the next chapter, we examine many ways in which religious systems feed back into the wellbeing and reproductive success of their constituents.

Chapter 2

Religion as a Cultural Solution to Social Living

with Azim F. Shariff

Scholars of religion have long assumed that religions offer benefits and fulfill the needs of individuals, and that these benefits can explain why religions exist. Religion's ascribed functions include pacifying existential angst (e.g., Darwin 2004 [1879]; Durkheim 2001 [1912]; Geertz 1973 [1966]; Russell 1961: 575–576), creating meaning in a natural world inherently devoid of meaning (Bering 2011; Inzlicht et al. 2011; Rappaport 1979), and coping with death anxiety (e.g., Becker 1973; Jong et al. 2018; Spiro 1987). But religions are more than answers and cures for the psychological concerns of individuals. Religions also solve social and ecological problems faced by groups of people, and religions have probably adapted responsively to serve these roles from their beginnings. In this chapter we explore evolutionary analyses of religion that aim to explain how religions solve many of the social and ecological challenges that human communities recurrently face.

First, we discuss the major distinctions between cultural functionalist theory and evolutionary functionalism. Evolutionarily minded social scientists are often faced with charges of endorsing functionalism, which continues to be a "dirty word in the social sciences" (Sharrock et al. 2003: 15; cf. McCauley and Lawson 1984). Here we focus on a number of commonly expressed objections to cultural functionalism and how, in both theory and practice, evolutionary functionalism overcomes them. We then review some of the evidence that demonstrates the conditions under which religions provide solutions to social and ecological problems faced by actual communities. Finally, we discuss avenues for further research and stress the importance of maintaining the theoretical and methodological pluralism that currently flourishes within the evolutionary study of religion.

Cultural Functionalism vs. Evolutionary Functionalism

In anthropology, functionalism has come in many forms over the years, ranging from the more sociologically oriented structural-functionalist schools of Radcliffe-Brown (1965) and Durkheim (2001 [1912]) to the cultural materialist and ecological schools of Harris (1966) and Rappaport (1979, 1984 [1968]). Malinowski (1944: 159), the titular founder of cultural functionalism, defines function as the "satisfaction of a need." He offers five components that comprise his vision of culture, three of which are key to understanding his thought:

- Culture is essentially an instrumental apparatus by which man is put in a position to better cope with the concrete specific problems that face him in his environment in the course of the satisfaction of his needs.
- It is a system of objects, activities, and attitudes in which every part exists as a means to an end.
- Such activities, attitudes and objects are organized around important and vital tasks into institutions such as family, the clan, the local community, the tribe, and the organized teams of economic coöperation, political, legal, and educational activity.

(Malinowski 1944: 150)

Malinowski considers the essential core of cultural domains to be functional; they contain within them the means to overcome "environmental problems" in order to "satisfy...needs," and "every part exists as a means to an end." Therefore, any successful functional analysis of a cultural system, such as religion, entails understanding the constituent parts' relationships and what their particular ends are, even if those ends are merely to fulfill the other components' functions. However, critics have identified a number of problems with such functionalist accounts of human social systems.

For example, many take issue with cultural functionalism's heavy reliance on interpretation (e.g., Sperber 1996: 47–49). Harris's (1966) classic explanation of the sacralization of cattle in India, for example, is a regular target for such critiques. Harris argues that the taboo against killing cattle exists because the benefits of keeping cattle alive for things such as milk and dung for fuel outweigh the benefits reaped by eating them. Bloch (1983: 133) critically points out the *ad hoc* nature of the explanation: "Harris notes that cows are holy in India and then looks around for

anything that will show the belief to be reasonable in terms of the economy." Indeed, strong correlative interpretivism and weak methodology
characterize much functionalist research in anthropology throughout the
middle of the twentieth century. Evolutionary functionalists, however,
have made use of a vast array of research methods to avoid the pitfalls and
limitations of interpretive ethnographic inquiry, as evinced by the studies
reviewed below (as well as a host of others we do not discuss).

The apparent lack of agency in functionalist accounts has been another
target for criticism (cf. Elster 1979: 28–35). As a response to this critique,
rational choice theorists have emphasized individuals' beliefs and desires
in the process of decision making. However, the classic (but often confused) distinction between *teleology*—referring to an intentional function—
and *teleonomy*—referring to functions that result from blind evolutionary
processes—has to be taken into consideration here (Pittendrigh 1958).
Individuals' intentions and decisions may indeed functionally influence
their wellbeing (see Spiro 1987: 109–144), and their internal cognitive
states can, at times, accurately represent the fitness value of a particular
strategy. That is, proximate intentions can align with ultimate explanations. Alternatively, the proximate, conscious goal can be quite removed
from the ultimate, teleonomic purpose for a given behavior (or ritual,
teaching, etc.). In short, the conscious intentions that motivate behavior
can vary widely, but what matters for evolutionary functionalism is *how
the behavior affects fitness*—whether genetic or cultural (for excellent discussions of this distinction with respect to the evolution of conservation
practices, see Hames 1991, 2007; Smith and Wishnie 2000).[1]

---

1. Another common problem identified with functionalism stems from an alleged
essentialization of culture. For instance, Collier et al. (1997 [1982]: 73) note that "The flaw
in Malinowski's argument is the flaw common to all functionalist arguments: Because a
social institution is observed to perform a necessary function does not mean either that
the function would not be performed if the institution did not exist or that the function
is responsible for the existence of the institution." In other words, Collier et al. take issue
with the idea that an institution is inextricably linked with its function or that there is
some causal role that a function plays in the formation of an institution. Moreover,
the authors suggest that functionalist analyses essentialize the *social context* with the
institution. Of course, an institution can exist longer than its constituent participants
and its function can change, and humans are particularly adept at finding ways to solve
problems by formalizing behaviors which work around them. Analytically, however, all we
need to see are an institution's effects to *claim* that it has a function, regardless of whether
or not it is true. This problem with functionalist institutional analysis is that institutions
are thought of as essential to a society. Evolutionary analyses (*pace* Gould) similarly tend

A third criticism of many functionalist accounts is the apparent lack of a "feedback mechanism" to sustain the movement of elements within the system. In other words, in order to be convincing and complete, functionalist accounts require a force external to the system to reconstitute, maintain, and reproduce elements within the system (Elster 1979: 28–35, 1982; Sperber 1996). The combination of natural selection and genetic transmission is one obvious feedback mechanism, but as Stinchcombe (1968: 86) has pointed out, other forms of selection and transmission—for example, cultural evolution—can serve as feedback mechanisms as well (Chapter 9). What functionalist accounts often lack is attention to the ecological pressures that led to the emergence of an institution, and the fitness effects that could explain its persistence (Chapter 10).

Again, methodologically, cultural functionalism has been systematically interpretative; one studies an institution and discovers the problem it solves, and this analysis is carried through to other domains of a population's experience. However, researchers must empirically demonstrate that the institution or trait under examination produces benefits that are not available to those who lack that institution or trait. The problem for those who study religion, however, is finding a sufficient control sample (cf. Sosis and Bressler 2003; Sosis and Ruffle 2003). As such, we are often limited to evidence that allows us to abductively conclude that particular traditions benefit individuals and communities in particular contexts. Currently, we lack a complete evolutionary functionalist analysis of any religious system; however, there is nonetheless plenty of evidence that suggests religion is adaptive in specific ecological contexts. Though this evidence relies primarily on the cultural evolutionary processes by which information—in the form of beliefs, rituals, and teachings—is selected and transmitted, the approach we advocate mimics that employed by naturalists to understand why organisms have the particular features that they do.

Here, we review the arguments and evidence for six of the most prominent hypotheses that propose that religion functionally enables, sustains, and facilitates large group-living among humans. We also note open questions that remain and avenues of future research that could address them.

---

to essentialize functions for traits, as traits will often serve different purposes in different contexts. Likewise, anyone with a modicum of understanding of the ethnographic record cannot deny the diversity in content of religion, and careful arguments must address the possibility that different religions overcome or address problems posed by local environments.

Monitoring and Punishing Selfish Behavior

While many non-state societies have traces of moralistic deities (Boehm 2008), anthropologists have maintained for at least half a century that morally involved "high" gods—creator deities that govern the world and a pantheon of subsidiary spirits—are found predominantly in societies with complex state-level organization (Swanson 1960; Wallace 1966). In the absence of highly effective secular institutions such as policing and court systems to regulate behavior, groups of this size face considerable challenges in controlling free-riding and cooperative defection. Genetically evolved mechanisms, such as kin-based altruism and reciprocity with non-kin, are only able, on their own, to sustain very small groups—much smaller even than the towns that sprang up 9000–11,000 years ago in the Levant (Dunbar 2003; Henrich 2004). With increasing population size, anonymous encounters become increasingly frequent, and with them opportunities to engage in self-interested, other-damaging, unethical behavior *without* sacrificing one's reputation.

Many researchers have argued that commitment to omniscient, morally judging supernatural agents facilitated cooperation by discouraging believers from cheating in these otherwise anonymous situations (Lahti 2009; Johnson 2005, 2016; Rappaport 1979; Sanderson 2008b; Schloss and Murray 2011; Shariff and Norenzayan 2007; Stark 2001). Furthermore, knowing that a potential interaction partner fears supernatural reprisal builds faith that this partner will behave with moral constraint, and thus heightens trust among people. These hypotheses have received ample empirical support from several different fields. First, psychological studies have shown that people primed to think about God and other supernatural agents are more cooperative, more honest, and more generous to strangers in anonymous situations (Ahmed and Salas 2011; Henrich et al. 2010; Johnson 2005; Piazza et al. 2011; Randolph-Seng and Nielsen 2007; Shariff and Norenzayan 2007). Second, cross-cultural studies show that people are more likely to behave honestly towards others when they think their morally concerned gods are punitive and knowledgeable (Lang et al. 2019; Purzycki et al. 2018). Third, people do indeed use other people's religiosity as a powerful cue of trustworthiness (Gervais et al. 2011; McCullough et al. 2016; Purzycki and Arakchaa 2013).

The threat of supernatural punishment, in particular, seems to have a much stronger effect than the promise of supernatural reward. Controlling for relevant variables, people who see God as more punishing than loving and comforting are less likely to cheat in academic settings (Shariff and Norenzayan 2011). Moreover, countries that have higher rates of belief in hell and lower rates of belief in heaven tend to have lower crime rates (Shariff and Rhemtulla 2012). In fact, there are indications that emphasizing God's forgiveness over his vindictiveness actually *encourages* norm violations (DeBono et al. 2017).

Anthropological work has shown that societies where cooperation was especially important and difficult to sustain with basic kin selection and close reciprocity—such as larger societies, or those that faced acute resource shortages—were more likely to develop beliefs in "high" gods (Roes and Raymond 2003; Snarey 1996). These findings suggest that supernatural punishment may have emerged to facilitate the management of limited resources. And considered together, the results emerging from this line of research suggest that, of the multitudes of forms supernatural deities have taken or could have taken, the most popular varieties—powerful, omniscient, and morally involved gods—evolved because of the moral cohesion that they offered large groups of people. These types of gods thrived because the societies they were attached to managed to succeed where less cohesive groups could not. These successes are measured in the individual benefits accrued by a cooperative distribution of those limited resources that could have otherwise been squandered by self-interest.

Resource Regulation and Management

One avenue by which regulated behavior among individuals fosters group-level success is the wise management of shared resources—preventing the "tragedy of the commons" (Hardin 1968). Durkheim (2001 [1912]) noted that this type of resource regulation was an example of religion's "secular utility." In a well-known example—mentioned above— Marvin Harris (1966) argued that cattle are sacralized in India because the benefits from the prohibition of slaughter outweigh the benefits of eating cattle. According to Harris, this institutionalized prohibition makes ecological sense for Indians engaging in the practice; if cattle are sacred and not to be slaughtered, then Indians maintain the secular utility of keeping cattle alive for plowing, milk, and dung for fuel. However, Harris's analysis did not attempt to demonstrate that, when controlling for ecological conditions, people who slaughtered their cattle enjoyed less caloric intake, had lower fertility, suffered more poverty, or scored more poorly on any other indicator of fitness than Hindus who sacramentally conserved them.

Other studies have attempted to more precisely specify the effects of sacred values and practices on resource commons. Roy Rappaport's (1984 [1968]) classic study *Pigs for the Ancestors* argued that ritualized mass pig slaughters among the Tsembaga Maring of New Guinea are timed at points when pig population sizes become too cumbersome and parasitic on resources used by humans. The pig slaughters, which occur on a cycle of 12 to 15 years, coincide with the temporary lifting of prohibitions against warfare. This ritual cycle, according to Rappaport, "helps to maintain an undegraded environment, limits fighting to frequencies that do not endanger the existence of the regional population, adjusts man-land ratios, facilitates trade, distributes local surpluses of pig in the form of pork throughout the regional population, and assures people of high-quality protein when they most need it" (ibid.: 224). Subsequent theoretical models have offered only mixed support for Rappaport's claims about the social utility of these rituals (e.g., Anderies 1998; Foin and Davis 1984; Samuels 1982; Shantzis and Behrens 1973). However, rigorous quantitative empirical testing still remains to be done—assuming that contemporary political and economic conditions among the Maring allow for the collection of relevant data.

Some studies have produced reliable empirical evidence of higher returns for religiously sanctioned resource management (e.g., Cox et al. 2014; Hartberg et al. 2016). In a landmark study, J. Stephen Lansing (Lansing 1987, 1991; Lansing and Kremer 1993) argued that the island of Bali's temple-focused religious system teleonomically and strategically mediates water distribution to artificially terraced rice paddies operated by cooperative units of people (*subak*). *Subaks* are farming collectives that engage in public rituals devoted to a host of deities. In these collectives, farmers resolve essential conflicts of water use for rice paddies by timing water flows with ritualized appeals to supernaturally sanctioned irrigation practices. These practices affect the nutrient content of the water, regulate pests, and maximize sunlight exposure to plants, but these benefits must be coordinated by individual farmers whose interests correspond to where their farms are located on the terraces. For example, if unregulated, by the time water would reach downstream paddies, their nutrients would already have been used by upstream plants. And, while keeping water in holding tanks upstream can maintain the nutrient richness of the water, downstream farmers still need water for their paddies. *Subaks* ritualistically coordinate the timing of water release and Lansing and Kremer (1993) demonstrated that by virtue of the religiously facilitated wide-scale coordination of competing *subaks*, each *subak*'s yield is better on average than it otherwise would be (see Chapter 10 for further discussion).

In both of these ethnographic cases, individuals might forego exploiting particular resources (e.g., water or pigs) at a personal cost. However, the payoffs of more sustained cooperative relations are evident in both examples. Unfortunately, studies as detailed and comprehensive as Rappaport's and Lansing's are rare. This lack of empirical data is particularly unfortunate because, as global markets increasingly engulf local economies, the need is greater than ever to understand any time-tested cultural strategies for resource acquisition and management that may have previously stabilized and ultimately sustained human communities.

Signaling Rituals

Many researchers refer to religion as a "social glue" that binds people together (e.g., see Graham and Haidt 2010).[2] Religious groups also typically provide their adherents with social and resource benefits, which are susceptible to exploitation (e.g., Sosis 2009b). How does religion accomplish this binding, and how do individuals determine whom to trust in times of need? In religious contexts, ritual behavior is a strong candidate. As discussed in the previous chapter, rituals can specifically serve as proxies for reputation, credibly indicating trustworthiness thanks to their public visibility and their somatic, economic, social, time, or opportunity costs. Costly ritual performances not only credibly convey commitment to the supernatural agents that receive the sacrifice, but also to the communities that proclaim belief in the agents. Such rites can therefore serve as an effective cultural bulwark against cooperative exploitation if costs are high enough to prevent likely defectors, who probably lack the concomitant beliefs and commitment, from performing them and so receiving social benefits.[3] A number of studies support the signaling theory of religion (e.g., Power 2017a; Soler 2012; Sosis and Bressler 2003; Sosis et al. 2007; Chapter 8). These studies suggest that, indeed, religious rituals function to

---

2. Indeed, the likely Latin derivation of the word "religion," *religare*, means "to bind," although it is unclear if the binding refers to the gods, community, or both.
3. In Henrich's (2009) model of credibility enhancing displays (CREDs), the signals of commitment need not be costly to the honest signaler, only too costly for a dishonest signaler to fake.

communicate commitment to other people and thus may be reliable indicators of trustworthiness. This trustworthiness translates to the payoffs associated with increased cooperation, which maintains important social relationships and, in turn, increases social cohesion and wellbeing.

Yet, while these studies may explain the ultimate effects that rituals have on building trusting and cohesive societies, we have little understanding of the proximate psychological mechanisms responsible for equating costly, ritualized displays of commitment with trustworthiness. Can factors other than ritual mediate perceptions of trustworthiness in a religious context? What are the factors involved in changing the perceived cost of ritual acts? These questions probably point to human social institutions, which facilitate shared expectations and cultural meanings. The operative word here is "shared." Nonetheless, as discussed below, various traditions appear to measure sharedness and conformity in different ways.

Cohesion Rituals: The Case of Synchrony

What are the proximate mechanisms that enable religion and ritual to elicit behavioral conformity? One answer may lie in the music, dance, chanting, and other coordinated physical activities that centrally feature in many rituals. Recent research on "synchrony," in which multiple people engage in rhythmically coordinated behaviors such as singing or dancing, suggests that such coordinated movement positively affects cooperation and prosociality (Lang et al. 2017; cf. Wood et al. 2018). In a seminal paper, Wiltermuth and Heath (2009) showed that subjects instructed to move in time with other research participants (as opposed to engaging in the same behaviors but doing so out of sync) reported higher levels of similarity, connection, and trust with their group members, as well as showing higher levels of coordination and self-sacrifice for their group. Paladino and colleagues (2010) found that subjects who watched targets having their cheeks brushed while having their own cheeks brushed simultaneously felt more resemblance with and attraction for their sensation partners. Even further, subjects actually tended to perceptually confuse themselves with their partners, perceiving agency over the other person and experiencing "body illusions" in which their own sensations were projected to the location of the other person. Notably, participants in the synchronous condition also showed more conformity in their responses to follow-up questions than those in the asynchronous condition.

Similarly, synchronous behavior has been shown to increase both pain tolerance and, perhaps as a consequence, work output (Cohen et al. 2010). Further, neuroimaging research has revealed that the intense audio-visual sensory experiences that often accompany religious rituals actually inhibit self-related processing (Goldberg et al. 2006). The ability of synchrony to promote the importance of the group while de-emphasizing the individual probably explains its persistence across a vast variety of religious rituals—from the whirling of Sufi dervishes to the coordinated movements of Muslim prayers (Raka'ah) to the collective hymn singing characteristic of Christianity. Of course, religions are not the only institutions to have leveraged the socially cohesive effects of synchronous behaviors. As Wiltermuth and Heath (2009) point out, modern militaries continue to put recruits through marching drills even though marching is no longer used in actual military engagement. This seeming anachronism may be due to the remarkable group-bonding effects of synchronized marching (McNeill 1995). Various forms of dancing, such as the coordinated step dances of primarily African-American fraternities and sororities (Malone 1996), probably achieve the same type of social bonding, as might subordination postures in worship (Goodman 1986). Such examples suggest that when individuals have a means by which to coordinate, the benefits of cooperative functioning are increased. This ingroup solidarity is further stimulated and maintained through religion's handling of outsiders.

Management of Competitors, Defectors, and Other Threats to Influence

As religious systems bind in-group members, they also often endorse mechanisms that mitigate potential disruptions to social order caused by insiders (real or scapegoats) or outsiders. For example, Steadman and Palmer (2008: 163–184) have argued that witch hunts around the world have been directly tied to perceptions of threats to the social order. They predict that "witch-killings occur only when there is a significant threat to the social hierarchy of the killers and those supporting them," noting that the rash of witch-hunts in Europe "began and ended with the Reformation and Counter-Reformation" (ibid.: 168). Of course, perceived threats to social order are especially useful for increasing social solidarity through rallying and mobilizing others.

Religious nonbelievers can also be seen as threats to the social order. In modern societies, disparagement of atheism can be understood as a "self-protective" device on the part of religions aiming to discourage defection from their cultural system (compare this to examples in Chapter 3). From the perspective of religious prosociality, however, anti-atheist prejudice can also be understood as a reaction against a moral threat. If cooperation and trust rely on the shared religious beliefs of those surrounding you, then members of society who explicitly reject these beliefs are immediately morally suspect. This theory fits recent empirical findings. Examining the virulent anti-atheist prejudice in North America—polls consistently show atheists at the top of lists of most disliked groups (Edgell et al. 2006)—Gervais et al. (2011) have found that these intense negative attitudes are driven by a profound moral distrust. In their studies, anti-atheist prejudice appeared most prominently in high-stakes trust situations. Participants were not overwhelmingly concerned about being served food by an atheist (a situation with low stakes for misplaced trust), but were highly unwilling to hire one for babysitting (a high-stakes trust situation). When given a scenario briefly describing a man of dubious moral character, participants were as likely to implicitly identify him as an atheist as they were a rapist.

Research also finds that anti-atheist prejudice does not exhibit the typical signature of standard "social identity" driven ingroup-outgroup psychology. As Gervais et al. (2011) discuss, these standard models fail to account for the domain-specificity of the antipathy (confined to trust-based situations), or the lack of a corresponding ingroup preference on behalf of non-believers. Instead, distrust of nonbelievers or adherents of different religions can be seen as the direct—and selected-for—outcome of the emphasis religions put on a trusted community of common believers. In a sense, these are flipsides of the same cultural adaptation.

Open questions remain. How does the distrust people feel toward nonbelievers compare to that they feel toward believers from other religions? Consistent with theoretical predictions that the fear of or commitment to any God is preferable to the fear of or commitment to none, preliminary research indicates that people are more inclined to trust a believer from another religion than a nominal but nonbelieving adherent of their own (Shariff and Clark 2012; cf. Gervais et al. 2011). Again, those who reject beliefs effectively reject the moral order fostered by religious ingroups.

The bulk of the research on attitudes about atheists has, however, primarily been conducted with Christian participants. One open question is whether adherents of orthopraxic religions, which emphasize shared religious behavior more than belief (see Box 2.1), would feel similar distrust of atheists. Might the level or kind of prejudice differ in, say, Judaism, which has a long history of non-belief and secularism (Biale 2011) or any cases where even violations of the sacred are an inherent part of the tradition (see Chapter 3)? Finally, what role will the rapidly increasing number of atheists in developed societies (Pew Research Center 2020) have on anti-atheist prejudice, and on religion, in general? Gervais (2011) showed that subjects who were led to believe that atheists were more rather than less prevalent in their communities subsequently showed higher levels

---

Box 2.1 Religious conformities: *Doxa* and *praxis*

One popularly entertained idea is that religions function to maximize ideological conformity. However, with the notable exception of a few evangelistic world religions, such as Christianity, Islam, or Buddhism, having faith or belief in the same religious concepts as others in the community (i.e., orthodoxy) has not been seen as vital in most religious traditions that have ever existed (see Chapters 3 and 4). These traditions often instead emphasize behavioral consistency and participation—that is, *practice* (orthopraxy)—as the mark of religiosity, rather than consensus in belief (see Fernandez 1965). Generally, only universalizing, evangelizing, or expansionist religious traditions—those that seek to subsume a wide variety of diverse groups through conversion—see faith as indicative of religiosity. Thus, different contexts influence the criteria for being religious. For example, Kavanagh and Jong (2020) show notable distinctions between orthodoxy, orthopraxy, and personal motivations for religious commitment in contemporary Japan, suggesting that decontextualized, "theocentric" approaches to religion will only continue to mislead researchers studying Japanese culture. Similarly, Cohen et al. (2003) predict that an emphasis on practice—and not on faith—is probably associated with ethnicity-bound traditions. Indeed, members of religious groups that see themselves as differing from others by virtue of some internal essence (see Gil-White 2001) may feel less need to demonstrate ideological conformity to each other than adherents of universalizing traditions—again, such as Christianity, Islam, and Buddhism—of which anyone can theoretically become a member. In support of this thesis, Cohen et al. (2003) show that that Protestants are significantly more likely than Jews to emphasize faith as an indicator of religiosity. The recurrent distinction between orthodoxy and orthopraxy offers a compelling illustration of the principle that different adaptive solutions culturally evolve in response to distinct social needs and pressures.

of trust in atheist individuals. As the "otherness" of atheists decreases, so too might prejudice directed against them. That said, it remains possible that the rise of a more coalitional form of atheism, which could unify non-believers into a coherent ingroup, may provoke more aggressive responses.

Marriage and Other Regulations on Sexuality and Reproduction

Religion may also be credited with the salutary effects that monogamous marriage norms have had on societies. Polygyny is common among other primates, and has been a demonstrable feature of human mating patterns throughout history—the vast majority of societies in the anthropological record permit men to take multiple wives (White 1988). The historical transition from nomadic hunter-gatherer lifestyles to permanent settlements, however, amplified the destabilizing effect that such polygyny norms had on human groups. As wealth inequality between men grew, so did the inequality in the number of wives that men could acquire. The ability of a handful of wealthy, high-status men to monopolize a disproportionate share of mating opportunities led to a large and particularly socially disruptive underclass of unpaired men. Facing restricted sexual opportunities, unpaired men of reproductive age are liable to engage in increasingly desperate, risky, and often violent behavior (Wilson and Daly 1985). Historical anthropological records show that polygynous societies have consistently had higher rates of crime and warfare than predominantly monogamous ones (Bacon et al. 1963; White and Burton 1988). Even today, societies with higher rates of polygyny show higher levels of murder, rape, and robbery after controlling for relevant variables such as per capita GDP and economic inequality (Kanazawa and Still 2000).

Modern monogamous marriage norms, which originated in ancient Greece 2500 years ago and spread via Christian expansion and, more recently, European colonialism, are thus likely to be adaptive cultural innovations that offer increased stability to large, unequal groups (Henrich et al. 2012; cf. Fortunato and Archetti 2010; Fortunato 2015). Societies that adopt monogamous marriage norms are likely to effectively suppress any anti-social consequences of polygyny by redirecting men's energetic investments away from acquiring more wives and toward paternal care for offspring, thus making such societies more competitive in the cultural evolutionary market (Henrich et al. 2012).[4]

Though monogamous marriage norms are likely to have strengthened groups, they ran counter to the evolved sexual strategies of individual men—and were particularly unappealing for high-status men who had the greatest opportunities for polygynous pursuits. This makes monogamous marriage a hard sell, especially for those with power. Tying these norms to religion would have been a particularly efficacious way of ensuring they had the strength to restrict behavior. Research has shown that norms are more likely to be adopted when they are backed by religious edict (Bushman et al. 2007).[5] Moreover, in societies with weak legal enforcement, religion served not only as the primary moral authority, but also the only one whose sanctions could be mostly trusted to apply equally to those at the top of the hierarchy (whose behavior, in this case, needed the most regulating).

Today, there is ample evidence for the relationship between religion and monogamous sexual behavior. In America, religious adherents have on average had significantly fewer lifetime sexual partners than have the non-religious (Billy et al. 1993). They also have lower rates of premarital sex (Beck et al. 1991; Herold and Goodwin 1981; Zelnik and Shah 1983), are more likely to get married (Thornton, Axinn, and Hill 1992), report higher marital satisfaction (Call and Heaton 1997; Wilson and Filsinger 1986), and have fewer extramarital affairs (Atkins, Baucom, and Jacobson 2001; Reiss et al. 1980). While these findings generally support a role for religiously regulated monogamy in facilitating positive mating outcomes, future research would do well to explore historical trends for evidence that the spread of religions with monogamous marriage norms indeed longitudinally predicted increased levels of sexual monogamy and, in consequence, indicators of social stability.

---

4. As Buss and Schmitt (1993) argue, the high rates of singledom, divorce, and adultery in modern Western societies make it difficult to argue that these are purely monogamous societies. However, monogamous marriage norms limit the number of women that can be *explicitly* tied to one man, leaving unmarried women at least theoretically available to other men.

5. Aside from just monogamy norms, the enveloping of other important group-beneficial norms in the power of supernatural sanction has probably been a highly effective and frequently used cultural strategy for ensuring compliance. Violating sacred values, after all, is a much weightier offense than breaking secular norms.

Religious norms and regulations for mating may have also contributed to the success of culture groups through maximizing fertility. Today, fertility rates have declined across the world, but they have done so at a slower rate among the religious—and particularly more conservative and orthodox religious sects (e.g., Berman 2000). At both the individual and national levels, religiosity is one of the strongest predictors of family size, even after controlling for important related variables (see Blume 2009; Frejka and Westoff 2008; Kaufmann 2010; Lehrer 1996). One provocative suggestion as to why the religious have lagged behind the general trend of reduced fertility is that religiously backed norms maintain entrenched gender roles, while simultaneously promoting a "cult of motherhood and fertility" (Beit-Hallahmi 1997: 167). According to this explanation, restricted access to education and economic autonomy prevents women in conservative religious communities from exercising as much control over their reproductive decisions and from seeing as many alternative opportunities to motherhood as their secular counterparts. While there is some support for this suggestion, especially among rural populations (Amin and Alam 2008), this important topic is ripe for further research (Shaver 2017). Although historically these high rates of fertility probably allowed religious groups to outcompete less fertile ones, they may today be a double-edged sword, given that high birth rates in modern times are tied to cycles of poverty and economic stagnation. This change reinforces the principle that religious systems are responsive to local adaptive challenges, not universal templates, making occasional strategic mismatches likely if not certain (Chapter 1).

Discussion

The above is not meant to be an exhaustive list of cultural adaptations that religions offer to solve problems of group living. Many other probably important group functions that religious rituals and proscriptions may serve have scarcely been mentioned—mostly due to lack of available research. For example, researchers have begun to discuss the idea of a *cultural immune system* (Sørensen 2004) consisting of cultural practices that are devoted to avoiding and managing the spread of virulent pathogenic diseases. The preferential culinary use of spices with anti-bacterial properties in areas of high pathogen load is one often-cited example (Sherman and Billing 1999; see Henrich and Henrich 2010, for another example), though this has been recently challenged (Bromham et al. 2021). It is very likely that many religiously sanctioned dietary and cleansing rituals serve similar disease-avoidance purposes. Though anthropologists have devoted much effort to cataloguing the great cross-cultural variety of these types of rituals, few have adopted the functionalist perspective featured here. Doing so in the future, however, may provide a critical tool for understanding the ultimate, culturally adaptive, reasons why these and other rituals and edicts exist in the first place.

Researchers must resist the pull of naïve "panadaptationism," however, when investigating the culturally evolved group utility that religions provide. Not every feature of every religion evolved to serve the group. For one thing, as briefly discussed in the introduction to this chapter, many aspects of religions may have developed to directly serve the individual. Moreover, many aspects of religions can be destructive to both groups and individuals. Cases such as Jonestown and Heaven's Gate illustrate the disastrous results for constituents when the costs of commitment so drastically outweigh the benefits of devotion. Indeed, religious traits that convey no adaptive advantages to either group or individual can persist for generations without being extinguished, simply because they effectively sustain belief in a broader religious system that may offer other, unrelated benefits (see Shariff 2008).

Finally, as changes occur to the socio-cultural environment in which religions exist—including the growth of competition from other religions, ideologies, and social institutions—hitherto adaptive elements can become adaptively inert, or even detrimental, to the welfare and survival of the group and group members. As typically conservative and tradition-rich institutions, religions may be slow to adapt to changes, leading them to lose market share to competitor institutions as they fail to maintain the devotion of their adherents. The future, ultimately, will belong to those religions that combine the best group- and individual-level cultural adaptations for the current environment and provide the most flexibility and optimal solutions to both the persistent and the novel challenges of modern life.

We have thus far argued that religious systems are characterized by a universal adaptive coupling of belief and ritual behavior and offered a few examples to illustrate how religion provides benefits for individuals with implications for survivorship and reproduction. Some ethnographers and other researchers, however, have claimed that supernatural beliefs and practices are absent or somewhat lacking in many traditional societies. If so, this would pose a significant challenge to our systemic approach; given that all human societies face problems of coordination and cooperation and various economies pose different versions of these problems, religion should be both ubiquitous as well as accommodating to these problems in significant ways. In the next chapter, we address this concern by examining the nature of supernatural beliefs in several populations that allegedly lack religion or critical elements of religious expression.

Chapter 3

Resistance, Subversion, and the Absence of Religion in Traditional Societies

Anthropologist Jack Goody (1996: 679) noted that "Both gods and doubts are widespread, transversal (if not universal) aspects of culture, the result not of inbuilt processes but of the interaction between language-using human beings and their social and natural environment." There are two important points Goody conveys here. First, doubt—that is, reluctance or resistance to adopt received wisdom (see Box 3.1)—exists in all societies. Second, doubt does not exclusively spring from some internal faculty, but rather is the output of a complex set of inputs to an organism that produces, manipulates, and transmits ideas. In other words, doubt emerges as the product of a systemic process. One implication of this view is that, much like the case we made for religion in the previous chapter, doubt can express itself differently across contexts; if humans' social and natural environments vary, it follows that doubt—as rising from their interaction—should exhibit itself in a corresponding fashion. Here, we point to ways in which people variously express religious doubt across traditions.

While doubt may be universal, how ubiquitous atheism and skepticism are within and across small-scale societies remains unclear. This uncertainty stems partly from a lack of data from appropriate samples; most research on secularization focuses on state-level societies (e.g., Norris and Inglehart 2012; Solt, Habel, and Grant 2011) and most research on religion (or its absence) in small-scale societies is anecdotal, thus lacking precise, comparable measures of commitment. Nevertheless, the ethnographic record makes clear that people express doubt about received cultural wisdom in various ways around the world. If we wish to come to terms with the presence and ubiquity of doubt in any precise fashion, then, we need a thorough sense of how people express it, an understanding of how this expression varies, and ways of measuring that variation.

Here, we restrict our discussion to religious commitment and non-commitment—that is, to individuals' beliefs about spiritual agents and human behaviors performed to influence the dispositions of these agents (Chapter 1; Spiro 1987: 187–222; Wallace 1966). This restricted focus helps us avoid classifying social belief systems such as Communism as religion by virtue of their ideological dogmas. Similarly, we do not equate religious faith with "ultimate concern," *à la* Paul Tillich (1957). Our focus is on popular beliefs and practices rather than doctrine. In what follows, then, "religious doubt" refers to a sense of uncertainty about the existence of spiritual beings and/or lack of confidence in the efficacy of practices associated with these beings (see Box 3.1 for definitions).

While not crucial to our presentation, we do assume that belief and behavior are dynamic (see Chapter 6). Behaviors can further stabilize ideological commitment and generate or strengthen beliefs just as much as beliefs can increase the motivation to act in particular normative ways (Sosis 2003). Acknowledging this dynamism highlights the weaknesses in some definitions of irreligion; one can be ideologically an atheist, for example, but nevertheless a serious, devoted practitioner of behaviors associated with gods. For example, the ritualistic study of Talmud is currently flourishing among atheistic secular Israelis (Freedman 2014: 210–211). Likewise, one can be a firm believer in the existence of gods and spirits while refraining from participation in expected ritual activity or behaviors. Indeed, as noted in the last chapter, anthropologists (e.g., Fernandez 1965) and social psychologists (e.g., Cohen, Siegel, and Rozin 2003) have long recognized that different religious groups place variable emphasis on beliefs versus practices (Chapter 4). Some emphasize ideological consensus (i.e., believing the same things, or orthodoxy) while others emphasize behavioral consensus (orthopraxy), leaving beliefs are relatively free to vary.

This chapter unfolds as follows. We begin by considering the universality of religion. Various scholars have argued that some traditional[1] societies are devoid of religious commitments or even a system of religion; we contest these claims and look closely at several alleged examples, specifically the Hadza and Pirahã. We then consider popular and scholarly claims that Buddhism is atheistic. Lastly, we examine ethnographic data

---

1. We use "traditional" to broadly refer to relatively smaller societies that are less integrated with and/or rely less on markets and large, specialized bureaucracies than those in highly urbanized state systems (see Mattison and Sear 2016).

on societies that foster religious traditions that challenge, subvert, and even resist the religious social order. These religions provide a very different model of religion than is generally familiar among Western societies.

How "Non-religious" are Traditional Societies?

Rappaport (1999) noted that "No society known to anthropology or history is devoid of what reasonable observers would agree is religion" (1). Yet, in fact, not all scholars agree on this point. Recent years have seen a remarkable influx of new or reiterated claims about the absence of religion, or some facets of religion, in various traditional societies. These claims address the conceptual and/or factual aspects of the matter.

On the conceptual side of the slate, some scholars simply claim "religion" *proper* is particular to only a few societies. Sperber (2018: 42), for example, doubts "that all or even most human societies have had a religion in any useful sense of the term." Boyer (2018: 121) elaborates: "Religions appeared with large-scale kingdoms, literacy and state institutions. Before

---

Box 3.1 Doubt, atheism, nonbelief, and non-commitment

We refer to *doubt* as a motivational force that leads one to reluctance or resistance to received wisdom and practices. If we take Bertrand Russell's (1961) colloquial distinctions as a starting point, *atheists* accept two propositions. The first is that we can know if gods exist. The second is that what we do know points to their lack of existence. *Agnostics* reject the first proposition, and the second by implication, positing that there is neither enough reason nor evidence to answer the question (ibid.: 577–584). In this view, then, agnostics doubt while atheists confidently reject. What brings people to these positions, of course, is complicated, particularly if we take Goody's views seriously; just as the processes that lead to a rejection of theism are manifold (Norenzayan and Gervais 2013), the kinds or types of rejection of or resistance to religion are multitudinous (Blanes and Oustinova-Stjepanovic 2017). The ethnography of doubt or apathy, therefore, must examine how people variously express different shades of *nonbelief* (e.g., atheism, agnosticism, and apatheism). *Non-commitment*, then, can vary between and include both *nonbelief* (i.e., the mental processes involved in assigning truth value to something) and nonparticipation.

them, people had pragmatic cults and ceremonies, the point of which was to address specific contingencies, misfortune in particular" (see also Boyer 2020: 459, who suggests that "religions" are "doctrines supported by organizations").[2] For Boyer and Sperber, religion appears to be synonymous with the spiritual traditions of complex, literate, large-scale societies. Despite the very high probability that the majority of individuals in all societies hold beliefs about spirits and gods, perform behaviors thought to please them, and avoid and/or discourage behaviors thought to displease them, only a small minority of people are taking part in "religion," according to this view.

For centuries (see Tylor 2006 [1873]), political and religious leaders as well as scholars have asserted that traditional societies lack religions or are somehow less religious than large-scale societies. Christopher Columbus, for example, posited that the Canary Islanders "would become Christians very easily, for it seemed to [him] that they had no religion[3]" (Dunn and Kelley 1989: 69). A century later, missionaries made similar statements about indigenous Caribbean traditions. For example, Breton (1929 [c. 1635–1647]: 5) notes that "After having lived without any knowledge of God, they die without hope of salvation. *It would be better for us to say that they have no religion at all*, instead of describing as a cult of divinity all their trifling nonsense, superstitions, or more exactly sacrileges with which they honor all of the demons who seduce them" (emphasis ours).

---

2. Boyer (2020) suggests that previous research has erred on the side of over-elaboration of traditional religions. In other words, researchers portraying the traditions of small-scale societies tend to craft over-intellectualized worldviews on behalf of the people they study, even though they lack such a worldview. We agree with this observation, but as we do not equate "religious system" with "logically coherent religious worldview," we also do not need to equate "over-intellectualize" with "systematize." Moreover, we would not on the same grounds dispense with the idea that traditional societies have visual art, music, fashion, numeracy, or any other of the many human universals by virtue of a lack of specialization or explicit *emic* theory about them. Finally, this view also requires some connection between doctrine and its location; as most of the laity might have little grasp of the doctrine underlying even state-level traditions, why lay faiths would be characterized as "religious" requires an arbitrary connection. Elsewhere, Boyer (2011) argues that the term "religion" itself is useless and "like aether and phlogiston, belongs in the ash-heap of scientific history." By sticking with our earlier conception, we are more aligned with Rappaport's sentiments.

3. "Ellos deben ser buenos servidores y de buen ingenio, que veo que muy presto dicen todo lo que les decia, y creo que ligeramente se harian cristianos, que me parecio que ninguna secta tenian" (Gillett and Gillett 1892: 22).

Another missionary (Bouton 1635: 1) suggests that "they do not trouble themselves with knowing what becomes of [the souls of the dead]; at least we have never been able to draw this information out of them." Note, however, that he readily admits to having little experience with the people themselves, and grants that he and his colleagues might "learn more if we were to live among them or they among us. At the present time they are greatly separated from us by inaccessible hills, so that we see them rarely and only when they come by sea to trade with the French" (ibid.). So, in addition to sheer lack of interaction, missionaries might dismiss what ritual activity they did witness as "trifling nonsense," thus minimizing any association with "anything heavenly."

The assumptions or claims that traditional societies lack a genuine or "full" religion have not gone away. For example, some social scientific discussions of contemporary small-scale populations make similar claims, although they stem from different motives than early missionaries' observations. Other researchers similarly characterize traditions such as Buddhism as "non-theistic" religions when considerable evidence points to the contrary. In the remainder of this section, we discuss these examples and attend to some counterevidence to such claims.

The Hadza

The Hadza are one of the most intensively studied small-scale populations in the world. Located in Tanzania, some Hadza communities have retained their foraging lifeways, while others have been incorporated into the market economy. But even Hadza foragers are increasingly influenced by market economies and tourism, and their territories continue to be pressured by neighboring groups. Celebrated ethnographer James Woodburn (1982) notes:

> The Hadza link death and burial with their major religious celebration, the sacred epeme dance performed in pitch darkness each month ... Failure to hold the dance is believed to be dangerous. Performing the dance is believed to maintain and promote general wellbeing, above all good health and successful hunting.
>
> (Woodburn 1982: 190)

He wagers that these traditions "might provide a starting-point for elaboration into a set of systematic beliefs about fertility and regeneration in death but the evidence does not, I think, support the idea that such a set of systematic beliefs has already developed" (ibid.: 204). Here, Woodburn suggests a kind of primitive religion that does not quite yet have the degree of formalism in terms of beliefs that fully established traditions would.

Following this, anthropologist Frank Marlowe (2010: 61) notes that after asking one man "if there was only one god or several, he thought about it for a while, then said he was not quite sure. This sums up much about Hadza religion." However, he continues:

> I think one can say the Hadza do have religion, certainly a cosmology anyway, but it bears little resemblance to what most of us in complex societies (with Christianity, Islam, Hinduism, etc.) think of as religion. There are no churches, preachers, leaders, or religious guardians, no idols or images of gods, no regular organized meetings, no religious morality, no belief in an afterlife—theirs is nothing like the major religions. All the beliefs and rituals associated with the *epeme* dance and *epeme* meat eating are at the heart of Hadza religion.
>
> (Marlowe 2010: 61)

Marlowe contrasts the religiosity of the major world traditions with Hadza beliefs and practices, as though what "most of us in complex societies" know as religion is some kind of reliable measuring stick. Yet, posing a similar question about the nature of the Trinity, to a lay Catholic, for instance, is likely to yield a similar uncertainty if not a similar kind of verbal shrug. In the same spirit, others have characterized the Hadza as being "minimally religious" and "having little belief in omniscient, moralizing gods" (Apicella 2018; Smith et al. 2018).

Others who have focused specifically on Hadza religion, however, suggest a rich religious life including multiple rituals, spirits, cosmological beliefs, and practices (Power 2015; Power and Watts 1997; Skaanes 2015, 2017b, 2017a). Data from the solitary study (Apicella 2018) that collected discrete quantitative data on the topic suggest that the vast majority of the sampled Hadza believe in at least two deities (only two were asked about, however) (Figure 3.1). Of the believers, 82 percent also said that *Haine* (represented by the moon) and *Ishoko* (represented by the sun) are the same god, only 7.4 percent of the sample claimed that these gods do not exist, and 5.9 percent claimed not to know if either exist. Forty-eight of those who answered (85.4%) claimed to engage in rituals devoted to *Haine*, whereas virtually the same proportion (85.7%; $n = 35$) reported engaging in rites devoted to please *Ishoko*.

A more specific look at these beliefs suggests that the Hadza largely conceive of these deities as punitive, moralistic, and knowledgeable (Apicella 2018). Figure 3.2 illustrates the distributions of these data (see Purzycki et al. 2016a for codebook). Here, modal responses for both deities are positive for the knowledge and punishment scores; whereas the mode for moral interest questions is positive for Haine (dark grey) but negative for Ishoko (white) and the distribution is roughly uniform across answer options. Furthermore, there is no reliable indication that exposure to Christianity has influenced these beliefs (Purzycki et al. 2022; Stagnaro, Stibbard-Hawkes, and Apicella 2022).

As for Hadza ritual behaviors, *epeme* and the *maitoko* are of central importance. The notion "*epeme*" can variously refer to the ritual itself, individuals who have been successfully initiated into the otherwise secretive ritual practices, prestigious parts of meat surrounded with taboos and norms regarding their consumption, and a deity. Here is where accounts tend to emphasize different things, thus creating a conflicting portrait of the tradition. For example, some of Apicella's informants suggest that the Hadza engage in this tradition "for themselves, not a god ... [Moreover,] nothing bad will happen if they do not do the dance, it can be used to

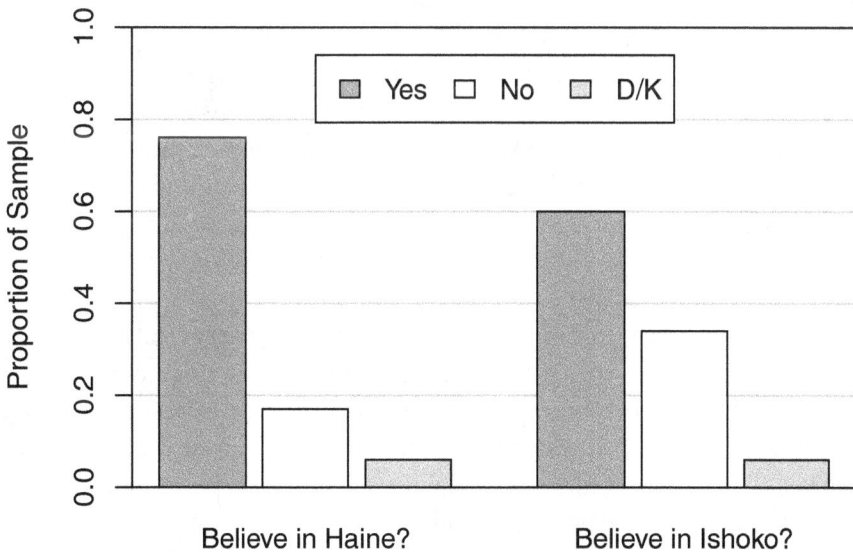

Figure 3.1 Distribution of belief in *Haine* and *Ishoko* among a Hadza sample (*n* = 68). D/K refers to "I don't know." Values are from Apicella (2018).

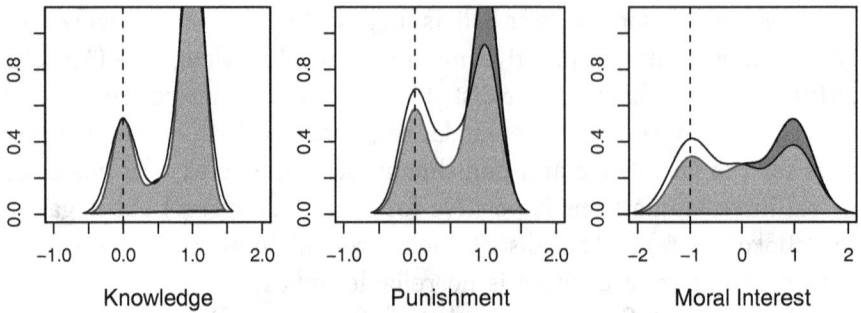

Figure 3.2 Density plots of Hadza claims about the breadth of knowledge, punishment, and moral interests of *Haine* (dark gray) and *Ishoko* (white). Scores for knowledge and punishment are the means of two binary questions (no = 0; yes = 1) and the moral interest scores are means of three (no = –2; I don't know = 0; yes = 2). Reference lines denote the minimum possible values. Sample sizes vary across questions and deity (min = 32, max = 44).

bring rain and good fortune, to heal the sick, and to make people happy" (Apicella 2018: 137). However, Skaanes (2017a) details how people dance for spirits where "a dancer communicates for whom it is that he is going to dance. This makes the spirit of the person he dances for enter the body of the dancer through his head, and the dancer becomes a vessel for the spirit of the one in whose name he dances" (ibid.: 108).

Interestingly, it appears that there is more consensus regarding the nature of participation in the ritual. First, simply being present requires a certain level of maturity, and there are ritual specialists who have performed specific behaviors of initiation in order to participate. Second, relationships forged in the *epeme* ritual predict sustained cooperative behaviors between individuals across camps (Hill et al. 2014), and individuals within camps can formally express others' transgressions during the epeme ceremony (Skaanes 2017a: 107).

In summary, then, contrary to some portraits and interpretations, Hadza traditions—many of which are conducted in secret—are demographically structured in important ways, create and maintain relationships, and are deeply intertwined with the Hadza cosmos and social order. In other words, the Hadza are indeed a religious society with many indicators of spirits and practices that can foster cooperative relationships that help maintain their communities. We find a similar case among the Pirahã of Brazil.

The Pirahã

The Pirahã have gained some notoriety through the various publications of ethnolinguist Daniel Everett (2005, 2008, 2009). In a chapter entitled "Material Culture and the Absence of Ritual," Everett (2008: 71–84) characterizes the Pirahã as having a "relative lack of ritual," which he refers to as "a set of prescribed actions with symbolic significance for the culture" (ibid.: 81). Even if we maintain Everett's definition, he provides various points of evidence to the contrary. For instance, the Pirahã make necklaces "to ward off spirits and to look more attractive" (ibid.: 74). Moreover, the Pirahã always bury their dead. According to Everett, burials are "an area where we can expect some ritual, though there is little that we can describe with this term" (ibid.: 81–82). Yet the Pirahã do have "loosely followed traditions surrounding the burial" and sometimes "the dead are buried in a sitting position with many of their belongings placed beside them" (ibid.: 82). While both burial traditions and the wearing of protective necklaces consist of sets of "prescribed actions with symbolic significance for the culture," Everett demurs on classifying them as "ritual."

Rather, Everett ponders that "the activity closest to ritual among the Pirahãs is their dancing [which brings] the village together. They are often marked by promiscuity, fun, laughing, and merriment" (ibid.: 83). There is also a "dance in which live venomous snakes are used." In it, a man dresses up as an evil spirit and emerges from the jungle while singing about his lack of fear and dwelling place in the jungle. He then proceeds to throw the snake at observers who "scramble away quickly" (ibid.: 84). Everett suggests that "Such dances might be classified as a weak form of ritual, in the sense that they are witnessed and imitated and clearly have value and meaning to the community" (ibid.). Yet, Everett also observes that "On many rainless nights, a high falsetto voice can be heard from the jungle ... it is taken by all the Pirahãs in the village to be a *kaoáíbógí*, or fast mouth [spirit]. The voice gives the villagers suggestions and advice, as on how to spend the next day, or on possible night dangers" (ibid.: 139). Everett entered the jungle to confront the man doing this, who on the following day denied it, under the assumption of some form of spiritual possession. This description ends with Everett musing: "Very puzzling, I thought" (ibid.).

Elsewhere, Everett (2005: 632) claims that the Pirahã "have no creation stories or myths." However, there is evidence from other ethnographers, and Everett himself, suggesting that there are many stories and characters about a mythic time (Everett 2009; Gonçalves 1990, 2000; Nevins, Pesetsky, and Rodrigues 2009a, 2009b), including rituals conducted under the auspices of spirits, and an active shamanic tradition. According to Gonçalves (2000), the Pirahã religious worldview includes a multi-tiered cosmology, including an afterlife in which spirits "compete for the responsibility to appear in [a] shamanic ritual" for naming people. The Pirahã spiritual landscape is full of various spirits and mythical beings. Other sources suggest that there are two major festivals that take place, both of which have the expressed "intention of provoking sounds, making a noise, sufficient for the demiurge Igagai, dwelling on the second celestial level, to hear them, becoming aware of their existence and of the exact place where they are found" (ibid.):

> The Pirahã's worry that they may not being located by Igagai can be interpreted as a fear of a repetition of what is contained in a mythic fragment narrating the destruction of the world. This destruction was due in the final instance to the fact Igagai was unaware where the Pirahã were. It was only through the crying of women, who were alone and without fire, that Igagai was then able to hear and locate them and start reconstruction of the world.
>
> (Gonçalves 2000; cf. Nevins, Pesetsky, and Rodrigues 2009b)

By Everett's estimation, Gonçalves's work is "the most reliable ever done by an anthropologist, but one simply cannot come to the best conclusions about Pirahã meanings working through the medium of the very poor Portuguese of Pirahã informants. Gonçalves based much of his research on interviews with two Pirahã informants whose Portuguese was somewhat better than that of most Pirahã" (Everett 2005: 632). Gonçalves acknowledges that he had to piece together what he calls "a cosmology without myths" and "where the ideas of the Pirahãs about the cosmos gain consistency is in ritual and the dreams that are in fact [believed to be] lived experiences. It is this thinking that they elaborate via ritual discourse and dreams that would be the equivalent of myths in other Amazonian cultures" (cited in Everett 2009: 431). Everett concludes, "the Pirahãs are repeating back amalgams of many of the stories that they have 'pieced together' over the years from caboclo [ethnically mixed] traders who share in the myths that pervade almost all Amazonian societies. These are not indigenous" (ibid). Here, Everett concludes that the Pirahã had to learn these myths from outsiders, but the requirement that myths be exclusively indigenous is entirely arbitrary. The Pirahã do entertain such stories, and having them suggests how embedded they are in a greater Amazonian tradition (see Nevins, Pesetsky, and Rodrigues 2009b: 392–394).

If we focus on beliefs in spiritual beings and rituals devoted to them, the Pirahã are far from non-religious. Moreover, their ritual lives strongly suggest patterned behavior under the influence of spirits, including possession and transformation. These rites are not merely "a set of prescribed actions with symbolic significance for the culture" as defined by Everett. Rather, they are practices that are clearly aimed at influencing spirits' temperaments. In summary, the Pirahã, too, are religious.

Are Small-Scale Societies Lacking "Moralistic" Traditions?

These examples are not unique (e.g., see Izquierdo, Johnson, and Shepard Jr. 2008; Johnson 2003 for similar discussions of researchers' attitudes toward the Matsigenka of Peru). Moreover, a related debate concerns not whether some small-scale populations lack religion, but whether they lack some specific component of religion. In fact, one of the most contested current debates in the evolutionary science of religion concerns whether or not small-scale societies had "moralistic" or "prosocial" religions prior to contact with the Abrahamic or other world religious traditions (Beheim et al. 2021; Boehm 2008; Johnson 2015; Norenzayan et al. 2016; Purzycki 2011b; Watts et al. 2015). On one side of the debate, Ara Norenzayan (2013: 127) suggests that "ancestral religions did not have a clear moral dimension." On the other side, Dominic Johnson (2015) rejects the idea that the gods of small-scale populations lack moralistic supernatural punishment. Both draw upon the same cross-cultural work (e.g., Boehm 2008; Peoples and Marlowe 2012; Swanson 1960), arriving at different conclusions. If we define morality as norms of prosocial behaviors with a cost or benefit to others (Alexander 1987; Purzycki et al. 2018), do traditional religions truly lack "a clear moral dimension"?

The San peoples of the Kalahari are often purported to maintain a religious tradition that lacks morality. Lorna Marshall (1962) writes that "Man's wrong-doing against man is not left to ≠Gao!na's [a deity] punishment nor is it considered to be his concern. Man corrects or avenges such wrong-doings himself in his social context" (245; cf. Katz 1982: 30). This oft-quoted passage (e.g., Norenzayan 2013; Peoples and Marlowe 2012; Wright 2009) portrays the San as ultimately self-regulating and therefore lacking any need for a punitive moralistic deity. However, there are a few compelling lines of evidence that warrant skepticism of this claim as a whole.

First, as we showed above, another small-scale foraging group, the Hadza, show signs that two of their deities are explicitly associated with spiritual punishment. In other words, with a similar economy and social scale, the Hadza have at least two deities with the properties denied of the San. Second, the San deity ≠Gao!na is reported to punish people both directly and indirectly. In the same article, Marshall (1962) reports that this deity can punish people for demonstrating their own dominance, taking honey, and accidentally shooting and eating a gemsbok that was ≠Gao!na in disguise. While these might not be construed as "moral," it is evidence that this god is thought to punish people for improper conduct. Moreover, wouldn't the San be able to just as easily "correct or avenge such wrong-doings themselves" like they do with other moral transgressions? Additionally, the San regularly plead with this deity to end suffering and to bring food and water to the community (Katz 1982: 30–31). Despite little evidence that ≠Gao!na is explicitly concerned with the kinds of moral expectations found in the Abrahamic traditions, he is a dominant, powerful agent that commands respect. As there is no reliable evidence beyond the speculation of ethnographers, the question remains open as to whether or not dominant, powerful deities that are explicitly moralistic are more effective at increasing cooperation than dominant, powerful deities associated with other forms of behavior.

The third line of evidence is the fact that *other* San spirits reportedly care about human moral behavior, intervene to mediate moral relationships (Lee 2003: 129–130), are the subject of a rich body of mythical morality tales (Guenther 1999), and are the targets of rituals conducted in an "emotional climate of 'dense moral interaction'" where local conflicts are resolved (Guenther 1979). These spirits, the //gauwasi, are either the children of the gods or spirits of deceased San. During the San trance dancing rituals, a "dancer may pointedly address himself to issues of tension in the group, and berate individuals or the group collectively for their quarreling and urge them to reconcile" (Guenther 1999: 195).

In addition to facilitating intragroup harmony, aspects of these rites also build bridges *between* camps and—as these rituals are thought to be quite effective for healing even by non-San—other South African ethnic groups. Katz (1982: 207) reports on one dance that was attended by neighboring camps "despite the fact there is a major, ongoing argument between the two larger camps over a prospective divorce, the wife coming from one of the camps, the husband from the other." This dispute was acted out, replete with name-calling and debate between the two camp members. After a while, "they agree[d] to resolve their differences, at least for a time," then proceeded to sit together, ultimately laughing and dancing in unison (ibid.: 208). In sum, not only do the San have very clear moral dimensions to their religious traditions, but there is evidence that their ritual practices can forge bonds beyond parochial boundaries.

Atheistic Buddhism?

Similar—and longstanding—claims exist regarding more popularly recognized traditions, such as Buddhism's alleged lack of deities, moralistic or otherwise. From general theorists William James (1958 [1902]) and Émile Durkheim (2001 [1912]) to generations of scholars of Buddhism (de Bary 1969; Rahula 1974), many continue to maintain the view that Buddhism is somehow an "atheistic religion" or lacking in spiritual agents. While most contemporary scholarship accepts that Buddhism is replete with spiritual devotions (Obeyesekere 1991; Orrù and Wang 1992; Pyysiäinen 2003), some nevertheless maintain the stance that Buddhism lacks gods "in the Abrahamic sense" (Schlieter 2014), calling contrary claims "merely an invention of 19th century Buddhist modernists" (Stausberg 2005: 150). As discussed earlier, the difficulty with making progress in such conversations is that scholars appear to be focusing on different analytical levels, ranging from doctrine to the laity to religious specialists.

Spiro (1982), for example, describes the Theravada Buddhism he encountered in villages of upper Burma (now Myanmar) as atheistic. Yet, he acknowledges that "[t]here are, to be sure, numerous gods in Buddhism" and "Buddhism might be called polytheistic" (ibid: xii). Indeed, he argues that gods become necessary in Buddhism because Buddhist explanations for suffering, which place "responsibility for suffering exclusively on the sufferer," are "less than satisfying emotionally" (Spiro 1996: 4). Consequently, offloading personal pain onto the supernatural realm provides a more appealing and compelling account of human suffering. Spiro's extensive ethnographic work in Burma details widespread beliefs in witches, nats, ghosts, and demons, and corresponding ritual activities that engage with these supernatural agents, including festivals, exorcisms, and possessions (Spiro 1982, 1996). Other traditions explicitly treat Buddha(s) as god(s).

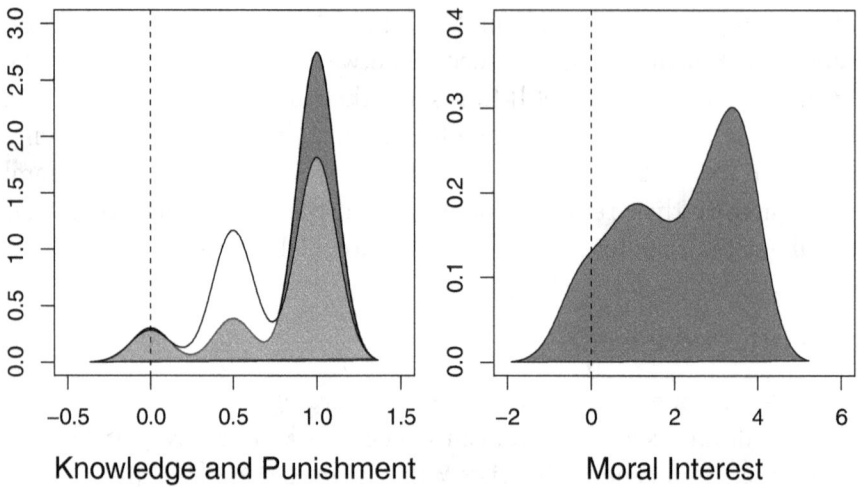

Figure 3.3 Density Plots of Tyvans' (*n* = 81) claims about the breadth of knowledge (left panel, dark grey), punishment (left panel, white), and moral interests (right panel) of *Buddha*. Scores for knowledge and punishment are the means of two binary questions (no = 0; yes = 1) and the moral interest scores are means of three items on a 5-point scale (0 to 4). Reference lines denote the minimum possible values.

For example, East Asian Pure Land Buddhists (Mochizuki 1999; Stevenson 2007) are committed to a doctrine of afterlife salvation through devotional practices explicitly devoted to Buddhas associated with heavenly domains. Among many of the Buddhist laity in the Tyva (pronounced TOO-vuh) Republic (Siberia), Buddha is a moralistic, punitive deity that has a hand in what happens to people after they die. In one study (Purzycki and Holland 2019), when participants were asked to freely list things that anger Buddha, most listed moral violations and lack of virtue. A majority claimed that Buddha knows more than normal humans—which technically is not far from orthodox Buddhism doctrine, which teaches that he attained Enlightenment. However, Tyvans also claim that he actively punishes people and maintains an interest in humans' moral conduct during their lives on Earth. Figure 3.3 illustrates the distribution of responses to these questions. Out of a sample of 79 individuals, 60 (76%) reported that they performed rituals devoted to Buddha. Berniūnas et al. (2020) employed comparable methods and found similar patterns among Mongolians, who share a deep cultural history with Tyvans. In summary, while official Buddhist doctrine may posit no deities, many devoted

Buddhists nevertheless regularly engage in rituals that propitiate spirits and even Buddha himself, whom they conceive of as a punitive, morally interested god.

Doubting, Subverting, and Resisting Tradition

Despite lingering questions raised by within- and across-group variation in the ethnographic record, the above examples suggest that it is unlikely that religious traditions—especially traditions that modulate interpersonal and intergroup relationships—are absent from non-state societies. In order to reach more substantive conclusions, researchers should actively examine this question through fieldwork, listening to what traditional people have to say about such matters. Nevertheless, as Goody suggested, doubt and resistance remain equally universal. What varies across groups is how people express doubt and resistance to tradition. In what follows, we examine evidence of resistance to religion in the ethnographic record of small-scale societies.

Azande Witchcraft

Consider, for instance, Evans-Pritchard's (1976) observations of the Azande, where skepticism toward witch doctors was quite common: "Absence of formal and coercive doctrines permit Azande to state that many, even most, witch-doctors are frauds ... Faith and scepticism are alike traditional" (ibid.: 107). Resonating with Goody's sentiments, Evans-Pritchard finds that commitment and rejection coexist, but in a curious way: the Azande do not reject witchcraft *in toto*. Quite the opposite; while the Azande are well aware of ritualized sleights of hand and therefore skeptical of many individual witch-doctors, they nevertheless continue to believe in witchcraft in general.

Much like Western notions of "luck," what helps maintain witchcraft beliefs are the vicissitudes of life. General misfortune and illness, coupled with the inevitable strife that comes with being a hypersocial animal, provides enough "evidence" of witchcraft. Yet, few if any Azande are confident enough to claim to know precisely how witchcraft works (ibid.: 31); they just know that ill-will between people can cause misfortune and illness and that witchcraft is made possible by a specific fluid in witches' bodies. However, the Azande can see this fluid only when processing the body of a deceased person, with the result that conclusive "evidence" must wait until the end of a witch's life.

Evans-Pritchard notes that if an Azande were asked if he were a witch, he would not respond with righteous indignation as he might if asked if he were a thief or murderer. Instead, in another example of self-doubt, an Azande might simply express hope that it isn't him who is causing misfortune to others, perhaps pointing to the lack of evidence of the witchcraft fluid in his deceased ancestors. When witchcraft becomes especially troubling—for it is always afoot—people consult a variety of oracular devices to learn the source of witchcraft. They might publicly announce that the oracles have informed them who the source of witchcraft was, but they do not publicly identify the suspected witch out of courtesy, giving the witch the opportunity to apologize and make amends (ibid.: 39). When the alleged witch is confronted, he typically apologizes and expresses that if he is a witch, he does not mean to intentionally cause harm, and proceeds to ritualistically "cool" any witchcraft fluid inside of him. Despite widespread belief in Azande witchcraft, the tradition thus remains shot through with ignorance, self-doubt, and suspicion of ritual experts.

Ilahita Arapesh

Like the Azande, the Ilahita Arapesh of Papua New Guinea simultaneously evince commitment to and rejection of the supernatural realm. In a series of extraordinary ethnographies, Donald Tuzin (1976, 1980, 1997) describes the Tambaran, a secret male cult of the Ilahita and other Arapesh communities. The Tambaran consists of a brutal five-stage male initiation rite, lavish male feasts, and various sacrifices to the spirits. For Ilahita males, the Tambaran is "a total way of life" (Tuzin 1980: 325). The Tambaran cult terrorizes both women and young male initiates, and often denies them much needed food, especially meat. Tuzin documents that the men were fully aware that the Tambaran was a fiction and its spirits were not real. Indeed, the men expressed considerable guilt and remorse about deceiving the women. Husbands, to alleviate their guilt, would often secretly provide their wives with meat that should have been offered to the Tambaran spirits, telling their wives that the spirits were no longer hungry.

The Tambaran cult was ultimately dismantled by the Ilahita. Specifically, the men publicly admitted to the women that the Tambaran spirits were not real and that the entire cult had been an elaborate deception. Fearing that the women would react to this revelation with anger and indignity, the men instead were surprised to learn that the women were well aware that the Tambaran had always been a hoax, and they had only played along to satisfy the men. Thus, we are presented with a remarkable spectacle: a religious system that all adult parties involved seemed to understand as a fabrication.

However, the situation was not so simple. As Tuzin describes, "[t]he men's confession also carried a warning, which was that in a truer sense the Tambaran was not a hoax at all. The spirit venerated in the cult was and is real; its power was lethal in the past, and it could kill again" (Tuzin 1997: 1). The death of the Tambaran was partially fueled by a Christian Revivalist movement, whose beliefs and doctrines ultimately reordered Ilahita lives. The Revivalists did not claim that the Tambaran spirits were not real; rather, they depicted them as quite real, but Satanic. As is often the case, religion created the problem and offered the solution: Jesus was superior to and would protect the Ilahita from the Tambaran's demonic spirits.

Clowns, Tricksters, Fools, and their Festivals

Many traditions around the world incorporate a certain level of tolerance for rejection—if not outright desecration—of their own values and customs in the form of mythical tricksters, sacred clowns, and festivals of disorder. In myth, tricksters are clever-but-foolish, taboo-breaking but likable anti-heroes who are typically responsible for the creation of humans and their more important cultural developments like language, hunting technology, and ritual traditions (Erdoes and Ortiz 1999; Hyde 1998).

In practice, ritual clowns disrupt sacred ceremonies, defile sacred artifacts, violate norms, and generally represent agents of chaos and disorder. Among the Mexican Mayo, for example, clown "behavior involves a fascination with oral behavior, eating bread, feces, etc., and with anal behavior, with goosing or jabbing other [clowns] in the anus and with 'defecating' upon sacred objects" (Crumrine 1969: 7). Throughout Polynesia, ritual clowns traditionally ridiculed chiefs and ritual specialists with impunity (Hereniko 1994). Many Native American traditions include clowns who disrupt ritual orders, perform rituals in reverse fashion, and adopt contrary lifestyles in everyday life as part of their sacred roles (Plant 1994, 2010). As Bricker writes of the Native Americans of highland Chiapas, although they "do distinguish between sacred and profane acts and have a clear sense of what is sacrilege and what is not, this distinction is not equivalent to a distinction between the solemn and the comic, as is often the case in our own society. Thus humor and religious ritual need not be mutually exclusive with respect to setting" (Bricker 1973: 10).

In a similar way, many festivals celebrate disorder, indulgence, and the rejection of normalcy. The Western European "Feast of Fools" consisted of chaotic church masses replete with cross-dressing, singing obscene songs, eating blood sausage and gambling at the altar, and the throwing of animal excrement at passersby (Bourke 1891: 11–23; cf. Harris 2011). Writing about the corrosive quality that humor had on the hierarchy of medieval Europe, Bakhtin (1984: 88–89) says that "laughter make[s] no exception for the upper stratum, but indeed it is usually directed toward it ... One might say that it builds its own world versus the official world, its own church versus the official church, its own state versus the official state ... [laughter has an] indissoluble and essential relation to freedom." Persistent repression of humor in the history of Western religious traditions suggests that even the powerful can fear mirth (Sanders 1995; cf. Resnick 2016).[4]

Such figures and events may reinforce adherence to the very norms they violate (conversely, normalcy may also reinforce the importance of rebellion; Turner 1969). They are demonstrations of how not to behave normally; they are exhibitions of excess, gluttony, indulgence, sexual freedom, and violations of general expectations. However, clowns and tricksters who have license to be critical of the otherwise infallible, and to point out the folly in taking things and people—including oneself—too seriously, may function more to equalize others and humanize those in power than to reaffirm their roles (Hereniko 1994). As these figures and events represent novelty, creation, and evolution, they are widely recognized as catalysts for change rather than maintainers of the status quo (Hyde 1998).

---

4. While the Hebrew Bible and Rabbinic literature are replete with humor including wordplay and examples of humans besting and entertaining God (Friedman and Friedman 2014), scholars also recognize the tension between the god of Abraham and humor, and point to a common pool of indices. For example, Ecclesiastes 7:4 states that "the heart of fools is in the house of mirth." Luke 6:22 notes that "Blessed are you who weep now, for you will laugh [in heaven]." Benedict of Aniane (747–821) writes that "the Lord condemns those who laugh now" and "there is never a time for laughter for the faithful soul" (cited in Resnick 2016: 93; Sanders 1995: 130). Writing in the 1120–1140s, Hugues de Saint-Victor (1648: 100), a Christian priest and theologian, observed that expressing joy may be good or bad, depending on its source, but laughter is always evil (*risus omnimodo malus est*).

Conclusion

In this chapter we have discussed the question of religious noncommitment in societies that largely fall outside the common sampling schemes of social scientists. We argued that, contrary to longstanding narratives, no society lacks religion; even prototypically nonreligious or minimally religious societies or atheistic traditions are in fact replete with rituals directed toward spiritual beings. When researchers privilege targeted inquiry over casual observation it is clear that these societies exhibit forms of religiosity. We also discussed some ways in which people variously express doubt and resistance to tradition, showing that the two appear to go hand-in-hand. Resistance and doubt in traditional societies offer many rich opportunities for further inquiry.

In fact, we think it is no exaggeration to say that just about every aspect of the social science of (non)belief in traditional societies needs more attention if it is to be of use to understanding the human experience. While ignorance, doubt, and apathy are ubiquitous, atheism and agnosticism as formal identities are not likely to be present in traditional societies; atheism as an organizational identity probably exists primarily as a response to, and therefore in competition with, theism. Similarly, atheism is not likely to arise in traditional societies that primarily emphasize behavioral commitments over ideological orthodoxy. Rather, in a context of competition, material incentives (e.g., not having to pay ritual costs) and ideological motivations (e.g., religious institutions are corrupt and deceitful) are likely to contribute to the rise of atheism or non-commitment.

Take, for example, one ethnographic case study of atheists in India (Copeman and Quack 2017). In response to the religious tradition of cremation and the expenses of mortuary rites (including the feeding of upper caste Brahmins), atheists have organized to donate their bodies to science, rhetorically packaging these donations as signals of greater virtue and selflessness than what the religious alternatives offer. Moreover, when benefits from a secular source outweigh those from a religious source, we should expect a reduction in religious commitment, unless religious systems acclimate to the novel conditions. Among the Shuar of Ecuador, access to secular medicine appears to be decreasing the likelihood of soliciting shamans as the first choice for healthcare (Blackwell 2009). Additional cross-cultural work is needed to explore the impacts of secular medicine on traditional healing practices, particularly including religious beliefs and practices.

Doubt is inherent in the belief systems of both small- and large-scale societies, although, as we have discussed, the nature and expression of doubt is likely to differ across societies. Having established that beliefs in supernatural worlds and rituals directed at spiritual agents are cross-culturally ubiquitous, we now turn to the cognitive underpinnings, ecological impacts, and developmental plasticity of such beliefs.

Chapter 4

What Do Gods Want?

Renowned zoologist E. O. Wilson remarked that "religions are like other human institutions in that they evolve in directions that enhance the welfare of the practitioners" (Wilson 1978: 182). As we have been arguing in the last few chapters, if this is the case, religions must have some way to flexibly respond to novel threats to the "welfare of the practitioners" and to overcome forms of doubt. This chapter details how one important component of religious systems—namely, appeals to gods' concerns—can adaptively align themselves to particular environmental conditions.

Humans are probably the only species on Earth capable of pondering the existence of "spiritual agencies," as Darwin put it (Darwin 2004 [1879]: 117). However, we do not limit our representations of these agents to their minds, bodies, or movements. We also commit ourselves to these agents, refraining from or performing a host of behaviors to appease them. These mental and behavioral commitments to supernatural agents form the core of religious systems, which in turn help solve the coordination and cooperation problems human societies ubiquitously face (Chapters 7 and 9; Alcorta and Sosis 2005; Rappaport 1999; Sosis 2009a).

This chapter focuses on three interrelated topics or questions that bear on humans' mental representations of gods: (1) the nature of our ability to attribute mental states to supernatural agents; (2) the way knowledge attributed to supernatural agents motivates behavior; and (3) why such knowledge and concomitant behaviors vary across communities in specific ways. To summarize our argument, supernatural agents vary widely in form across cultures: some are people-like, others are animal-like, and some are conceived of as bodiless forces. Yet, it is intuitive for people to think that these entities have wills, knowledge, and desires. This intuitiveness makes their existence seem plausible. As we suggest below, the knowledge and concerns attributed to gods seem to be constrained between two poles. Some supernatural agents are believed to be omniscient, but in fact these agents are primarily concerned with human moral behavior. Other agents are believed to possess limited social knowledge and are not concerned with human morality *per se*, but rather are strictly concerned with policing proper ritual performance.[1] Both forms of interest, we argue, function as impediments to various kinds of selfish behavior. Societies develop toward one or another of these poles of supernatural belief depending on their ability, constrained by ecology, to monitor the behavior of their human members.

Representing Supernatural Minds

The Mindreading System and Attributed Domains

Supernatural agent concepts are found in every human society. From gods and ghosts to ancestors and animal spirits, supernatural agent beliefs exhibit not only many essential similarities but also remarkable differences across cultures. The similarities frequently suggest pan-human cognitive biases, whereas the differences are often considered to be merely cultural byproducts of evolved cognitive mechanisms (Atran 2002; Atran and Norenzayan 2004; Boyer 2001; Kirkpatrick 2006, 2008). One such bias is the ability to explain events and rationalize behavior in terms of supernatural agents. We therefore begin with a sketch of the human attribution of mental states to other entities and objects in the world. In contrast to the dominant view in the cognitive science of religion (Boyer and Bergstrom 2008), we have argued that, in the context of religion, such attributions show evidence of functional design (Chapter 2; Sosis 2009a). Here we further develop this argument by exploring the variation in the types of knowledge attributed to supernatural minds around the world.

Detecting mental states has often been characterized as an exclusively human characteristic, although there are indications that other primates have the ability to do so as well (Call and Tomasello 2008). This ability to detect and represent mental states, as noted in Chapter 1, has come to be known as "theory of mind" or ToM (Premack and Woodruff 1978). Even though we ultimately lack direct, solid evidence of other people's minds

---

1. Note that when it comes to what gods care about, ritual and taboo are closely related. While rituals are prescribed behaviors whereas taboos are proscribed behaviors, they are both linked to particular supernatural agents and they both convey solidarity and group identity (see Chapter 9).

and their contents, we nevertheless cannot help but attribute internal motivational states to them—indeed, to nearly all animate entities. British psychologist Simon Baron-Cohen characterizes the mindreading complex as composed of subsystems that infer internal motivational states driving the observable behavior of other animate entities. One such subsystem is the intentionality detector, which "interprets motion stimuli in terms of the primitive volitional mental states of goal and desire" (Baron-Cohen 1995: 32). The intentionality detector "is activated whenever there is any perceptual input that might identify something as an agent ... This could be anything with [apparently] self-propelled motion. Thus, a person, a butterfly, a billiard ball, a cat, a cloud, a hand, or a unicorn would [activate this mechanism]" (Baron-Cohen 1995: 33; see Gelman et al. 1996). Baron-Cohen suggests that the intentionality detector's "value lies in its generality of application: it will interpret almost anything with self-propelled motion, or anything that makes a non-random sound, as a query agent with goals and desires" (Baron-Cohen 1995: 34).

Barrett and Keil (1996; Barrett 2004) argue that we have a mental mechanism, similar to Baron-Cohen's intentionality detector, which interprets objects and events in terms of agency. They refer to this mechanism, as discussed in Chapter 1, as the hyperactive agency detection device (HADD). HADD is hyperactive insofar as it attributes agency even to agent-less events and things such as rustling bushes, moving dots on a computer screen, surprising events, and, most importantly for our discussion, the gods and spirits of the world's religious traditions. HADD can of course be overridden by post hoc conscious reflection. What makes Barrett's account significant for religious cognition is that the hyperactivity of this device triggers the ToM mechanism to explain events and other phenomena in agentive terms. The subsystems of the mindreading system, including HADD or the intentionality detector, share most of the features of Fodor's conservative definition of cognitive modules (Baron-Cohen 1995: 57–58; Fodor 1983, 2000). As input-only mechanisms with operations we cannot consciously manipulate (i.e., it is difficult not to detect internal states upon seeing animate entities with the minimal features/inputs that trigger the device), our ability to attribute mental states to other things allows us to "make sense" of much of our world without noticeable effort. It is at this modular level of human cognition that we interpret our world by way of the "intentional stance" (Dennett 1971, 1987).

It is not, however, at this level of processing that we categorize *specific* mental states. In addition to detecting others' mental states, we also attribute particular domains of knowledge and feelings to other minds (Bering 2002; Bering and Shackelford 2004; Johnson 2005). What makes the human mindreading system particularly remarkable is that it works together with our learned repertoire of recognizable beliefs, desires, and perceptions, as well as our inferences about physical objects. While there is evidence suggesting that non-human primates have the ability to mentally represent others' mental states, it is uniquely human to be able to identify in others and state the differences between melancholy, boredom, vindictiveness, schadenfreude, and so forth. Our external environment provides information about our internal environments; we learn how to make distinctions between types of mental states and accredit others with identifiable concerns and understandings. As such, we can attribute very specific kinds of mental states to others that are exclusive to the human experience (e.g., she is performing calculus in her head). Moreover, we attribute particular domains of knowledge to others as well (e.g., he knows a lot about computers). Domains consist of closely related units of information. One intriguing aspect of religion is that people have even less definite evidence of the contents of supernatural agents' minds than we have of one another's, yet throughout the world people act in ways that seem to reflect strong confidence about such agents' concerns and wishes.

Spiritual Forces and Anthropomorphism

The central religious concepts of many traditions are not supernatural humans (see Guthrie 1980, 1995), but rather supernatural forces. These forces are nevertheless portrayed anthropomorphically. Vine Deloria Jr. notes that:

> The overwhelming majority of American Indian tribal religions refused to represent deity [sic] anthropomorphically. To be sure, many tribes used the term grandfather when praying to God, but there was no effort to use that concept as the basis for a theological doctrine by which a series of complex relationships and related doctrines could be developed. While there was an acknowledgment that the Great Spirit has some resemblance to the role of a grandfather in the tribal society, there was no great demand to have a "personal relationship" with the Great Spirit in the same manner as popular Christianity has emphasized personal relationships with God.
>
> (Deloria 1992: 79)

Rather,

> the most common feature of primitive awareness of the world [is] the feeling or belief that the universe is energized by a pervading power. Scholars have traditionally called the presence of this power mana, following Polynesian beliefs, but we find it among tribal peoples, particularly American Indian tribes, as wakan [Sioux], orenda [Iroquois], or manitou [Ojibwe]. Regardless of the technical term, there is general agreement that a substantial number of primitive peoples recognize the existence of a power in the universe that affects and influences them.
>
> (Deloria 1979: 152–153; see Powers 1975: 45–47)

Such forces are characterized as creative and intelligent, and are often attributed with intentionality in order to transmit ideas more effectively. From a cognitive perspective, however, it is not surprising that Christian missionaries translated such concepts regularly as a personified "god." The Sioux concept of *wakan tanka*, often translated as "sacred vastness," "big holy," or "great incomprehensibility", was "the sum of all that was considered mysterious, powerful, or sacred":

> Wakan Tanka never had birth and so could never die. The Wakan Tanka created the universe. ... Rather than a single being, Wakan Tanka embodied the totality of existence; not until Christian influences began to affect Lakota belief did Wakan Tanka become personified.
>
> (DeMallie 1987: 28)

However, it seems likely that it was not Christian influence that resulted in Native Americans talking about sacred forces as though they were anthropomorphized and/or attributed with mental states, because anthropomorphization comes naturally to humans' cognitive appraisals of supernatural concepts. Evolutionary theorists exhibit the same anthropomorphic tendencies when they talk about "selection," knowing full well that nature lacks intentionality and or discriminating "taste" for the more fit.

In animistic traditions, there are certainly supernatural agents, but not necessarily "culturally postulated *superhuman* agents" (McCauley and Lawson 2002: 8; emphasis added). In Tyva, for example, there are many mineral springs (*arzhaannar*), each of which has its own "spirit master." Indeed, all features of the natural world are believed to be animated by such agents, which take various forms. One of Purzycki's informants noted that:

Everyone prays to the *arzhaannar*. Because they are alive. All of the *arzhaan-nar* have their spirits. The spirit of Adargan Arzhaan of Sagly [a village in southwestern Tyva] is a small marmot. It appears to shamans and lamas. It protects that place. So a man should pray to it. They say there is a bird in this *arzhaan*. It also appears. We notice it in the night when it makes noise. All of these *arzhaannar* have their spirits. That is why every Tyvan prays to his *arzhaannar*, his lands. If we take, for example, Ubsa-Khol [a lake on the border between Tyva and Mongolia], its spirit is a big bull. Each place has its spirit. That is why a Tyvan prays when he is on the road, even if he can't see the spirits. It's the Tyvan people's good ritual.

(Purzycki 2010: 29–30)

In this case, the spirit masters of these various places are all represented as animal spirits that endow the features of the natural world with life. Despite these spirits' invisibility, people pray to them in recognition of the protective power they hold over their particular domains.

Spiritual Agency and "Correct" Beliefs

In his classic text *The Golden Bough*, James Frazer notes the difficulty of attributing belief in God to those he refers to as "the lower races":

If we civilised men insist on limiting the name of God to that particular conception of the divine nature which we ourselves have formed, then we must confess that the savage has no god at all. But we shall adhere more closely to the facts of history if we allow most of the higher savages at least to possess a rudimentary notion of certain supernatural beings who may fittingly be called gods, though not in the full sense in which we use the word. That rudimentary notion represents in all probability the germ out of which the civilised peoples have gradually evolved their own high conceptions of deity; and if we could trace the whole course of religious development, we might find that the chain which links our idea of the Godhead with that of the savage is one and unbroken.

(Frazer 2006 [1890]: 51)

Looking past Frazer's ethnocentric language, we find here not a dismissive denigration of "savage religion," but an argument that Europeans' "high" conceptions of the gods were simply more refined versions of the same concepts found in non-Western societies (see Chapter 3). He sees an "unbroken chain" that links the two traditions. We posit that this chain—though not by any means unilinear or unidirectional—is the attribution of mental states to agents without readily apparent bodies.

Our religious thinking can be influenced by mundane cognitive operations. Attributing agency to otherwise non-agentive things may be the best bet for an organism's fitness, because failing to detect agency when an agent is in fact nearby—for example, a predator rustling in the bushes—may mean the organism's demise (Guthrie 1980, 1993, 1995). However, as discussed above, the bulk of our agency attribution is not religious in nature. What is more, we readily talk about omnipresent, omniscient gods as though they are not much different than people. Such inconsistencies in thought are considered "theologically incorrect" (Barrett 1998, 1999; Barrett and Keil 1996) insofar as they depict the gods as though there were nothing particularly supernatural about them at all.

Theologically incorrect thinking is the output of other "best bet" computations (see Andersen 2019). As such, the distinction between theologically correct and incorrect religious ideas tells us more about the human mind (and perhaps about particular dogmas) than about the nature of religion as a universal human cognitive product. After all, we effortlessly attribute agency to material as well as immaterial objects. Statements such as "the University doesn't like it when we drink alcohol on campus" or "the government just wants your money" reflect such a tendency. Our propensity to anthropomorphize has arguably even made it possible for corporations (root: *corpus*) to have the status of a legal person, a practice which originates in Roman law (Bakan 2004). Not only do we naturally think of collections of people as single agents, but we also design laws enforcing such a conception, giving the individual members of an organization limited personal liability for its collective decisions.

What, then, distinguishes "religious" agency attribution from everyday agency attribution to other bodiless agents such as institutions? One possible answer is that, even though we may readily think in terms of their agency, we can recognize that corporations, universities, and the like are composed of individuals but lack most features of people, whereas religious concepts are not as easily unpacked. In other words, the agency of institutions is a perceived emergent property of a collection of bodies. While there is nothing particularly extraordinary, then, about construing a group of real, physical people as one metaphorical "person," there is something quite remarkable about believing in an agent that is nowhere grounded in the empirically verifiable world.

Many researchers in the cognitive science of religion characterize religious concepts as essentially "counterintuitive," putatively violating deep assumptions about essential ontological and physical categories (Box 6.1; Atran 2002; Boyer 1994a, 2001; Pyysiäinen 2004). This "minimal counterintuitiveness" (Boyer 2001) in turn is held to account for the differences between normal agency attribution and its "religious" counterpart. However, these approaches seem to be working from some flawed premises (Purzycki and Willard 2016). For instance, they assume that we do not normally attribute agency to plants or artifacts, yet in fact we explain what plants and artifacts "do" in terms of agency all the time. Consider the following statements inspired by Dennett's (1987: 59) discussion of the intentional stance:

1   My jade plants appreciate the love I give them.
2   My jade plants prefer Mozart to the Melvins.
3   My jade plants know of all the bad things you did as a child.
4   My jade plants know where the sun is.
5   This block of Wisconsin Cheddar appreciates your fine tastes.
6   The thermostat knows how warm it is in here.
7   "Lightning ... always wants to find the best way to ground, but sometimes it gets tricked into taking second-best paths" (Dennett 1987: 65).

Attributing mental states to a plant because it moves toward sunlight or grows better when it is loved (1) or "listens" to Mozart or the Melvins (2) is perfectly intuitive when explaining movement and change with a preference and interpreting two sequential events as linked by a causal force (presumably "listening" to one or the other makes the plant grow better). Attributing mental states to a stationary block of cheese (5), on the other hand, applies agency to an inanimate entity, rendering the statement counterintuitive. By contrast, the thermostat (6) is inanimate yet has perceptible effects on the world; it seemingly acts on its own (preprogrammed) accord, as does lightning (7). Attributing agency and mental states to these entities is thus more intuitive. Indeed, there might be an intuitive–counterintuitive continuum (Norenzayan et al. 2006; Purzycki and Willard 2016): while (1), (2), (3), and (4) attribute agency to plants and are therefore counterintuitive in the technical sense, (1), (2) and (4) make intuitive sense, whereas (3) does not. Why? It is the particular *domain* of knowledge attributed to the jade plant in (3) that makes the statement so striking, not the attribution of mental states to the plant. Suggesting that a plant is cognizant of all the awful things one did as a child does not necessarily violate our basic ontological intuitions; rather, it attributes a particular domain of knowledge to plants that they (or any other kind of agent) are not normally accredited with.

It is not, then, the simple attribution of agency to an agentless object that renders an idea counterintuitive (in the technical sense). Since humans are not capable of knowing everything that someone else did wrong, attributing such knowledge to plants is a violation of our expectations about the knowable (i.e., "counterschematic"; see Chapter 6; Barrett 2008a; Purzycki 2006, 2011; Purzycki and Willard 2016). Likewise, if we accredit dogs with the capacity to have such knowledge, it is a violation of our inferences about the knowable, not about animals. Granting non-agents knowledge or agency is thus not necessarily counterintuitive without qualifying the kind of agency and the domains of knowledge in question. As we discuss below, it is these attributed domains that make supernatural agents particularly salient concepts, not their disembodied or otherwise non-normal natures.

To summarize thus far, there is considerable variation in how supernatural agents are represented; some agents are conceived with bodies, others are not, and some supernatural agents are conceived with bodies in some contexts while in other contexts they are believed to be bodiless. It does not appear to be the case that counterintuitiveness or attributions of agency in general make ideas about such agents religious. What makes supernatural agents specifically religious (i.e., worth committing to) are their attributed domains of knowledge and concern. In other words, as discussed below, in contrast to other non-agents to which we attribute agency, such as institutions and fictional characters, supernatural agents possess relevant, typically hidden social knowledge and are conceived of as acting upon this knowledge. It is this knowledge and concern which informs—and is informed by—religious behavior.

Variation in Domains of Supernatural Agents' Knowledge and Concern

Omniscience with Heightened Concern: Prosocial Behavior

> Believing that there are many spirits makes more sense than believing in one god. There are a lot of rivers and mountains. How can one god watch over everything?
>
> —Anatoli Kuular, Tyva Republic (Levin and Süzükei 2006: 29)

Just as we attribute particular domains of knowledge to other humans, we do the same to our deities. While some supernatural agents know everything we do and think, others are not concerned with such matters and have limited knowledge. We can test one another's knowledge about particular domains, but we have no concrete evidence regarding the minds of supernatural agents, let alone what types of knowledge they possess. We find, however, that there are patterns in the mental contents attributed to deities. Some have argued that throughout history people have committed themselves to "the gods," rather than countless other supernatural beings (e.g., cartoon characters, leprechauns, goblins, etc.) precisely because the gods are uniquely accredited with access to valuable social information (Atran 2002; Boyer 2001; Chapter 5).

Recent evolutionary theories of religion claim that supernatural agents that evoke religious commitment and devotion are particularly concerned with certain types of social knowledge. This knowledge primarily consists of breaches of prosocial responsibilities (i.e., moral behavior). As such, commitment to supernatural agents may function to inhibit self-interested behavior, and thus in turn contribute to the evolution and persistence of human cooperation (Bering and Johnson 2005; Johnson 2016; McKay et al. 2011; Norenzayan and Shariff 2008). Populations differ both in the sets of values they maintain and importance they attribute to different types of prosocial behavior, so we would expect the concerns of supernatural agents to vary accordingly. What the gods know is an interesting question, but what they are *concerned* with is more likely to motivate us to act in socially prescribed ways. The Abrahamic god (i.e., the god of Jews, Christians, and Muslims) might not like it if you steal, for instance, but if you live in a small community where little value is held on the accumulation of personal property, then your deity may be more concerned with punishing stinginess than theft.

Boyer (2002: 75) argues that it is the perceived access of supernatural agents to socially relevant (i.e., socially strategic) information that makes them salient in our minds. Boyer makes a distinction between agents with "perfect" and "imperfect" access to such information. While there is cross-cultural variability, Boyer suggests that supernatural agents are typically granted "perfect access" to socially strategic information—a very specific domain of all conceivable knowledge. Various studies have examined the distinctions between what people are supposed to attribute to God, known as theological correctness, and how people actually think about God. Whereas people typically say that God is omniscient and omnipotent when asked about this explicitly, more subtle measures show that people tend to implicitly attribute certain human limitations to God, such as the inability to be in two places at once (Barrett 1998; Barrett and Keil 1996).

Indeed, in the response-time task (discussed below in Chapter 5), we found that individuals took a significantly longer time to respond to questions regarding God's knowledge of positive, prosocial behavior than those regarding negative, antisocial behavior. Moreover, socially insignificant knowledge (e.g., whether God knows how many pickles are in Seth's refrigerator) yielded even longer response times (Purzycki et al. 2012). Despite God's proclaimed omniscience, we seem to process God's knowledge about negative social information more quickly than other kinds of knowledge. This suggests that our minds can stray from doctrine in systematic ways (i.e., we are highly predisposed to associate supposedly omniscient gods with knowledge of moral information).

Not all supernatural agents, however, are concerned with the general moral behavior of people. For example, when religious traditions are bound to local ecologies, there is a greater stress on sacralizing particular domains that require resource management (e.g., Lansing 2006; Lansing and Kremer 1993) and defense (Sosis 2011). Supernatural agents in these traditions are acutely concerned with costly ritual behaviors directed toward themselves rather than with, say, policing people's everyday interpersonal behavior. At a glance, this suggests that there may be no pan-human cognitive bias for supernatural agents concerned with specifically prosocial behavior after all. Yet, as our experiments (see Chapter 5) suggest, we are quick to respond to omniscient agents' knowledge of moral information, even when the agents are not seen as interfering with human behavior. Moreover, cross-cultural evidence suggests that, when asked, individuals are more inclined to posit that gods of all kinds care about immoral conduct than about other kinds of behavior (Purzycki 2011b, 2013a; Purzycki et al. 2022). Culturally variable expressed beliefs, then, may conceal deeper, universal biases in reasoning. Such biases represent the universal association between morality and spiritual minds.

Box 4.1 The ongoing study of gods' minds

The study of beliefs about gods' minds and how individuals process their features has been flourishing and diversifying. The things that people claim their gods care about are certainly broader than merely "faith," "morality," or "ritual," and current research is mapping the variation that exists. Broadly put, gods appear to be *explicitly* concerned with believing in them, human morality, and ritual practice—as focused on in this chapter—but also resource preservation, etiquette, and drug use, among other things (Bendixen and Purzycki 2020; Purzycki and Baimel 2016; Purzycki and McNamara 2016; Shaver, Fraser, and Bulbulia 2016). These culturally postulated concerns are likely to co-occur with the tendency to ascribe moral concern to gods, which we discuss in the next chapter (Purzycki 2013a; Purzycki et al. 2022). Beyond this work, studies that attend to gods' minds have increased in prevalence and profile in the field. In addition to the studies assessing the cross-cultural role of the effects of morally concerned gods in adults (Lang et al. 2019; Purzycki et al. 2016b) and historical populations (Beheim et al. 2021), researchers have also examined how children conceptualize God's knowledge (Heiphetz et al. 2016), how adults process notions of omniscience (Lane et al. 2012, 2014), and how different attachment styles (Johnson et al. 2015), cross-cultural conceptions of minds (Willard and McNamara 2019), and cultural modes (McNamara and Purzycki 2020) can lead to different kinds of inferences about gods' concerns or personalities.

Imperfect Access with Acute Concern: Ritual and Other Behaviors

We nevertheless find significant variation across populations regarding the way people represent their deities' knowledge and concerns. Barrett (2002) offers several predictions regarding the relationship between the knowledge and ritual behavior of supernatural agents. If spirits, for example, have imperfect access to human affairs and "can only discern intentions based on a person's actions, then the particular action will have relatively greater importance" than a person's intentions (ibid.: 104). On the other hand, "having the right intentions" will be more important during ritual performances directed toward omniscient gods. We suggest that, cross-culturally, omniscient supernatural agents will be primarily concerned with general moral behavior, whereas supernatural agents who are limited in their social knowledge of human affairs will be conceived of as acutely concerned with the performance of ritualized acts that are costly to perform. Again, in terms of the functioning of religious systems, what spirits and gods know may not be nearly as important as what they care about (cf. Purzycki et al. 2018).

For instance, in the highly complex traditional Lakota (Sioux) religion, if one dreamt of the *Wakinyan* (lightning/Thunderbirds) or one of their associates (e.g., rabbits, barn swallows, etc.), one had been chosen by the Thunderbirds to become a *heyoka*—or sacred clown (see Plant 1994; Wallis 1996 for further discussion). Thomas Tyon noted that "the Wakinyan often command the man who dreams of them to do certain things" which are typically quite embarrassing for the initiate. If they fail to do whatever they are instructed to do by the Thunderbirds, "Wakinyan will surely kill them" by lightning strike (Walker 1991: 155–156). In sum, the Thunderbirds will present the dreamer with an embarrassing scenario that he or she must act out in public (see Chapter 3 for discussion of "sacred clowns"). In some cases, the conditions and people in the dream are also revealed, making the act quite specific. In this particular case, the supernatural agents—the Thunderbirds—are primarily concerned with whether or not the "chosen" individual carries out the act as detailed in the dream, and lives as a clown until his or her tenure is completed. Individuals fulfill the wishes of the Thunderbirds to avoid reprisals from them. In this case, then, personified concentrations of the Sioux supernatural force *wakan tanka* (discussed above) are accredited with acute concerns and knowledge about the ritual behaviors of those "chosen" to be clowns—but not about those persons' moral behaviors toward others.

In Tyva, there appears to be no consensus regarding the breadth of knowledge of local "spirit-masters," let alone what they are (e.g., dead ancestors, creations of nature, etc.). Most Tyvans suggest that spirit masters only know what happens in their areas of governance, and just a few claim they are globally omniscient (Purzycki 2012). However, there is virtual unanimity when it comes to the question of what spirits *care* about. When freely listing things that please or anger spirit-masters, Tyvans typically claim that these spirits are concerned with ritual practices and maintaining the natural resources over which they lord (Purzycki 2010, 2011, 2013). One pays respects to (i.e., "feeds") spirit masters by making offerings of food, money, and/or tobacco, as well as by tying a prayer ribbon to the place where they are honored.

In both the Sioux and Tyvan cases, we see the attribution of agency to vague and often inconsistently conceived bodies. A Thunderbird is often described as "shapeless, but He has wings with four joints each; He has no feet, yet He has huge talons; He has no head, yet has a huge beak with rows of teeth in it" (Walker 1917, cited in Brown 1989 [1953]: 39). The spirit masters in Tyva will frequently manifest themselves in various, often shifting, physical forms. The Abrahamic god is often conceived of as being everywhere, but is attributed a body, not only in present day thinking (Barrett and Keil 1996), but in sacred scriptures as well (e.g., Exodus 33:18-20).

Conceptualizations of these supernatural agents are particular to their respective traditions. Each tradition, however, delimits the range of worldly affairs that these entities are particularly concerned about. Such specific, culturally contingent domains of concern are not essential components of our basic ontological categories, nor can they be produced by innate modules. When we entertain the concept of God, Thunderbirds, or spirit masters, our theory of mind encourages us to attribute a mind to these entities. God concepts and the anthropomorphic spirit masters may violate default expectations about people, and the Thunderbirds and animal spirit masters may violate default expectations about animals. Experimental studies suggest that these violations make such concepts easier to remember than intuitive ideas (Boyer 2000; Boyer and Ramble 2001). However, these supernatural agents vary considerably in their forms, concerns, and abilities. This variance represents differences in our cognitive models or schemas of our particular deities (for further discussion of the distinction between templates and schemas in the context of understanding religious concepts, see Chapter 6; Barrett 2008a; Purzycki 2011a; Purzycki and Willard 2016). So where and why do we find these divergences between what supernatural agents care about?

Emphases on Faith, Practice, and Social Complexity

In the previous chapter, we argued that religious belief and doubt are evident in all societies. Despite the inherently individual nature of belief and doubt, the general contents of religious beliefs are typically largely shared between an individual and his or her community. Thus, even a doubter doubts the specific beliefs of his or her own society, not those of another. As we discuss in more detail in Chapter 7, this perceived sharedness has mediating effects on judgment and compliance (Zou et al. 2009), and it also affects behavior toward in-groups (Purzycki and Lang 2019) and out-groups (Sechrist and Stangor 2001, 2007). However, more specific interpretations or details of religious beliefs may vary, sometimes widely, between individuals within the same group (Rappaport 1999). This inconsistency in beliefs (heterodoxy) may be offset by an emphasis on consistency in behavior (orthopraxy). Recall from the previous chapter anthropologist James Fernandez's (1965) crucial distinction between what he calls social and cultural consensus. Social consensus is an emphasis on the shared "agreement to orient action towards one another":

> This acceptance and agreement involve the acceptance of a certain set of signals and signs which give direction and orientation to this interaction permitting the coordination and co-existence of the various participants. A good example of social consensus is found in ritual action.
>
> (Fernandez 1965: 913)

Cultural consensus, on the other hand, is an emphasis on shared beliefs or the measurable degree to which individuals share cognitive models (Romney et al. 1986), such as their shared conceptions of what concerns the gods.

In general, most societies seem to value social consensus more highly than cultural consensus. For instance, in his analysis of the Fang of Central Africa, Fernandez (1965) observed very little cultural consensus regarding the claimed function of their religious rituals. In fact, among his informants he found "a feeling that too great a concern with [cultural consensus] might actually interfere with social consensus—the readiness to orient actions toward one another and engage in ritual activity" (Fernandez 1965: 914). A similar preference for ritual consistency over identical beliefs has been observed in American Jews in comparison to Protestants (Cohen 2002; Cohen et al. 2003). Nevertheless, ritual actions and the communities they support are less likely to endure without appeals to spiritual agents, even in small-scale contexts (Sosis and Bressler 2003). The reason for this keystone-like role for supernatural agents in ritual systems may be their particular concerns and knowledge of socially salient information.

We suggest that two primary domains of behavior that supernatural agents are concerned about—general moral behavior and ritually prescribed behavior—correlate with emphasis on cultural versus social consensus respectively. These polarities may also correlate with group size. Human communities are vulnerable to individuals who may exploit others for personal gain. If some members of a group shirk their duties, yet reap the benefits of others' work, the community may ultimately become overrun by exploiters. Costly religious rituals linked to gods who care about general moral behavior—generosity, honesty, respect for property, and so forth—may filter out free riders, increasing the overall quality of cooperation within the group (Alcorta and Sosis 2005; Bulbulia 2004a, 2009; Bulbulia and Sosis 2011; Henrich 2009; Sosis 2003, 2005a; Sosis and Alcorta 2003; Sosis and Bressler 2003). Accordingly, it has been shown that religious communities are able to maintain larger stable group sizes than their secular counterparts (Dunbar and Sosis 2018).

Thus, although not without serious problems (Beheim et al. 2021; Chapter 3), the common view is that social complexity and the probability of having a god that cares about morality are positively correlated. Stark (2001) demonstrates that moralizing gods are found primarily among large societies with higher degrees of economic specialization (i.e., sedentary agricultural societies). The more complex a society is, the more likely a population is to worship a high, moralizing creator deity (Johnson 2016; Lahti 2009; Rappaport 1999; Sanderson 2008b; Swanson 1960; Wallace 1966). As group size increases and occupations become more specialized, religion also becomes more diversified, institutional, compartmentalized, and doctrinal (Boyer 2001; Whitehouse 2004). While there is variation in religious thought and practice in non-state societies, there are fewer competing traditions than in state-level societies. As the size of a population grows, social accountability is impaired, and thus the form of a population's religion must change to counter the problems of religious diversity, anonymity, and accountability. It becomes more taxing for communities in larger populations to monitor commitment. Someone may reap the benefits of group cooperation, and when threatened with sanctions for not reciprocating, he or she may simply seek opportunities elsewhere. Yet badges of religious affiliation can be reliable signals of trustworthiness to individuals, even though members might not know each other, or may not even be of the same tradition (McCullough et al. 2016; Sosis 2005a). Omniscient deity concepts are probably attempts to curb such problems of social complexity. Indeed, recent results suggest that the more individuals claim gods know, the more likely they are to play fairly towards geographically distant individuals (Purzycki et al. 2018), a stronger effect than even their beliefs in the supernatural punishment of the same gods. Hence, emphasis on cultural consensus at the expense of social consensus probably emerges in contexts where religious traditions are:

- intertwined with imperial expansion;
- not an ethnically based religion;
- not rooted in a specific ecological area; and/or
- in competition with one or more dominant traditions.

Conclusion

This chapter began with a description of the pan-human ability to attribute mental states to all sorts of entities, including gods, ghosts, and spirits. There is abundant variation in the kinds of supernatural agents humans believe in, but limited variation in the types of knowledge attributed to them. The knowledge and concern attributed to supernatural agents seem to vary across two domains: moral actions and ritual actions. Any evolutionary account of religion must be able to explain the considerable cross-cultural variation in religious expression and belief. While religious systems can become maladaptive (e.g., suicide cults, exclusive reliance on faith healing, etc.), their capacity to overcome problems of defection will generally sustain adaptive variation (see Chapter 9). Ecological variation in the feasibility and reliability of monitoring the behavior of other group members will influence the concerns of a community's supernatural agents. The concerns of supernatural agents, whether moral, ritual, or both, will be systematically associated with other elements that comprise the religious system, including the importance of faith, practice, ethnicity, proselytization, and ecology. Given particular constraints, the religious system will respond to diverse socio-ecological conditions and generally adapt to ensure group cohesion and prosocial behavior.

While the contents of appeals to gods vary cross-culturally, at the heart of their conception is the fact that the gods are agents. They are therefore very likely to have intuitive properties associated with agency cognition. In other words, despite localized kinds of concerns, people may nevertheless think about divine minds like they think about other minds. One important dimension of agency cognition is its association with morality and moral domains (Boyer 2001). We now turn to this deep relationship in a discussion of experiments we conducted that predicted and found a particular efficiency when processing omniscient minds' access to specifically moral information.

Chapter 5

What Do Gods Know?

People often think of the Abrahamic god as having an infinite mind, that is, God is omniscient. But gods are not the only entities to which we attribute omniscience. For example, readers of George Orwell's *Nineteen Eighty-Four* (2003 [1949]) typically attribute omniscience to the creepy government, led by Big Brother, that monitors even mundane activities like brushing one's teeth.

However, even if we claim that God or Big Brother "know everything," omniscience might not be all that salient when we actually think about such entities. Certain kinds of information about supernatural agents might be more cognitively accessible than information about their omniscience. Thus, despite declarations to the contrary, people who believe that God is all-knowing may not reason in ways that are consistent with such beliefs. The study we discuss here (Purzycki et al. 2012) explored these potential inconsistencies.

As discussed in the previous chapter, scholars have long recognized our curious propensity to talk and think as though many things, including even inanimate objects, have intentions, personalities, and perceptions (Dennett 1987; Guthrie 1995). From machines (e.g., "my car doesn't want to run today") and human organizations (e.g., "the government is watching you!") to features of the natural world (e.g., "this storm wants me to turn the car around"), humans undoubtedly excel at detecting minds even where they are not present. Cognitive scientists have proposed a variety of cognitive devices (e.g., theory of mind, hyper-sensitive agency detection, etc.) that may be responsible for detecting other minds—even when those minds that do not necessarily exist (Chapter 1; Baron-Cohen 1995; Barrett and Keil 1996; Guthrie 1980). Such devices, researchers argue, make thinking about other real minds possible, but these devices also probably help us reason about and detect supernatural minds. In other words, our ability to think about other minds makes it possible—and perhaps even easier—to believe in gods. Indeed, many recent studies have shown that the more difficulty people have with thinking about others' minds, the less likely they are to be religious (Norenzayan, Gervais, and Trzesniewski 2012; Willard and Norenzayan 2013; cf. Reddish, Tok, and Kundt 2016; Visuri 2020). This suggests that the cognitive systems responsible for mentalizing are an essential component of religious thought, which makes some sense in at least two ways.

First, people appear to focus on gods' minds in religious discourse (Boyer 2001). Central to religious systems around the world are beliefs about gods, ghosts, and other spirits. Also important are the contents of these supernatural agents' minds—their knowledge, desires, likes, and dislikes. Throughout the world people claim that their gods desire the particular rituals they perform and abhor the foods from which they abstain. People burn incense and pray to gods because they think the gods can hear them and maybe even smell the incense. In sum, people frequently mentalize when they engage with their gods (see Schjoedt et al. 2009).

Second, cognitive systems for detecting other minds may be linked to cognitive systems for regulating our social behavior, and religion undoubtedly affects our social behavior (e.g., Lang et al. 2019; Purzycki et al. 2016b; Sosis and Ruffle 2003). The cognitive link between detecting agency and social regulation should seem quite intuitive. People may have evolved the ability to mentalize because doing so made navigating social environments easier; our ancestors who could accurately anticipate and predict others' behavior probably had a distinct advantage over those who could only respond reactively (after the fact) to others (Baron-Cohen 1995). There may therefore be deep cognitive links between mentalizing systems and what might be called "moral cognition," or mental systems that regulate our social behavior. One may trigger the other. If we anticipate negative social consequences for doing something nasty to someone else—maybe our victim will directly retaliate, or his extended family might refuse to aid us in the future—we might reconsider engaging in such behavior. This ability to carefully regulate our decisions and behavior with reference to potential social consequences is central to what we usually consider moral cognition. Indeed, these two systems—detecting agency and social regulation—may have co-evolved (Gray, Gray, and Wegner 2007; Gray, Young, and Waytz 2012).

Yet it is one thing to say that your real, flesh-and-blood mother wants you to share with your brothers, and another to say that an invisible god is watching your behavior and cares about what you do. Mothers are often concerned with making sure we are kind to others—nothing surprising there. And, as children, we can generally see and touch our mothers. Gods are much different; believing that some entity without a clearly defined body is paying attention to us is, as far as we know, unique to our species. That a non-obviously-existing entity knows what you are up to and cares about your actions is remarkable. Even in the case of a government "watching you," we can at least point to some individuals and/or machines doing the work of monitoring us. Pointing to the presence of a god is not so straightforward, and when people do "point" to gods, they use different criteria to argue for their existence than they would if they were arguing for the existence of their mothers or governments (e.g., Luhrmann 2012). Yet all around the world, people claim that their gods care about what they do. As we asked in the previous chapter, what specific actions do gods around the world care about?

In normal human conversation, people express the belief that gods are concerned about human morality, ritual, environmental preservation, and etiquette (J. Barrett 2008b; Boyer 2001; Purzycki and McNamara 2016). Why gods' interests are generally limited to these areas is not well understood (cf. Bendixen and Purzycki 2020). One way forward is to assess what functions religions might serve (Chapter 2). Many researchers consider religion to be something that helps us make sense of the world, brings us comfort, and gives us meaning in life (Barber 2011; Inzlicht, Tullett, and Good 2011). It may. But evolutionary researchers also seek to assess whether or not—and if so, how—religion serves functions related to human fitness, particularly survival and reproduction (Bulbulia et al. 2008; Shaver et al. 2019, 2020; Sosis and Bulbulia 2011). According to this view, on which we elaborate more in Chapter 8, religions operate as behavioral frameworks or niches that solve the challenges of social living.

One important challenge that people everywhere face is building and maintaining stable cooperative relationships. In small-scale communities, the context in which most of our evolutionary history has occurred, people are remarkably interdependent, and they rely on reciprocal relationships to help them when in need. In such communities, if you are a chronic rule-breaker and fail to engage in cooperative behavior, you might be ostracized or suffer other punishments as a consequence. Thus, some researchers have suggested that natural selection may have favored strong cognitive connections between gods and social regulation, because these connections would have contributed to cooperation that aided survivorship and reproduction. Accordingly, gods function as ways to help us avoid very real punishment; religion reduces the costs involved in secular punishment (such as ostracizing or expelling rule-breakers, which can be a messy process) precisely because gods get us to behave. We posited that a deep connection between agency and moral cognition would be more likely to prevent such costs, where agency detection alone might not suffice. This prediction is an extrapolation of what has become known as the supernatural punishment or supernatural monitoring hypothesis (Atkinson and Bourrat 2011; Johnson 2005, 2016; Lang et al. 2019; Norenzayan 2013; Purzycki et al. 2016b; Schloss and Murray 2011). To assess the idea of a deep link between agency and moral cognition, we examined how intuitive it is for people to associate gods and god-like beings with knowledge of specifically moral information.

Hypotheses

Is there a cognitive link between moral information and thinking about other minds? If so, it should be evident in how quickly and easily we respond to questions about the moral knowledge that others possess. If our reasoning about gods' minds taps into moral cognition, we should find it easier to cognitively process information that explicitly links these two. In other words, people should be better prepared to answer "Does God know that Benjamin hurts people?" than "Does God know that Richard likes curry?" even though those people might believe that God knows the answers to both of these questions.

We designed our study to determine whether or not people could rapidly process certain classes of information about God's and other agents' knowledge. Even though people might think God knows everything, they should respond more quickly to questions about God's knowledge of moral information than trivial, non-social information if they strongly associate God with moral behavior. Moreover, we suspected that negative social information would be especially accessible. In other words, negative social information would have a particularly close relationship with what God knows, since people often assume that God can punish the violation of social norms.

We also predicted that, if our minds process God's knowledge this way, we are likely to similarly process an omniscient government's knowledge. For instance, while putting up cameras everywhere or monitoring phone calls might mean collecting a lot of mundane data, such practices are designed and rationalized to catch and prevent criminality. Whether such devices work is an important question, but not one addressed by our study. Rather, we examined how rapidly our minds process the relationship between moral information and omniscient beings. So gods and nosy governments might be designed to trigger our moral cognition, but what about an omniscient agent that does not interact with people or care about their behavior? We predicted that there should be no real differences in processing such an agent's knowledge across moral and nonmoral information. In other words, an apathetic omniscient being should not intuitively have better access to moral information.

Methodology

We conducted four experiments among four different samples of student participants. Participants sat at computers and answered a host of questions. The experimental questions asked about three types of information concerning people: nonmoral information, information about immoral behavior, and information about good or moral behaviors. We also included distractor questions[1] to ensure that participants were following instructions. To make sure they were the same length (i.e., shorter questions might elicit quicker responses), target questions all had ten syllables, and there were ten questions for each category.

Examples of "nonmoral" questions are *Does _____ know how fast Joey's heart beats?* or *Does _____ know how many freckles Sharon has?* Questions involving "immoral behavior" were questions like *Does _____ know that Jane has stolen a car?* and *Does _____ know that Jen lied to her mother?* Examples of "good or moral behavior" questions are *Does _____ know that Ann gives to the homeless?* or *Does _____ know that Sam always helps his friends?*

---

1. Because it was technically possible to just press a single button all the time (or answer in a patterned fashion), we included the distractor questions to test whether or not people were actually paying attention and to make sure that all questions had "no" responses. The distractor questions ranged from trivia you would hear in a pub quiz to bizarre questions that were difficult to understand. Our distractor questions took participants a lot longer to answer, which gave us confidence that participants were paying attention to all the questions in the experiments.

Purzycki recorded himself asking these questions and trimmed each sound file to ensure that they were of similar length. To be more certain that recording lengths were not likely to affect response time, we statistically analyzed all recording lengths to ensure they were the same length on average, which was confirmed. We then uploaded these files onto a program that randomly played questions and awaited a response. We encouraged participants to answer each question as quickly as they could, and they did so by pressing one button for "yes" and another for "no." As participants answered questions, the computer recorded in milliseconds how long it took them to respond.

Participants in the experiments answered questions about either God, Santa Claus, a fictitious surveillance government called "NewLand" (a bit like George Orwell's surveillance government), or a fictitious (as far as we know) omniscient alien species we called "The Ark."[2] God and Santa Claus are similar insofar as they are supernatural beings. NewLand is an omniscient government system without any special powers beyond punishing the bad and rewarding the good. NewLand has cameras everywhere and records what its citizens do. The Ark are an alien species (i.e., not really "supernatural" per se) that observe everything on Earth "down to the tiniest of details." However, we described them as completely non-interfering. In other words, while they may know everything that transpires on our planet, they never do anything about what happens here. NewLand and The Ark are "natural" insofar as they are not spiritual or spirit-like beings with supernatural powers.

Analyses and Results

Our analyses consisted of a variety of statistical tests to see whether or not response times were in fact different across category types. We were not really interested in the absolute response times to questions; it didn't matter that it took someone on average 1000 milliseconds longer to answer some questions than others. Rather, we were interested in the

---

2. While one of our reviewers worried that it's a bit too much like "Noah's ark" or the "Ark of the Covenant" and therefore may make people think about religion, we used it simply because an "ark" is a big boat and was the name of a ship in a science fiction television series in the 1970s. One way to check our results is to replicate our study and extend it by comparing the "Ark" with the same kind of alien species with a different name.

magnitude of differences. One standard way to transform data to capture this question is to take the natural logarithm[3] of a given value. So, we log-transformed the response times.[4]

Figure 5.1 shows a bar plot of these log-transformed average response times by experiment and question type, with 95 percent confidence intervals for those average speeds. In each experiment, participants responded significantly more quickly to moral questions than they did to nonmoral questions.

What is striking about these results is that response times for the God and NewLand experiments were quite close to each other; people were quickest to respond to the questions about immoral behavior, followed by the positive moral behavior questions. They responded more slowly to nonmoral questions about people. In other words, participants appear to process omniscient gods and governments in very much the same way. Responses to Santa's knowledge were also curious. We might say that Santa has better access to moral information than the average person, but just how omniscient participants think him to be is not quite clear. We found that participants answered 60 percent of the questions about Santa's knowledge of nonmoral information with a "no." However, there were no significant differences in response times between those who answered "yes" or "no" for these questions. Moreover, the response times to the "naughty" and "nice" questions were similar, but both were in stark contrast to the relative lethargy in answering the nonmoral questions.

---

3. Logarithms are ways to find out how many times you need to multiply a certain number by itself to get another number. Logarithms have various bases. So, the "base 10" logarithm of 100 is 2, because there are two 10s on the left-hand side of the equation ($10 \times 10 = 100$). So, $\log_{10}(100) = 2$, $\log_{10}(1000) = 3$, $\log_{10}(10,000) = 4$, and so on. Each time we add a zero to the target number, the answer increases by 1. Think of this like a rate of increase. We used the natural logarithm, which uses "Euler's number," a value of around 2.72 (often looks like $\log_e$ or "ln" for "*logarithmus naturali*"). In our study, if someone took 6,232 milliseconds to answer a question, this transformation converts it into 8.74 ($\log_e(6,232) \approx 8.72$). If they took 1000 milliseconds, the number becomes around 6.91. This condenses values to more manageable units (and makes graphs easier to understand). Transformations like this are very common. As long as every value gets transformed the same way and transformed data are not confused with the raw data, such transformations can help interpret results.

4. Note that participants could technically answer before the recordings of the questions were finished playing. The program we used would therefore create negative response speed values. There are no natural logarithms to negative numbers, so we added 1000 milliseconds to each response time and log-transformed those values.

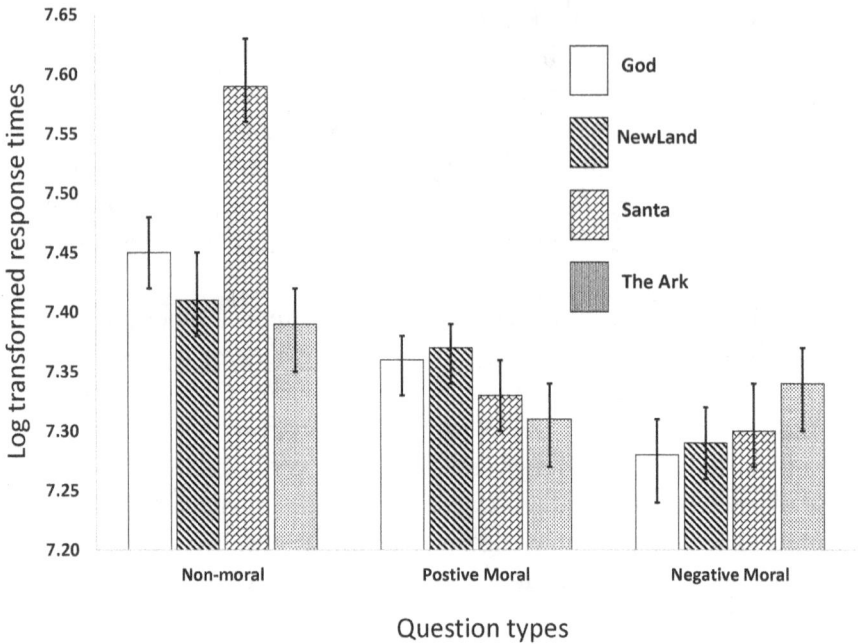

Figure 5.1 Bar plot with 95 percent confidence intervals for the mean log-transformed response time by question type across experiments. Notice the general trend of shorter response times in the negative moral questions.

Finally, even in the case of omniscient but noninterfering aliens, participants took more time to answer nonmoral than moral questions.

We ran further analyses to assess whether or not the familiarity of the agent (God, Santa, etc.) had any effect on overall response times. In other words, maybe participants were slower to answer questions about the Ark and NewLand because they had never heard of them before. We did not find this. We then assessed which specific features of these agents—supernaturalness and/or ability to punish—accounted for the results. We found that subjects gave slower responses to nonmoral questions when agents were both supernatural *and* able to punish. Overall, supernaturalness and punishment ability did not appear to alter the speed of responding to the positive moral questions, but they did appear to quicken responses to the negative moral questions. In other words, supernatural agents are predictably more associated with information about immoral behaviors. From a cognitive perspective, this might mean that pools of negative social information are particularly accessible when people reason about the minds of omniscient beings. So even when people affirm God's goodness or wax poetic about how well-versed God is in the number of hairs on a camel's back, quite possibly lurking beneath the surface is the unconscious conviction that what God *really* cares about is the kinds of things we don't want other people doing to us.

Discussion

As with any study, ours had blind spots and limitations. One methodological challenge was that our items were long by comparison to standard psychological response-time studies. Many researchers assessing implicit psychological biases use an instrument called an "implicit association task," which asks participants to match certain single words with others to form pairs (Greenwald, McGhee, and Schwartz 1998). In our study, participants answered relatively longer questions. Even though we found time differences in responses, we cannot be completely confident that we were in fact measuring the time people took to reason about these agents' knowledge.

One major limitation with the study sample was that it was drawn exclusively from university students in the United States. Of course, American university students are not a representative sample of the rest of the world (Sears 1986). Importantly, people do not obviously hold that all deities around the world are concerned with moral behavior (i.e., how we treat each other). Many are thought to be primarily interested in ritual, environmental preservation, or taboos (Bendixen and Purzycki 2020; Purzycki and McNamara 2016; Chapter 4). Would we find similar results among people whose deities are concerned with these other matters?

Some research suggests this might be the case. Purzycki followed up on this study at his field site in the Tyva Republic in southern Siberia. He found that when Tyvan respondents were asked to freely list what local spirits cared about, they predominantly claimed that the spirits cared more about ritual and resource management than about morality (Purzycki 2016). However, when Purzycki directly asked respondents whether or not these spirits knew and cared about specific topics—essentially forcing them to think about topics they would not have listed on their own—they were more likely to say that the spirits cared about morality-related topics than about non-moral topics (Purzycki 2013a). A similar, more recent study shows consistently affirmative responses to questions about whether gods care about moralistic punishment across 15 societies of various sizes and geographic regions (Purzycki 2022; Purzycki et al. 2022). While these studies did not measure response times, the results do suggest that humans subtly associate supernatural agents with moral information—even when these agents are not obviously or explicitly expected to care about moral behavior according to local doctrine.

This finding again raises the question of the source of this bias (see Gray, Gray, and Wegner 2007; Gray, Young, and Waytz 2012). Is it simply because gods and spirits have agency that people are quick to associate them with moral information? In other words, do we just default to associating gods with moral concern simply because we think gods have minds, even when there is not a cultural expectation to do so? As we mentioned earlier, people attribute agency to all sorts of things. But do we subtly associate moral domains with anthropomorphized cars, the weather, and other things? Or do gods' alleged interests in our lives specifically trigger moral cognition? Experimental research is useful for teasing apart these complicated and often overlapping riddles.

Another way to address the source of this bias would be to assess how it develops throughout the course of an individual's life and the factors involved in its development. Exposure to consistent associations between God and morality probably help build a close conceptual relationship between moral and religious cognition. However, as mentioned above, it may go deeper than that; if our ability to reason about other minds co-evolved with moral cognition, we may be prepared to create the association between morality and other minds quite early, even in cultural contexts where people do not explicitly talk about their gods as concerned with moral behavior.

Moreover, if gods subtly trigger moral cognition—even when people don't explicitly think of them as caring about morality—why aren't they all simply concerned with how we treat each other? Decades of research reveal a link between morally concerned deities and various aspects of our social and natural environments. These studies suggest that some beliefs and practices function in ways that resolve social problems that develop as a result of our interaction with the natural world. Gods that explicitly care about morality appear to pop up predominantly in societies with relatively large populations (Johnson 2005; Stark 2001; Wallace 1966), societies suffering from water scarcity (Snarey 1996), and herding societies where people vie for land (Roes and Raymond 2003). While important, all of these studies rely upon cross-cultural or cross-national data that were not necessarily collected to answer such questions. Perhaps now more than ever is a good time to investigate such questions ethnographically by asking living people about what they think. Observing actual people's behavior in natural settings will inevitably shed light on these and other important questions about why gods matter so much in people's lives. Moreover, doing such work systematically would allow researchers to see how much variation and sharedness matter in religious traditions. The next chapter hones in on this particular aspect of religious systems.

Chapter 6

The Context of Supernatural Minds

Scholars have devoted a significant amount of attention to the question of whether or not religion is adaptive (Bulbulia et al. 2008; Pyysiäinen and Hauser 2010; Sosis 2009a). Many evolutionary explanations claim that religious concepts in particular are byproducts of psychological mechanisms that evolved for other functions (Atran 2002; Boyer 2001). Such a view has since entered popular scientific portrayals of religion as well (Dawkins 2006; Dennett 2006). Research that focuses on the structure of supernatural agent concepts (e.g., Beebe and Duffy 2020; Boyer and Ramble 2001; Swan and Halberstadt 2019) still has yet to examine how these concepts fit into local, real-world religious systems (cf. Purzycki 2013b) and whether or not such systems elicit adaptive responses for their adherents.

Answering the question of the adaptiveness of any trait, however, relies on an understanding of the context in which the trait reputedly provides a selective advantage for the individuals who bear it (Chapter 8). Claiming that the porous nature of blood cell membranes is adaptive, for example, is inadequate without addressing the internal requirements and constraints of the cell and the external context in which the cell exists. Similarly, examining the adaptiveness of the circulatory system without addressing the internal requirements of the organisms that possess it would be unthinkable among contemporary biologists. We hold the same of religion.

Throughout this volume, we have embraced this view with respect to religious systems, positing that it consists of complex interrelations between necessary components that ultimately function by and large to provide benefits for individuals. In this chapter, we focus primarily on the interrelationship between the structure, sharedness, and social contexts of supernatural agent concepts. Sharedness—the recognition of engaging in the same practices and entertaining the same beliefs—emerges from costly rituals and taboos that are motivated by socially accepted, expected, and articulated rationalizations (i.e., beliefs). Moreover, the social environment delimits the range in which these rituals and taboos are collectively deemed appropriate. The present chapter attempts to account for religious variation with particular reference to evolved minds and the necessity of entertaining religious concepts. We situate supernatural concepts and their underlying structures in socioecological contexts and argue that beliefs in these concepts are not merely byproducts of evolved minds, but are necessary constituents of religion's adaptive functioning. Specifically, such concepts are regularly invoked as a means to communicate sharedness with others. This sharedness facilitates intragroup coordination and cooperative endeavors that affect survivorship and reproduction (Alcorta and Sosis 2005; Bulbulia 2004a; Irons 2001; Norenzayan and Shariff 2008; Sosis 2003; Sosis and Alcorta 2003).

The Internal Context of Religious Beliefs

Mental Organs

While the modular structure of the human mind is often stressed as an important factor in religious evolution, there is little consistency in different scholars' concepts of cognitive modules (see Anderson 2007; Barrett and Kurzban 2006; Chomsky 1980; Fodor 1983, 1998, 2000, 2005; Pinker 2005a, 2005b) or our basic, evolved ontological domains (see Atran 1989, 2002: 96; Boyer 1994a, 1994b, 2001; Keil 1989; Sperber 1985, 1996: 131; see especially Pyysiäinen 2004: 39–52 for detailed accounting of these inconsistencies).

For example, as hinted at in Chapter 4, some approaches assume a set of basic, innate ontological categories: people, animals, plants, and artifacts. These models suggest that our minds are equipped with templates that consist of inferences about various entities in the world. For example, people and animals have mental states, animals have an essential and immutable species membership, plants are immobile, and artifacts have an essential function (Boyer 1996, 2001; Boyer and Ramble 2001; Keil 1989). The primary utility of these templates is that they provide us with predictions about objects in the world with little, if any, explicit instruction.

Cognitive scientists of religion maintain that these templates provide the foundation for the development of religious concepts. Religious ideas, it is argued, consist of either a violation of default expectations (e.g., a plant that levitates) or the application of an assumption from one template to that of an object in another domain (e.g., a plant that thinks). When we hear such ideas, known as "minimally counterintuitive concepts" (MCIs), they arouse our interest because they allegedly violate some of our most basic assumptions about how the world works. Boyer and Ramble (2001) demonstrated that such domain-level violations are recalled at a significantly better rate than intuitive concepts (such as "spruce tree that requires sunlight and water to grow"). This suggests that these violations enhance memorability. However, statements with too many violations ("maximally counterintuitive" statements) are not retained as well as MCIs (Norenzayan et al. 2006). While there are many problems with this paradigm (Box 6.1; Bendixen and Purzycki 2021; Purzycki and Willard 2016), one limitation stands out as important for our immediate purposes, namely, that MCI theory fails to account for intra- or inter-cultural variation in religious concepts. Cognitively, this variation is best represented by informational schemas, not deeper faculties.

Schemas, like templates, are informational structures that shape, reflect, and inform perception, but they are more specific in content and flexible than templates precisely because they are not innate. Schemas are often socially constructed categories that allow us to navigate diverse socioecological environments. We have schemas for "favorite movies" just as we might have schemas for "surrealist painters" and "unanswerable questions." Schemas are quite flexible and often in flux (see Bechtel and Abrahamsen 2002: 15; Brewer 2000; D'Andrade 1995: 142; Strauss and Quinn 1997: 48–84). As such, they change and allow individuals to acclimate to new environments, connect new conceptual structures to extant schemas, and readily create novel associations. While we have a PLANT template, we also have a "willow tree" schema, for instance. Because willow trees are categorized as plants and species membership is immutable, we know that when willow trees move, it is because of something external rather than internal. Such inference-making is systematic, predictable, probably statistically universal, and made possible by virtue of our templates. However, because we also possess schemas, we further recognize that willow trees have long tendril-like branches, typically grow in sandy soils, and can grow to great heights—traits they do not share with all other members of the innate category plant. Such concepts require observation and experience.

The concept of a "fluorescent pink willow tree," then, violates only our willow tree schema, and not obviously the plant template. While such counterschematic notions (Barrett 2008a; Purzycki 2006, 2011) may be the stuff of fables (e.g., giant people and beanstalks), very seldom do they form beliefs worthy of our devotion and rarely are they used to rationalize religious behaviors. Indeed, MCI theory posits that counterschematic notions—such as a "river of chocolate," for example—are unlikely to become religious concepts precisely *because* they are merely counterschematic (i.e., they are in principle empirically verifiable). On the other hand, the notion of a "river that listens to people" might be a potential religious concept according to MCI theory, since it transfers agency to a feature of the natural environment and so violates deep categorical or ontological assumptions. The notion of a "river that knows your future," however, ostensibly has an ontological violation *and* violates our schema of "accessible knowledge." In contradistinction to MCI theory, we suggest that the latter—schema violation—is often more pivotal for the religious valence of a concept than ontological violations are. For instance, sects or denominations of the same religious tradition often maintain their distinctiveness through schematic differences, such as the power of saints (Catholics vs. Protestants) or whether or not the hadith are divinely inspired (Sunni vs. Shia).

Moreover, successful religious concepts might be intriguing to potential believers because they challenge deep assumptions about objects in the world, but successful religious concepts are also emotionally salient. Ghost concepts are not scary because minds without corporeal bodies violate the person template; they are scary because of their harmful intentions. The ghost's violation of the person category grabs our attention, but the emotional response effectively serves to provide an automatic judgment about the stimulus (e.g., if afraid, then avoid; see Frank 1988). Counterontological and counterschematic concepts that elicit emotional responses are, then, the best candidates for religious concepts. Emotion-triggering MCIs are not only easier to retain, but they also motivate others to take the initiative to transmit them (see Bell and Sternberg 2001; Heath et al. 2001). In a series of experiments, Nairne et al. (2009) found that subjects had better recall of words when treatments were framed as fitness-relevant (e.g., hunting, gathering) than when framed as fitness-irrelevant. These results suggest that transmitting emotion-triggering religious concepts (e.g., the spirits know if you are honest) that are framed in terms of fitness effects (e.g., you will be punished if you are dishonest) may be maximally retainable. It is the transmission of these concepts that alters the nature of individuals' interactions with each other (see Purzycki and Willard 2016 for a more thorough review). Simply put, by virtue of their strangeness and association with emotion-triggering content, religious ideas are more

---

Box 6.1 Counterintuitiveness and MCI theory

Compared to typical, mundane notions, religious concepts are no doubt strange. Some versions of MCI theory posit that these concepts' strangeness has a particular form, namely, that they violate default inferences that are—for all intents and purposes—innate or naturally formed very early in life with little direct tutelage, hence "counterontological." Methodologically, however, most MCI studies simply create lists of statements that researchers presuppose are MCI items. Any memory advantage of those concepts lends support to the theory, despite not actually knowing whether it is an innate ontological template or an acquired schema that has been violated in each instance. In other words, the concepts used in most MCI research might violate habituated associations, but not necessarily default inferences. Many memory studies (e.g., Beebe and Duffy 2020; Porubanova and Shaver 2017; Purzycki 2006) add various additional components to the kinds of concepts participants are supposed to remember (e.g., humor, disgust, fitness relevance, etc.). These studies tend to find that emotional content drives retention, yet determining whether or not "MCI" is a useful construct remains a deeper, unresolved issue. Purzycki (2013) analyzed Tyvan folktales and freely listed spirits and found very little explicit evidence of concepts that resembled MCI concepts. Instead, Tyvan folk and religious concepts very clearly consist of *schematic* violations (e.g., a girl with deer antlers or a fish-scaled bull). In short, we've grown increasingly skeptical of MCI theory's utility to either characterize religious concepts or account for their distributions (Bendixen and Purzycki 2021; Purzycki and Willard 2016). In fact, many scholars are now (re)turning to examining the importance of schemas and cultural variation (see Chapter 10).

---

interesting than mundane ideas. In addition to finding them "catchier," however, people also *use* religious concepts.

Types of Religious Concept

Sperber (1997) and Barrett (2004) distinguish between *reflective* and *nonreflective* beliefs. *Reflective* beliefs are those generated by way of conscious weight assignment and distribution, debate, and deliberation. *Nonreflective* beliefs are those generated by our deeper mental faculties with little reflection. Barrett discusses these distinctions in light of religious thought: "God exists as three persons" is an example of a *reflective* religious belief, whereas "God has desires" is an example of a *nonreflective* belief. That agents have desires is an intuitive computation generated by our theory of mind mechanisms (Baron-Cohen 1995). Agents think, feel, and perceive—activities that innately seem to require bodies. Hence, the idea that agents without bodies can do these things might violate our *non-reflective* understanding of agents (i.e., people and animals).

However, as Barrett's example of the Trinity shows, many religious concepts are the targets of reflective belief. For the present analysis we might distinguish between two types of reflective beliefs: *assumed* and *invoked*. *Assumed* beliefs are presuppositions that provide the foundation for other propositions. For example, one first requires the assumed belief that God exists in order to believe that God loves you and can answer your prayers. *Invoked* beliefs, on the other hand, are reflective propositions that are communicated between individuals. They can signal ideological solidarity or affiliation (e.g., "God knows that you are lying to me" or "the spirits don't like to be disturbed"), rationalize one's behavior (e.g., "I drink this wine to be one with Christ"), or manipulate others (e.g., "God wants you to behave").

Invoked religious concepts are primarily the schematic elements of religious concepts. They vary widely in content and frequency across populations and can adapt quickly in fluctuating social environments. That is, they are less enduring and more liable to change. *Assumed* beliefs (e.g., God exists), by contrast, should be more stable over time, since they are not as readily available to scrutiny as *invoked* beliefs. Schemas allow us to readily conceive of new associations (e.g., "God wants a lollipop" or "God wants another day off"), but the expectations of our social environment constrain the public acceptance of such novel associations.

To summarize, the best candidates for religious concepts are emotion-triggering with some form of categorical uniqueness, represented either at the domain- or schema level. While schemas are flexible, allowing one to effectively navigate multiple socioecological contexts by creating novel conceptual models and associations, templates provide necessary, stable inferences about objects in the world. Domain-level inferences are non-reflective, whereas schematic representations are necessarily reflective so they can be readily invoked in appropriate social contexts. Typically, however, in order to communicate religious claims, such invoked concepts require assumed beliefs and the presupposition of other notions and premises to be shared.

We argue that an ultimate function of articulating *invoked* beliefs in a religious context is to communicate and motivate solidarity in order to stimulate cooperative behavior; they are useful appeals. Why do church-goers repeatedly tell each other that God loves them but not that God exists? Why do Christians constantly remind each other that Jesus died for their sins? These are not merely reminders, of course, but rather they are acts of re-cognizing and reinforcing group membership.

Perceived sharedness in belief and/or behavior is necessary to reap the benefits of the religious system. In order to be of any adaptive utility, one's worldview—religious and secular—must have an appropriate degree of compatibility with others' in contexts where (a) such compatibility or lack thereof has fitness consequences, (b) a demonstration of sharedness and commitment is expected, and (c) such demonstrations have costs. As we cannot directly see peers' mental models and motivations, behaviors often need particular costs in order to demonstrate commitment to such models, regardless of belief. Rituals offer these qualities (Alcorta and Sosis 2005; Sosis 2003, 2006) and their performance can consequently produce adaptive outcomes. But we have little understanding of how shared perceptions are achieved. Nor do adaptive or byproduct accounts of religion inform us why the religious system's constituent parts recurrently coalesce across cultures (Sosis 2009a). As detailed throughout this volume, virtually all religions consist of an essential supernatural agent-ritual coupling (see Kavanagh and Jong 2020). Supernatural agent concepts, whether as gods, ancestors, spirits, totemic animals, or demons, are used in contexts where costly rituals need to be rationalized with appeals to unverifiable, highly ambiguous notions (e.g., Sosis 2020b). Standard psychological methods employed by cognitively oriented researchers are ill-equipped to address these concerns, but even dynamic systems approaches are likely to only get so far. There are undoubtedly complex principles at work that current approaches fail to address (see Chapter 8).

For now, how does the relationship between beliefs and behaviors produce adaptive outcomes? To answer this, we will examine various supernatural agent beliefs and their corresponding behavioral practices.

The External Context of Religious Beliefs

Religious Communication

Philosopher and early semiotician Charles Sanders Peirce (Houser and Kloesel 1992: 225–228) recognized three types of signs: symbols, icons, and indices. In Peirce's typology, symbols are established purely by convention, such as in language, where words have no intrinsic meaning but are conventionally associated with objects, qualities, and actions. Icons are signs that physically indicate what they represent, such as a map or phallus. Finally, an index is a reliable cue which indicates a particular state that is causally affected by its referent, such as a rash that directly indicates contact with poison ivy. There is a three-way relationship between signs, their referents, and our minds: "the sign is related to its object only in consequence of a mental association, and depends upon a habit" (Houser and Kloesel 1992: 225). As discussed in Chapter 1, habit is effectively a learned instinct that allows one to navigate his or her environment more efficiently.

The mental component in this relationship is an act of interpretation by an observer who interprets, say, the weathervane's direction as an indicator of the direction of the wind. Likewise, there are encoded messages in religious rituals that are interpretable by appropriately habituated (enculturated) minds. Rappaport (1999: 65–68) argues that religious rituals primarily convey two messages. One is indexical, indicating the current physical and mental states of the participants. The other is canonical, containing the moral rules of a community. All interpretations of the indexical and canonical meanings of rituals are schematic insofar as they are individually and culturally specific (e.g., "we kneel to remind ourselves of the suffering of Christ" or "we burn incense to greet our ancestors' spirits"), but they also have obvious "counterintuitive" components (Christ's death and resurrection, or the disembodied minds of ancestor spirits). The differences between the indexical and canonical are described as follows:

> Whereas that which is signified by the indexical is confined to the here and now, the referents of the canonical are not. They always make references to processes or entities, material or putative, outside the ritual, in words and acts that have, by definition, been spoken or performed before. Whereas the indexical is concerned with the immediate the canonical is concerned with the enduring.
>
> (Rappaport 1979: 179)

By participating in ritual, individuals are signaling that they accept the traditions (e.g., moral codes, social obligations, institutions, etc.) of the community and can be held accountable if these expectations are breached. Rappaport insightfully observed that whereas belief is a private, internal state, acceptance is a public, external state. Participating in a public ritual demonstrates acceptance of rites and the beliefs that underlie them and *"establishes an obligation* to abide by whatever conventions ... that order represents. The force of acceptance is, thus, moral, for breach of obligation ... is the one element present in all unethical acts" (Rappaport 1999: 395, italics in original).

A better understanding of religious behavior, then, entails an account of the relationship between the signal (e.g., eating a communion wafer), the referent or object of the index ("I accept this tradition and its adherents"), and the interpretation of the signal ("She is devoted to the tradition and therefore one of us"). Interpreters must encode participation appropriately ("the wafer is the body of Christ"), but there must be a collectively shared understanding of others' religious behaviors. In other words, such behaviors must indicate religious concepts which have the status of institutions (see below). It is religious beliefs' status as institutions that radically changes the dynamics of the religious system from one of personal reflection (i.e., belief) to that of acceptance of public mores. It is not necessary that an individual believe in order to accept. For example, one may be an observant participant in a religious tradition but believe the ideas are nonsense (e.g., Sosis 2009b). However, if one expressed contrary convictions or socially unacceptable motivations, then there would probably be social repercussions (see Chapter 3). Goody (1996: 678) suggests "that in polytheistic [traditions] doubt often leads to a search for new cults, whereas in monotheistic religions (religions of the Book) the alternative may be exit rather than voice." If "exiting" or "searching for new cults" is possible, then a doubting individual may take advantage of this bounty of religious specialization. However, if one is confined to one's small social group, rejecting the religious beliefs and behaviors of one's tradition is tantamount to rejecting his or her social group.

Religious Behaviors as Indices of Motivations and Institutions

Adherents often rationalize their religious behavior by referring to the will or interests of supernatural agents. For instance, Orthodox Christian firewalkers in Greece typically explain their behavior in terms of venerating saints (Xygalatas 2008). Pleasing the spirits is more likely to stimulate risky behaviors (or behaviors perceived as risky) than a secular motivation if one reasons that the consequences (i.e., negative fitness effects) of not participating or not believing are caused by supernatural beings and forces. In the spirit of Blaise Pascal, Guthrie (1993) argues that anthropo-morphism and belief in supernatural agents is cognitively the "best bet" as the benefits reaped from interpreting the world in anthropomorphic terms outweigh the costs of not doing so. The same can be said for engaging in religious behavior. Dimitris Xygalatas (personal communication) observes that some of the participants rationalize their behavior in terms of group identity and appeals to tradition (e.g., "My ancestors did this, and it is part of who we are"). Once secularized, however, such a potentially risky ritual is less likely to persist through time (Sosis 2000; Sosis and Bressler 2003). When ancestors can easily be honored in significantly less risky ways, individuals are likely to opt to do so. It is important to stress that the relationship between religious beliefs and behaviors is not necessarily unidirectional, but rather beliefs and behaviors mutually reinforce each other (Sosis 2003). Likewise, given how religious expression without its symbolic content often appears entirely outlandish, it is worthwhile to consider the institutional context of religious expressions.

Philosopher John Searle (1997) defines institutions (see Box 6.2) as the collectively held meaning ascribed to objects in the world. Institutions, according to Searle, are the transference of brute facts (X) to social facts (Y) in a particular context (C). In a Catholic service (C), for instance, a piece of bread (X) may represent the body of Christ (Y). "Catholic service" means the sum total of the thoughts, practices, institutional roles, and individuals participating in the ritual. Among Jews (C), a circular piece of woven material covering the head (X) may represent the fear of God (Y). Notice that there is individual variation in the acceptance of Y; a Catholic may not take the sacrament literally, just as Jews might associate wearing the kippah as a mere statement of religious affiliation rather than accepting the Talmudic rationalization.

Religious beliefs and behaviors are institutional signals insofar as their expressions resonate with receivers' understandings of them. Speaking in tongues to demonstrate one's allegiance with the Holy Spirit at a Catholic Mass would probably not be a successful signal of acceptance of Catholic doctrine as glossolalia is not an acceptable practice among traditional Catholics. The Mbuti Pygmies of the Congo voluntarily engage in stressful initiation rites, and those who do not participate are still treated as children and are not allowed to partake in adult affairs (Turnbull 1961: 226). Or consider the case of the Ainu. Outsiders to particular Ainu settlements needed permission from the headmen to use local resources. Watanabe (1972: 476) observes that "[s]uch permission was usually (but not always)

Box 6.2 A note on institutions

Searle's (1997) conception of institutions, of course, is not the only one (see, for example, Hill, Barton, and Hurtado 2009; Richerson et al. 2016). One conception in particular, offered by economist Douglass North, nicely fits with our discussion. He defines institutions as "the humanly devised constraints that structure political, economic and social interaction" (North 1990: 97) and suggests that the function of institutions is "to reduce the uncertainties involved in human interactions" (North 1991: 25). North also appreciates complexity, recognizing that institutions are reducible to smaller constituent parts (ibid.: 83–91). Collapsing North's economic-ecological conception with Searle's informational one offers a comprehensive definition of an institution as: *the contextually dependent* (C) *symbolic overlay* (Y) *of a set of interacting humanly devised, efficiency-seeking components* (X) *that reduce energetic costs and informational uncertainty.* Some have elaborated upon institutions' importance for understanding the symbolic aspects of religious traditions (e.g., Wood and Shaver 2018). Others (Turner et al. 2017) even emphasize "institutional evolution" as something that is a target of other, non-Darwinian forms of selection. For further discussion of these definitions and the implications for the evolutionary social sciences of religion, see Turner et al. (2020) and Purzycki (2020).

---

given on the performance of a ritual for local *kamui* deities, because assurance was required that the fisherman or hunter would be faithful to the local *kamui* deities." Those caught trespassing were required to appear before the headman and apologize to the spirits. Thus, collectively shared institutions provide the constraints within which an individual navigates social life and the framework from which sanctions are prescribed for improper behavior.

The Adaptive Religious System

Among traditional Mongolian cultural groups, ritual performances of epics were conducted—always at night—before hunting and war in order to please the spirits. These spirits were believed to ensure a successful hunt or battle. While one group, the Altai Urianghais, believed that "epic performances during summer months would antagonize the spirits," another group, the Baits, "believed that this restricted timing applied only to certain epics" (Pegg 2001: 112). Here we see between-group schematic variation in understandings of the appropriate epics to perform and the appropriate times to perform them. These variations are institutional insofar as they are collectively held. A factor that unites these traditions is that "[k]nowing of the impending performance, everyone in the area converged on the host's tent and food was served" (ibid.: 112). Thus, the recitation ritual facilitates prosocial behavior in the ways that evolutionary theorists of religious ritual have come to expect. If everyone is perceived to assist the hunters and warriors in their success by being present and pleasing the spirits when they could otherwise be doing something else, the resulting solidarity will allow them to reap the benefits of their devotion. These events were valued so highly among one group that "children were warned that falling asleep would be a sign of support for the epic's evil forces, and, more seriously, they would actually become the souls or spirits ... of enemy soldiers. Onions were put on their eyelids to help them stay awake. During the performance, it was forbidden to drink fermented mare's milk or milk-spirit and silence had to prevail" (ibid.: 113).

In this example, we see the commonly shared understanding that epic performances influence the spirits. We also see schematic differences in understandings of standard protocol for epic performance, but shared belief in the performance's causal efficacy. Participants engage in food sharing, and children are forced to stay awake. While applying onions to the eyes of a child might be rationalized as necessary to avoid supernatural sanctions or simply a matter of religious discipline, ensuring that one's children retain and appreciate this particular institution facilitates participation and so ultimately helps them later exploit the cooperation-enhancing, energy-saving affordances of the institution for themselves as adults.

Religious concepts thus serve to motivate *others* to engage in costly rituals and other behaviors. Of course, humans also engage in costly behaviors and rituals that are not rationalized with religious concepts, but the counter-schematic or counter-ontological strangeness inherent in religious concepts and their fitness-relevant framing makes them particularly cognitively salient and, as such, demands communication (i.e., the appeal) and subsequent declarations (i.e., the confirmation) of acceptance. Just as engaging in costly ritual is a reliable demonstration of solidarity, communicating acceptance of a god's punishment is a public demonstration of sharing worldviews and motivations with the already-committed. Religious rituals credibly signal commitment to one's group and acceptance—though not necessarily belief—in the group's doctrines, which in turn helps minimize free riding by filtering out the uncommitted (Alcorta and Sosis 2005; Bulbulia 2004a, 2008; Bulbulia and Mahoney 2008; Sosis 2005a, 2006; Sosis and Alcorta 2004; Sosis et al. 2007). Costs of behaviors thus help maintain the reliability of ritual signals, but costs vary across cultures and are reinforced by the institutional models within the communities that have them. The forms and rationalizations for such behaviors must be understood on the part of the receiver of the signal, meaning that such models must be shared. What makes these rituals particularly salient and difficult to fake is their costliness and the non-empirical, supernatural claims in reference to which they are conducted. Participants at the Phuket Vegetarian Festival pierce their cheeks, Sufis force skewers through their bodies and swallow swords, and Fijians and Greeks walk on hot coals—all to gain the favor of (different) supernatural agents. Beliefs about gaining the favor of spirits are about reaping net benefits otherwise unavailable. True to form, these processions are followed by feasting and other social engagements that maintain reciprocal relations and have lasting fitness effects. These religious systems are therefore explicitly and implicitly economic.

Religion is an adaptive system where each of its constituent parts comprises an ever-changing, adaptive amalgam of concepts and behaviors. Our species entertains religious concepts partly because our minds produce and preferentially retain concepts that are mysterious and emotion-triggering. Yet, religious concepts are emotional and also publicly proclaimed, which motivates others who would otherwise abstain from religious participation for lack of belief. Religious concepts are also intriguing enough to be salient and motivate physically and often materially taxing ritualized behaviors. Such behaviors indicate shared mental models and maintain social cohesion by reducing the prevalence of potential defectors in the social order (see Chapter 10). But as we have argued, ritual cannot do this work alone. The gods also play a pivotal role in maintaining the social order. In the previous chapter we examined one possible mechanism by which gods accomplish this effect: the moralistic biases humans exhibit toward knowledgeable and powerful supernatural agents. In the next chapter, we shift our scope to include the relationship between religious systems and their ecological contexts, while bringing behaviors and interpersonal relationships into sharper focus.

Chapter 7

Fostering Sharedness in
Religious Communities

As alluded to earlier, evolutionary and cognitive scholars have long debated whether religion is the product of dedicated adaptations or functionless byproducts (see Bulbulia et al. 2008; Sosis 2009a). Much of the debate divides neatly between cognitivists who support a byproduct view (Atran 2002; Barrett 2007; Boyer 2001; Kirkpatrick 2006), and behavioralists who take an adaptationist stance (Alcorta and Sosis 2005; Richerson and Newson 2008; Sanderson 2008a; Wilson 2002), although there are notable exceptions (Bering 2004; Harris and McNamara 2008). This chapter contributes to this discussion by arguing that religion is an adaptive system and exploring how religious systems function. Despite our partiality to adaptationist interpretations, we situate our argument within a cognitive approach in hopes of building a much-needed bridge between cognitive and behavioral approaches to religion.

We focus on the inter-individual processes of cultivating a sense of sharedness. Building on the work of Alcorta and Sosis (2005), we examine how: (a) the cognitive mechanisms responsible for religious beliefs flexibly adapt to accommodate the wide range of social environments that humans inhabit; (b) the beliefs and behaviors that comprise religion are attention-grabbing and emotionally salient; and (c) emotions can display and indicate an individual's physical and psychological state, and thus serve as honest signals of commitment. Together, these functions catalyze shared beliefs in coherent worldviews that are adaptively linked to particular, variable local contexts. We hold that the flexible cognitive, emotional, and behavioral mechanisms necessary to participate in this system were enduringly favored by natural selection because of the powerful benefits that flow from prosocial cooperation in communities with high sharedness in beliefs.

The Religious Mind

The Interaction of Nature and Nurture: Mental Organs and Cognitive Flexibility

As we discussed in Chapter 1, Chomsky reasoned that our minds are innately equipped with "mental organs" or "modules" that require external stimuli in order to function optimally in particular environments (Chomsky 1980). While there has been no shortage of debate among philosophers, linguists, cognitive scientists, and anthropologists regarding what exactly counts as a module (Atran 2002; Fodor 1998, 2000, 2005; Pinker 2005a, 2005b; Sperber 1996), one of Chomsky's lasting contributions to contemporary cognitive science and evolutionary psychology is his assessment of the language learning process. Learning, he argued, should be thought of as the *growth* of genetically endowed mental organs that are triggered and then influenced by the external environment. That is, Chomsky emphasized the interaction between genetically determined cognitive faculties and the contingent environments in which they operate (Chomsky 1980). One child grows up speaking British English and another Arabic because multiple innate but flexible cognitive mechanisms are biologically prepared to compute the *specific* linguistic information that the developing child encounters in his or her environment. Likewise, a child raised in a Christian environment is likely to grow up believing in the death and resurrection of Christ, whereas a child raised in an Islamic environment might grow up to believe that Muhammad spoke with the angel Gabriel. Religious beliefs are similar to unique languages, then, because they are formed by the interaction between genetically inbuilt but flexible cognitive mechanisms and the contingent social environment.

Sperber (1996) argues that cultural ideas that are easier to retain and transmit have a cognitive selective advantage and will become culturally prevalent. Therefore, he contends, we must understand why our evolved minds find some ideas catchier than others if we want to explain why some ideas survive whereas others do not. Sperber's epidemiological program has strongly influenced how cognitive researchers examine the structure of religious ideas. Indeed, it is now axiomatic in some circles that religious ideas are widespread because they violate the expectations of our basic organizational mechanisms. As we discussed in Chapters 4 and 6, such ideas might be "counterintuitive" and attention-grabbing and therefore "catchier" than intuitive ideas.

The acquisition of religious beliefs, however, is not simply an anarchic transfer of counterintuitive ideas between minds where merely the catchiest ideas survive. There are many avenues of transmission and kinds of learning biases (Kendal et al. 2018), often broadly divided between vertical transmission (from elder generation to younger) and horizontal transmission (from peer to peer), each of which faces respective constraints (Boyd and Richerson 1985). But despite numerous experimental studies on the memorability of counterintuitive ideas, we have little understanding of the distinct dynamics of vertical or horizontal transmission either in the lab (cf. Willard et al. 2016) or in natural settings (cf. Purzycki 2016). Nor do studies examine whether research subjects are *committed* to the counterintuitive ideas they are exposed to in research settings. Yet commitment, we maintain, is a crucial component of bridging the gap between the cognitive and behavioral aspects of religion. And since commitment can be understood as "belief" or acting as though one believes (Chapter 1), understanding cultural systems and rituals is vital for tracking how religious ideas are actually transmitted.

Again, our means of categorizing the world are flexibly informed by context and experience, so the default inferences of one category can be attributed to an object in another category (e.g., rivers having voices or forests that listen to you) if the social environment provides this information. Different environments produce different counterschematic concepts, resulting in extraordinary diversity in religious beliefs. Beneath this diversity, however, lies a similar, underlying, pan-human cognitive structure (Bulbulia 2004b) marked by its flexibility in response to variable conditions. Tomasello (1999: 206) notes that "truly cognitive adaptations, almost by definition, are more flexible than [modular accounts]. Although they may have arisen to solve one specific adaptive problem, they are quite often used for a wide array of related problems." As discussed in Chapter 6, we wager that the more flexible aspect of religious beliefs lies in the conceptual or schematic layer of cognition.

This view of human cognitive flexibility is solidly grounded in biology. Across species, adaptive mechanisms—physical and mental—are maximally beneficial for organisms when they have some degree of plasticity. For example, genetically fixed foraging instincts might subtly adapt to different environments among various subpopulations of the same species of bird. Humans, however, exhibit an exceptional, even extraordinary, degree of behavioral flexibility, which has allowed us to utilize virtually every environmental niche on Earth (Boyd, Richerson, and Henrich

2011). Our cognitive mechanisms are flexible enough to produce adaptive responses under diverse social and ecological conditions, and they are flexible enough to create and process religious ideas that are accepted and incorporated into diverse worldviews. These abilities are necessary, of course, for individuals to function optimally in any social environment. As we've stressed, *sharedness* is essential for achieving this optimal functioning in a community.

The Ontogeny of the Religious Mind

Some children spontaneously create imaginary friends (see Wigger, Paxson, and Ryan 2013). It could be that, because imaginary friends lack physicality, they are counterintuitive and are therefore "catchier" than other concepts (Sperber 1996). However, this account of imaginary friends would not explain why children generate such beliefs or actually believe in and behave as though they perceive some agent, rather than simply mentally storing away the bare concept of an imaginary friend. Children engaging in pretend play will also readily use sticks and rocks to represent counterintuitive creatures. These phenomena strongly suggest cognitive flexibility; if children are capable of *producing* (as opposed to simply "catching") religious-like ideas without explicit instruction, it suggests there is much more to religious beliefs than memorization.

Cognitive flexibility therefore poses a challenge to cognitive accounts of counterintuitive religious ideas. If a child is raised in a social environment where others grant agency to mountains and this belief is actively encouraged, such a belief may change the very nature of the template upon which such ideas are built. Cognitive flexibility is an adaptation that enables us to learn appropriate socioecological information within local environments, and social pressures often define what information is valuable. While the persistence into adulthood of individualized fantasy play would probably entail social costs, the rejection of commonly shared beliefs can also have negative social consequences for children and adults alike.

Beliefs that are endorsed and encouraged by the community may be internalized and become assumptions about the world. Internalizing such ideas and behaving in line with these assumptions makes adaptive sense if one is to successfully operate in a social organization composed of like-minded individuals (D'Andrade 1992; Ryan et al. 1993). But internalizing ideas is never enough to ensure positive social outcomes; the acceptance of ideas must be demonstrated and the culturally derived motivations for demonstrating them must be understood as well. Unlike purely rational self-interest, expressed motivations such as "participating in a community" or "ensuring the wellbeing of one's tribe" (see below) are typical, socially accepted reasons for religious participation. Demonstrating acceptance of religious beliefs defines who is within and outside the community, who shares ideological commitments, and who can be trusted (Rappaport 1999).

Public displays of acceptance often come particularly in the form of transitional rites of passage for young members of societies. While the young learn important aspects of traditions, they are also inculcated with a sense of the social—as well as the stakes in cooperative relationships. Among the Walmadjeri and Gugadja of Australia, for example, rites of passage involve genital mutilations, intensive religious instruction, blood rites, and extended pilgrimages to sacred sites. During subincision rites, an initiate "is repeatedly told to be good—not to go contrary to custom, not to quarrel, to conform; to pay attention to his elders ... to shoulder his responsibilities and fulfill his obligations; to supply food and to look after those who perform ritual" (Berndt 1972: 221). During circumcision rites among the Mbuti Pygmies of the Congo, boys are inducted as "blood brothers," forging life-long economic ties to each other. After the operation, boys "are made to sit down and join the others in singing one of the many work songs they will have to learn during the coming months" (Turnbull 1961: 221). These initiates endure considerable pain and religious indoctrination, but their successful completion of the rites is an unquestionable public demonstration of acceptance of societal norms and roles, and in both cases directly tied to cooperative relations. This demonstration is a critical social function of religious ritual, particularly at developmental transition points such as initiation. Alcorta and Sosis (2005, 2020) argue that the emotional intensity of initiation rites, coupled with explicit instruction about the sacred, facilitates, or even establishes, the transition into adulthood by collectively sharing cultural models about the world and the emotional motivations that ensure their retention. Other rituals serve similar adaptive functions once shared cultural models and motivations are institutionalized and codified in the young. The shared nature of institutions is a prerequisite to an individual's success as they grow into the recognized adult roles of their social group.

The Religious Community

On the Adaptive Value of Sharing Institutions

Our species has a remarkable ability to arbitrarily ascribe meanings and attributes to ordinary objects. As we noted in Chapter 6, philosopher John Searle distinguishes between brute and social facts, defining institutions as the shared transference of the former to the latter (Searle 1997). The oft-used example of paper currency serves quite well. Imagine a 50-dollar bill and a 100-dollar bill side by side. There is no inherent difference between the two pieces of reconstituted cotton and linen fiber covered with ink illustrations (brute facts). However, we ascribe them a particular conventional value: one is "worth" twice as much as the other (social facts). The active rejection of social institutions—once they are stable—can be particularly maladaptive at both individual and group levels. In market economies, an economic transaction is unlikely to transpire if one tries to pay for a meal with a tuft of cotton soaked in ink. The conceptualization and acceptance of our monetary system and similar social institutions are essential for successfully navigating modern social environments, and as such they bear on one's ability to acquire resources and attract mates.

We typically defer to people in positions of power to rationalize the legitimacy or illegitimacy of institutions. If we were to sneak into the mint at night and illegally print money using the exact same machinery, materials, and specifications used for legitimate paper currency, the resulting money would still be considered counterfeit by virtue of its not being "made" under the auspices of the designated authority, "the Treasury"—even though it would be physically indistinguishable from the real thing. Even if employees of the mint were to sneak in after hours to print money for their personal use and kept only what they would have been paid to work for the same amount of time, it would still be counterfeit—that is, illegitimate—money. Authority is what sets the values of the variables in the formula "A counts as B in C" and so licenses proper behavior within an institutional framework.

In turn, institutions serve as profound motivators of collective action. While institutions may provide internal rationalizations for behavior, it is quite clear that publicly asserting these rationalizations does not convince anyone of the merit of such institutions (although this may occur), but rather serves as a public demonstration of shared understandings that reinforces perceived solidarity within the social group. The question of whether or not belief in institutions is required for the perpetuation of them is thus rather moot. What matters is that the population acts as though they believe by actively participating in them. Not every Catholic, for instance, believes that consecrated wafers and wine are actually the body and blood of Christ (Pew Research Center 2019). This does not prevent the institution from perpetuation as though it were literally true.

As previously mentioned, many believers who claim that God is eternal and omniscient nevertheless often reason about God as though he were confined to the limits of time and space (Barrett 1998). The disparity between theologically correct (eternal/omniscient) and theologically incorrect (anthropomorphic) versions of God illustrates our point precisely (Slone 2004).[1] The fact that our stated beliefs (i.e., the theologically correct, omniscient version) are so dramatically inconsistent with how we think about God in real time suggests that our stated beliefs are better signals of group affiliation and devotion than our intuitive assumptions are (Chapter 5). The beliefs that serve as signals must be publicly demonstrated and cognitively palatable for receivers if signalers are to reap benefits from sending such signals (see Henrich 2009).

Supernatural Agents and Socioecological Variation

In *The Descent of Man*, Darwin observes that human beliefs in "unseen or spiritual agencies" are a universal means to make sense of the world around them (Darwin 2004 [1879]: 117). Darwin assumes that "making sense of the world" has adaptive value, an assumption still entertained

---

1. The problem of theological incorrectness (see Chapter 4; Barrett 1998, 1999; Barrett and Keil 1996; Slone 2004) suggests that there is a distinction between the invoked level of religious thought necessary for communicating group membership (e.g., "God knows everything and is everywhere") and a level of cognition that exhibits normal, real-time processing (e.g., "God couldn't help Lucy in Toledo and Fred in Wichita simultaneously"). Theologically correct concepts within religion, therefore, are external indexical badges of group membership. The fact that our stated beliefs are so dramatically inconsistent with how we think about deities in real time suggests that our stated beliefs are useful signals of group affiliation and devotion. Communicated beliefs serving as signals must be publicly demonstrated, understood, and deemed appropriate enough for receivers if signalers are to reap benefits from sending such signals. It is this collectively determined "cognitive palatability" that sets the parameters within which religious traditions operate over time. As such, invoking theologically incorrect versions of religious concepts (i.e., limiting God's abilities to the same temporal or spatial constraints that physical humans face) is likely to elicit sanctions on the part of one's community.

by many scholars today. However, the selective pressures that could have shaped our need for a coherent worldview are generally left unspecified. The notion that "God loves us" may be comforting, but this does not explain *why* many people find this idea comforting. Assuming for the moment that people do indeed strive to attain a worldview that makes sense, why do religious beliefs provide a satisfying worldview?

Religion provides a "satisfying explanation" for an individual when his or her own models of the world are successfully signaled and accepted by receivers, thus maximizing perceived solidarity and the benefits concomitant with this perception of solidarity. Religious views are satisfying when they are confirmed by one's peers; consequently, individuals constrain one another's religious beliefs. There is of course individual variation in religious belief within all religious communities, but all communities ensure that the range of beliefs remains within acceptable, usually socially enforced, limits. Those whose beliefs are outside the range of acceptability are typically denied access to group benefits. However, religions can and do change these limits in certain circumstances. Religious belief systems often change or mutate in particular when the benefits derived from sharing a given symbolic model of the world are no longer perceived to be worth the costs of participation. Note that this assessment targets the costs and benefits of participation in the entire system, not the epistemic value of the beliefs; thus, religious systems often undergo dramatic change or adopt new beliefs and values because the community that upholds them has stopped facilitating effective social coordination, rather than because the beliefs themselves—which were always extra-empirical anyway—have lost inherent credibility. That is, whether a religious worldview is "satisfying" is a function of the overall returns on participating in it.

Social organization also poses constraints on religious concepts (Sanderson 2008b; Wallace 1966). Conventional wisdom suggests that in small-scale societies, selective pressures for belief in one supreme moralizing supernatural agent are weak since social behavior in small communities is easily observed and moral reputations are easily communicated. The anonymity of individuals in large-scale societies, however, favors belief in an all-knowing supernatural agent that can encourage particular modes of conduct (Rappaport 1999). We might be less inclined to transgress social norms if we believe that a mysterious, punitive spiritual agent can punish us for doing so. Indeed, many researchers have argued that belief in supernatural agents with access to strategic information evolved to enhance prosocial behavior (Johnson and Bering 2006; McKay et al. 2011;

Rossano 2007; Shariff and Norenzayan 2007). As mentioned in Chapters 5 and 6, believing that supernatural agents are watching us has been shown to alter the way we make moral decisions (Bering et al. 2005) and influence our conduct in economic transactions.[2]

We find examples of spiritual sanctions for moral behavior with some interesting cross-cultural variation (see Chapter 3 for further discussion). The Yanomamö, for example, believe that in the afterlife, a spirit named Wadawadarwä directs those who have not been generous in life down a particular path "leading to a place of fire" (Chagnon 1996: 112–113). However, these beliefs are unlikely to prevent hoarding or stinginess since, according to the Yanomamö, this spirit is easily fooled: "We'll just all lie and tell him we were generous, and he'll send us to hedu [the sky]" (ibid.: 113). The Ju/'hoansi of the Kalahari (Lee 2003) seem to lack agreement on the nature of their two gods, but they are virtually unanimous in their belief that ancestor spirits cause most major illnesses and other misfortunes. These ancestors, according to one Ju/hoa, "expect certain behavior of us. We must eat so, and act so. When you are quarrelsome and unpleasant to other people, and people are angry with you, the //gangwasi see this and come to kill you. The //gangwasi can judge who is right and who is wrong" (ibid.: 129). Supernatural agents in these societies vary in form and the roles they play in human affairs, but both are associated with moral concern and have a role to play in the downstream outcomes of individual behavior.

Cross-cultural analyses indicate that supernatural agent concepts exhibit predictable socioecological variation (Chapters 4, 10; Sosis and Alcorta 2003), which suggests that religious beliefs are a product of the interaction between environmental (social and natural) constraints and our evolved cognitive architecture devoted to detecting mental states (Baron-Cohen

---

2. Originally, this paragraph ended with "People are even more generous with their money when primed with a drawing of two eyes (Haley and Fessler 2005)!" Since this chapter was originally published, others have conducted studies that examine artificial "observer effects" (e.g., Krátký et al. 2016). However, two noteworthy replication and meta-analysis studies (Northover 2017; Northover et al. 2017) suggest that, in fact, there is no reliable evidence of an effect of artificial surveillance on moral judgment and generous behavior in laboratory settings. While "There is no doubt people behave differently when they know, or at least believe, that they are being watched by others" (Northover et al. 2017: 150), experiments apparently do not systematically tap into this relationship. Other studies nevertheless find that *gods* believed to monitor behavior have a fairly stable cross-cultural relationship with generous or honest behavior (Purzycki et al. 2016b; Lang et al. 2019).

1995). To better understand cultural variation and the adaptive nature of religious beliefs, we should therefore examine socioecological factors. Consider, for example, the widespread belief that ancestral spirits cause illness. If such beliefs steer individuals away from reliable curing behaviors, then they are unlikely to be adaptive. However, when effective medications and treatments are unknown or unavailable, convincing someone else that your ancestral spirits have curing powers opens an opportunity for an exchange of resources (see Blackwell 2009). Believing in the efficacy of ancestral spirits may have significant consequences in such contexts on one's ability to survive and reproduce (McClenon 2002; Winkelman 2002).

On the other hand, not believing in supernatural ideas such as the ancestral spirits might be socially costly and serve as an indicator of outsider status. For example, in Malagasy communities where respect for the ancestors is traditionally manifest in nearly all spheres of life, the refusal to participate in ancestral ceremonies or adhere to ancestral taboos elicits conflict among kin, and can be stressful and socially isolating. As anthropologist Eva Keller details in her exceptional ethnographic work among minority Seventh Day Adventists in northeastern Madagascar, "nonparticipation in these rituals [ancestral exhumations] is one of the most important criteria by which the Adventists assess each other's commitment to the church" (Keller 2005: 175), but in the wider community nonparticipation and failure to secure the blessings of the ancestors "is considered a serious threat to someone's status as a socially meaningful person" (ibid.: 36). Moreover, the social costs of adopting Adventist practices directly impact community-wide cooperation. For example, Adventists' religious injunction against alcohol makes "it difficult for them to call on their non-Adventist kin to help them with a day's work, because these kin clearly expect to be offered large amounts of rum in return for their efforts" (ibid.: 197). Such social costs are traded off against the benefits achieved through in-group cooperation. Rather than relying on the merits of ancestral blessings, Adventists benefit, for instance, from the care and financial assistance that co-religionists offer during illness (ibid.: 217).

Religious ideas are not dormant assumptions that underlie worldviews; they motivate frequent expressions of acceptance of social institutions. Accusations of witchcraft or wearing an amulet to protect one from the "evil eye" reinforce an individual's beliefs, but also signal acceptance of such ideas by directing others' attention to them. If emotions are default decision-making programs (Frank 1988), then the employment of emotion-triggering religious ideas undoubtedly affects the way we interact with each other and serves to maintain the social structure, whether egalitarian or hierarchical, among individuals within a social unit (Alcorta and Sosis 2005). If idiosyncratic behaviors are associated with witchcraft, for instance, then people who exhibit those behaviors are avoided and ostracized by those who share this belief. Similar mechanisms are often exploited by religious authorities to organize others, maintain their own status, and enter into contracts between themselves and adherents (Watts et al. 2017). What these examples all show us is that, at the very least, religious beliefs systematically *point to* the costs and benefits of spiritual *and* social life; in exhibiting one's religious commitment one simultaneously enacts the costs and benefits of spiritual life and the social network in which one is embedded. To be reminded of the "evil eye" with an amulet is to be reminded of the repercussions of *not* having an amulet and the committed might be wary to associate with those who reject such beliefs. Appealing to a god when expressing local rules and regulations packages spiritual (e.g., supernatural punishment) and social costs (e.g., avoid skeptics or apostates) together. By extension, religious specialists and authorities master the art of organizing—and manipulating—these costs and benefits.

Specialists and Authorities

There are limits to what individuals will believe. If we were to claim that pink rabbits inhabit the moon, you are not likely to take us very seriously. On the other hand, if we were to suggest that we had the ability to cure your loneliness or illness, find a valued article that you lost, or remove soul-sucking spirits from your body, the ethnographic record suggests that you might be a little more credulous. Beliefs themselves might be generated or even perceived as violations of intuitive knowledge of the world, but in order for these beliefs to survive, others must accept them. One of the best predictors of which ideas survive is who proclaims the idea. If someone in a position of power announces, for instance, that their ancestral spirits have healing powers or that God told them to invade a particular country, the risk of social sanctions might prevent public denunciation of such claims. Humans may be disposed to readily accept, or at least evaluate less critically, the information offered by those in power, since the powerful may have greater access to important social information, and their ascendancy to leadership may be a direct consequence of their social knowledge. This "prestige bias" (Henrich and Gil-White 2001), is likely to have significant effects on whether or not counterintuitive ideas are accepted (see Willard, Henrich, and Norenzayan 2016). Religious leaders often have the power to impose social and economic costs on skeptics or non-participants. Moreover, regardless of the reliability of claims made by those in power, such social costs can encourage the acceptance of even patently false claims (Kiper 2020; Kiper and Sosis 2020).

In some cases, a religious specialist quite readily suggests that he or she possesses exclusive knowledge or has been "chosen" for a specific role. Such claims pique others' interest and, if propositions are accepted, garner prestige for the producer of such ideas. Dennett refers to this as the "shamanic-advertising hypothesis" (Dennett 2006; cf. Singh 2018). The Hopi, for instance, participate in highly secretive, rigidly hierarchical religious clans where conformity garners benefits and violations yield supernatural sanctions (Whiteley 1998). Each clan owns rituals and knowledge about how to control natural forces, and access to this knowledge is positively correlated with age. Institutional mechanisms serve to reinforce the status of those who have those have positions of power, but also entice others to strive for more insight into the nature of reality. Knowledge increases the prestige of the elders and their ability to influence others. Among the Netsilik, medicine men were both "respected and feared" (Balikci 1970). They also publicly competed over who had more power by doing seemingly extraordinary things: "[one] used to shoot himself with a gun ... [one] removed his own leg, other[s] preferred to pierce themselves with spears and grow beards in a second" (ibid.: 235).

Moreover, medicine men "lived in an atmosphere of suspicion and fear, dreading both the possible secret attacks of [their] camp fellows and the spirits who might initiate an evil action on their own." These specialists served to "enforce norms or re-establish harmonious relations between environment, people, and supernaturals," yet they clearly competed with each other both publicly and privately (ibid.: 237).

The Hopi and Netsilik exemplify the principle that influential religious specialists engage in competition over both material and ideological resources, using institutions and counterintuitive ideas as leverage to maintain and advance their status. Note, however, that the ideas advanced by these religious specialists do not typically become broadly held doctrines, but are instead associated idiosyncratically with unique performers. Their demonstrations are often materially costly and pose potential social costs if the displays are revealed as dishonest. These costs can become excessive if an "arms race" develops between individuals competing for limited social status. However, benefits accrue not only to successful leaders, but also to followers (Van Vugt et al. 2008; Van Vugt and Kurzban 2007). More specifically, when ritual experts organize communities around particular difficulties, community members can express—and build—their solidarity through ritual communication.

Confirming Sharedness with Ritual

Although there may be physical or mental health benefits associated with some ritual practices (Koenig et al. 2001; Wood 2017), the significant time, energy, and financial costs involved in any particular religion also deter those from joining who do not believe in the teachings. Hence, those who partake in the behaviors, badges, and bans can be trusted to accept the doctrines of the group, which often includes behaving altruistically to other group members. The resulting increased levels of trust and commitment enable religious groups to overcome the free-rider problems that otherwise typically plague communal pursuits, thereby preventing over-exploitation of common goods and other collective benefits (Sosis 2005a, 2006). Evolutionary biologist Jeffrey Schloss argues that "Costly signaling theory helps make sense of a distinctive aspect of religious belief that neither spandrel nor memetic accounts alone address: not why people believe, but why their beliefs motivate such substantial investments" (Schloss 2008: 201).

Rappaport (1999) claimed that religious rituals, badges, and bans are indexical signals; that is, they refer to what they denote by being truly affected by them, just as weathervanes indicate wind direction because the wind itself moves them. Rappaport argued that while ritual behaviors appear to be shrouded in mystery, their message to other adherents is clear: participation in a ritual performance indexically signals acceptance of (and not necessarily belief in) the moral values encoded in the ritual (see previous chapter). He maintains that, regardless whether individuals *believe* in the moral values encoded in a ritual performance, by participating they are signaling that they *accept* the moral code and can be held accountable for violating it. Rappaport insightfully observed that whereas belief is a private, internal state, acceptance is a public, external state (Rappaport 1999). Participating in a public ritual demonstrates acceptance of the obligations and claims that underlie the rite. Such demonstrations, however, generally come at a cost to the participant.

Recall the above-mentioned rites of passage. Sending one's child to engage in a dangerous, stressful initiation rite seems especially maladaptive given the risk of permanent damage or disfigurement to one of the most important instruments of one's genetic replication. However, it is for exactly this reason that allowing one's children to engage in traumatic rites sends an unmistakable signal of commitment to other group members (Sosis et al. 2007). Such "skin-in-the-game" demonstrations of sharedness are a critical component of the religious system and its ability to promote cooperative behaviors under diverse conditions. Less traumatic rituals can augment and reinforce these functions once shared cultural models are institutionalized in and reliably internalized by the young.

There is considerable experimental, cross-cultural, and historical evidence that costly rituals are associated with increased group solidarity and cooperation. These payoffs are especially important in high-stakes contexts such as intergroup competition. As mentioned in Chapter 1, one cross-cultural study found a positive correlation between the costliness of male rites and warfare frequency (Sosis et al. 2007). Warfare is widely recognized to pose significant coordination and cooperation problems, and accordingly it appears that costly rituals are one way in which groups increase male solidarity to overcome these problems. One illustrative case not represented in that study's sample is the Sundance of the Sioux of the Great Plains, who are well-known for their historical military prowess. After four days of "visiting ... relatives, courtships, minor rituals and feasting" (Lewis 1990: 52), and four subsequent days of fasting, the flesh of ritual participants is pierced with eagle talons. If tied to a pole, Sundancers rip these talons out by pulling themselves free. Alternatively, one might drag behind them bison skulls attached to thongs. Often dancers extend and intensify the pain as a test and demonstration of endurance.

This elaborate rite is explained by many Lakota as a sacrificial one; piercing ensures the wellbeing of one's family and nation. People can sponsor dancers by cutting away pieces of their own flesh. If dancers require assistance in tearing themselves free from the talons, family members donate a pony to those who help (Standing Bear 1975 [1928]). Sundancers are afforded a fair amount of prestige for piercing. Although they are piercing for the good of the Nation and must give away some personal possessions, they also reap benefits from such an investment in the form of gifts and status (Feraca 1998; Lewis 1990). Feraca (1998: 18) notes that "every candidate will pray for the general well-being of the people" but there are, of course, personal motivations as well, including impressing women, political publicity, and laying the groundwork to become a medicine man.

This ritual rests on the collectively held belief that suffering ensures group wellbeing. Bodily sacrifice to *wakan tanka* ("sacred vastness" or "big holy"), the creative force that is found in everything, ensures that prayers are heard and enhances the group's chance of success (Mails 1979; Standing Bear 1975 [1928]). This practice also reinforces the shared understandings of the cosmos and demonstrates acceptance of that shared understanding. In the case of the Sioux, this idea has payoffs in the form of group cohesion, cooperation, and social solidarity. These beliefs and behaviors have efficacy among adherents precisely because they actually do yield benefits.

The prosocial effects of ritual have also been demonstrated in experimental and historical studies in other settings not directly focused on war. For example, Sosis and Ruffle (2003, 2004) and Ruffle and Sosis (2007) found that Modern-Orthodox Israeli kibbutz inhabitants who participate in frequent public prayer—costly in terms of time investment if not physical pain—were more cooperative in an economic game than those who did not attend synagogue daily. As briefly mentioned in Chapter 1, in related ethnohistorical work Sosis and Bressler (2003) analyzed a sample of nineteenth-century American communes, finding that religious communes that imposed more ritual demands on their members survived significantly longer than less demanding communes. Signaling theory offers a parsimonious explanation for this paradox; the costly demands serve as both a gatekeeper against those who are not committed to the goals of the commune and as a mechanism to bond individuals in an experience of ideological and institutional sharedness.

Conclusion

The religious system plays a vital role in human sociality. The cognitive mechanisms that entertain widespread cultural and religious assumptions are remarkably flexible, enabling humans to respond adaptively under diverse conditions. Rituals, badges, and bans are collectively shared institutions that both internalize and publicly display commitments to counterintuitive ideas. Youth, for example, often endure costly religious rites of passage in order to demonstrate their initiation into the adult community. These rites signal to others not only the child's, but also the parents', solidarity with the rest of the community. People regularly engage in religious behaviors that entail short-term costs, but doing so enhances long-term relationships built on a foundation of trust and religious-institutional sharedness. This trust, perpetuated by ritual signaling, sustains communities and promotes social coordination and cooperative behavior.

Having covered religious cognition, emotion, beliefs, and ritual communication in the previous chapters, we now turn to further developing our examination of how religion fosters cooperation within religious systems, and the adaptive consequences of this cooperation. In order to appreciate the possibilities of the functional consequences of religious commitment, we maintain and elaborate our stance of looking beyond the human mind and see the interconnectedness of religion's constituent parts.

Chapter 8

Extending Evolutionary Accounts of Religion beyond the Mind

with Omar Sultan Haque

Scholars and lay people alike have characterized religion as serving a number of functions. Many have argued that because we are profoundly ignorant of the purpose, if any, of our existence, mythologies and religious beliefs developed to satisfy our curiosity by providing explanations for a complex and mysterious universe (e.g., Darwin 2004 [1879]: 117; Durkheim 2001 [1912]: 29–30; Geertz 1973 [1966]: 108). Some propose that religion's essential function is to allow us to cope with death and other forms of psychological suffering (e.g., Becker 1973: 203–204; Spiro 1987: 172), while others maintain that religion serves to establish and sustain the social order (e.g., Radcliffe-Brown 1965).

Within anthropology and related fields, such functionalist explanations have been in decline for decades. Recall our discussion from Chapter 2, where among other deficiencies, traditional functionalist theories often incorrectly assume that particular, contingent institutions are essential parts of the societies in which they operate (Collier et al. 1997 [1982]: 73). Moreover, functionalist theories typically lack any consideration of feedback mechanisms that can account for the maintenance of benefits to social actors, as discussed in Chapter 2 (Elster 1983, 2007; Sperber 1996). However, anthropologists, psychologists, and biologists who employ evolutionary models avoid such pitfalls by using explanatory frameworks grounded in the selective retention of useful effects (e.g., Dennett 1995; Owens and Wagner 1992; Smith and Winterhalder 1992). Boyer nevertheless correctly cautions those seeking evolutionary explanations of religion:

> Most attempts at an evolutionary account of religion have proved unsatisfactory because a single characteristic identified as crucial to the origin of religion is not in fact general. The attempt to find the single evolutionary

track for religion is another manifestation of a general urge to identify the single mechanism that motivates religious thought or makes it plausible to believers.

(Boyer 2003: 123)

We heed Boyer's cautionary advice and approach religion from a more holistic and multivariate perspective than currently offered by the evolutionary and cognitive sciences of religion. Indeed, we argue that an evolutionary approach to religion requires that religion be viewed as a dynamic *system*; isolating particular features of religion for analysis without understanding their influence on the full religious system can be misleading and generate trivial results. The present chapter examines the functional logic of religious systems and explains how they solve adaptive problems. As argued throughout the present work and beyond (Alcorta and Sosis 2005; Sosis 2009a, 2019) the religious system is composed of cognitive and emotional mechanisms that produce, retain, and motivate commitments to shared supernatural ideas, and behavioral procedures—rituals—that enact, reproduce, and encode these ideas. These components appear to lock into place and form a universal social system with remarkable cross-cultural similarities, as well as predictable differences. Here, we further elaborate how such a system evolves. In particular, we focus on how its constituent parts acclimate and adapt to socioecological changes in order to maintain a suitable social niche.

Byproduct Accounts

As we have discussed throughout this book, there has been considerable debate regarding whether or not religion meets the biological criteria for an adaptation (e.g., Bulbulia et al. 2008; Pyysiäinen and Hauser 2010; Sosis 2009a). Remarkably, most researchers on all sides of the debate are in agreement on the nature of religious cognition and its prosocial effects. Scholars involved in the debate primarily disagree on whether religion's prosocial benefits indicate that it is an adaptation, a functional byproduct of other adaptations (i.e., an exaptation), or a functionless byproduct with only prosocial effects. The *sine qua non* of any selectionist analysis is explaining how a particular trait increases its bearer's fitness—that is, its likelihood of transmitting genes into future generations. Adaptations—traits forged by natural selection—often have multiple effects and may be composed of a number of other traits that are either a direct result or an indirect result (i.e., a byproduct) of natural selection. Moreover, a trait's classification as an adaptation does not entail that it is necessarily currently *adaptive*. Adaptations to past environments can be maladaptive—meaning they confer a fitness *disadvantage*—in the present. For instance, our taste for rich, fatty foods and the overpowering urge to privilege learning over procreation are both probably adaptations, because they are universal traits that probably improved fitness in ancestral human environments; nevertheless, they are harmful to fitness today (Richerson and Boyd 2005: 148–190). By the same token, traits that are adaptive today may have been less so in past environments. Such traits may be *adaptive*, but they are not necessarily *adaptations*.

As discussed in earlier chapters, various authors have argued that religious concepts are byproducts of evolved cognitive architecture and that religion is therefore an evolutionary byproduct (Atran 2002; Barrett 2004; Boyer 1994a, 2001; Dawkins 2006; Dennett 2006). These scholars argue that religious concepts co-opt psychological mechanisms that evolved for purposes unrelated to religion, and these concepts tap into emotional and other strategic systems to powerfully motivate behavior. Boyer (2003), for instance, argues that because religious concepts exist by virtue of "neural systems" that function for very specific purposes outside of religion, religious thought is a byproduct of these systems. Atran (2002) acknowledges that religious behavior may result in fitness benefits for participants, but, similar to Boyer, he asserts:

> religions are not adaptations and they have no evolutionary functions as such. There is no such entity as 'religion' and not much sense in asking how 'it' evolved. Unlike the case for language, for religion there is no integrated set of cognitive principles that could represent a task-specific evolutionary design.
>
> (Atran 2002: 264–265)

In other words, there is no domain-specific module (or set of genes) for religion. Therefore, the question of whether or not it is an adaptation is meaningless (Kirkpatrick 1999).

Byproduct accounts that employ this reasoning are prevalent in the evolutionary and cognitive science of religion literature. Some of the more influential hypotheses associated with this paradigm propose that:

- Supernatural agent concepts emerge from mind-detection mechanisms (Barrett 2004; Guthrie 1980, 1995; Chapters 1 and 4).
- Religious concepts predominantly consist of ideas that violate default assumptions about objects, artifacts, plants, animals and persons in our world (Atran 2002; Barrett 2004, 2008a; Boyer 1994a, 2001; Boyer and Ramble 2001; Norenzayan et al. 2006; Pyysiäinen 2004; Chapters 4 and 6).
- Supernatural agent concepts exploit emotional attachment systems (Kirkpatrick 2005; Granqvist and Kirkpatrick 2008; Granqvist et al. 2010).
- Ritual behavior is a byproduct of hazard precaution systems (Boyer and Liénard 2006, 2020; Liénard and Boyer 2006).

The general logic of these accounts is that because features of religion are analogous to or exploit extant psychological systems, religion is not trait selected for its advantages.

While such views might offer compelling mechanistic explanations of certain features of religion, we contend that they cannot explain four key aspects often encountered in religious systems. First, they fail to account for the recurrent cross-cultural coalescence of many of religion's core features. Second, they specifically fail to account for coupling of supernatural agent concepts with rituals, a combination essential to all religious traditions. Third, they fail to account for patterned cross-cultural differences in religious traditions. Fourth, byproduct accounts derived from cognitive studies that focus merely on the mental representations of religious concepts and ritual operate in an analytical vacuum at the expense of accounting for what religion actually does.

Adaptationist Accounts

Humans are composed of many systems, which are themselves composed of even smaller sub-systems. While our stomachs are evolved adaptations for food-processing, the stomach itself is composed of numerous systems of cells, their interactions, and the emergent properties of their collectivity we call "tissue." Not only do we consist of various interacting systems, but we also regularly participate in systems far larger than ourselves. No one who embraces evolution by natural selection would argue that the immune system is *not* an adaptation, yet we find no one claiming that there is a particular locus of this adaptation, since the system is composed of a number of interacting units that must function together to maintain the defensive capabilities of organisms against infectious microorganisms. Moreover, no one would deny that our own immune systems are any less adaptive because they served different functions or had different forms in our evolutionary past.

Similarly, what we have been calling the "religious system" is composed of constituent parts. These constituent parts consist of evolved cognitive, emotional, developmental, and behavioral traits. At its most basic level, this system is composed of ritual behaviors and the supernatural agents to which people appeal. Yet, this system of course has its own constituent parts, such as myths, symbols, taboos, sacred values, all of which must operate together in order for individuals to reap the benefits of participation (see Chapter 9). Adaptive accounts of religion do not disagree with the central—often empirically supported—assertion of byproduct theorists: namely, that religious concepts are made possible by evolved psychological mechanisms that evolved as a consequence of selective pressures probability unrelated to religion. However, an adaptive approach goes a few steps further. First, it gives equal attention to human universals and cross-cultural variation, both of which are explicable by evolutionary analysis. Second, it emphasizes the functional *effects* that coupling religious concepts, emotions, and behaviors has over time on human social interactions. Third, it emphasizes the remarkable recurrence, convergence, and non-random distributions around the world of these features.

Religious Ritual as a Signal of Commitment

Psychologists Steven Pinker and Paul Bloom suggest:

> Supplementing the criterion of complex design, one can determine whether putatively adaptive structures are correlated with the ecological conditions that make them useful, and under certain circumstances one can actually measure the reproductive success of individuals possessing them to various degrees.
>
> (Pinker and Bloom 1992: 457)

Indeed, there is a significant amount of evidence that affiliation with a religious community is positively correlated with fertility (Blume 2009,

2010; Bulbulia et al. 2015; Frejka and Westoff 2008; Kaufmann 2010). The mechanisms driving this effect, however, are unclear (Shaver 2017). Quite possibly, individuals with a genetic predisposition toward religiosity find like-minded individuals with whom to mate. The norms and practices of religious communities may then serve as solutions to coordination problems for persons who prefer a monogamous, high-fertility mating strategy. Indeed, attitudes towards sex and mating behaviors are very strong predictors of attendance at a house of worship (Weeden et al. 2009). Religious communities may, then, provide places for individuals to find like-minded individuals, such as others with similar mating strategies. This approach, however, fails to explain how religious non-kin and non-mates are also remarkably cooperative with each other. Consideration of religion as a form of communication helps provide a more fruitful approach.

We undoubtedly share forms of communication with our nonhuman relatives. Animals regularly communicate with others using various signals (Hauser 1996; Searcy and Nowicki 2005). As mentioned in Chapter 1, Otte (1974: 385) defines signals as "behavioral, physiological, or morphological characteristics fashioned or maintained by natural selection because they convey information to other organisms." These signals can vary in form, content, cost, intensity, frequency, and reliability. Human facial expression of emotion, for instance, is a reliable, difficult-to-fake signal of an internal emotional state (Frank 1988; Pinker 1997), but of course there are individual differences in the intensity of expression of emotions. Organisms regularly engage in behaviors that reliably and flexibly convey various messages.

For instance, as discussed in Chapter 1, Zahavi and Zahavi (1997) argue that organisms perform risky behaviors in order to reliably demonstrate their fitness. The so-called "handicap principle" predicts variation in the ways animals signal their fitness to potential mates, same-sex competitors, and/or predators. These signals are generally reliable because they come at a cost to individuals bearing them and thus accurately communicate the message that they are designed to convey. Humans, for instance, regularly engage in conspicuous consumption in order to "sufficiently put [their] opulence in evidence" (Veblen 2007 [1899]: 53; see also Miller 2009) just as male bowerbirds collect and arrange attractive colorful trinkets to display hard-to-fake information about their attributes, and so can attract females. While humans can convey their opulence by spending their resources on symbols of wealth (e.g., fast cars, jewels, etc.), bower birds demonstrate their fitness by using energy and time expenditures to amass a hoard of apparently useless objects. The real utility of such behavior, of course, lies in its social payoffs (e.g., prestige and mates, respectively).

As discussed above, signaling theories of religious behavior contend that religious rituals also act as signals of an individual's solidarity with a religious tradition, and more importantly, with the specific individuals engaged in that tradition (Alcorta and Sosis 2005; Bulbulia 2009b; Irons 2001; Sosis and Alcorta 2003). Cooperative relationships face the inherent problem of exploitation by cheaters: those who free-ride (i.e., profit at others' expense) can take advantage of others' good-faith contributions to the common good (Axelrod 1984; Dawkins and Krebs 1979; Iannaccone 1992, 1995). Religious rituals, as discussed in Chapter 2, are one mechanism that minimize such free-riding and can serve as a reliable means to communicate trustworthiness (Sosis 2005a, 2006).

Tan and Vogel (2008), for example, found that religiosity predicts trustworthiness and willingness to trust others in economic games. If people are perceived to be trustworthy, then cooperative relations are probably more reliable and their benefits higher. Of course, costly signals are used as signals of commitment in atheistic and secular contexts as well. Tattooing onto one's body, for example, the logo of the atheist "Brights" movement, one's fraternity letters, Captain Beefheart lyrics, etc., are all demonstrations of costly commitment in secular contexts. However, what costly religious signals do is communicate commitment to social contracts perceived to be mediated by sacred and often eternal beings. There is ever-growing evolutionary modeling (Dow 2008; Henrich 2009; Wildman et al. 2020; Wildman and Sosis 2011) and empirical evidence (Purzycki and Arakchaa 2013; Power 2017a, 2017b; Ruffle and Sosis 2007, 2020; Soler 2012; Sosis et al. 2007) that supports the hypothesis that ritual's adaptive function is to strengthen social bonds through such costly signals.

As mentioned in Chapter 7, Sosis and Bressler (2003; Sosis 2000), for example, demonstrated that religious communes outlive secular communes, and that among religious communes, but not secular communes, costly rituals are positively correlated with commune longevity. In subsequent work, Shaver et al. (2018) showed that costly obligations could *not* explain variation in cooperation and trust among Greek fraternities or other secular social groups within a U.S university. Religious concepts— gods and spirits—are therefore probably necessary for costly ritual signaling to solidify prolonged cohesion; secular rituals do not seem to offer as strong a "social glue" (Nielsen 2018) when they refer to concepts, such as economic systems (e.g., Sosis and Bressler 2003), that can be empirically disconfirmed. Successful religious concepts are by nature unverifiable and thus provide people with a stable, albeit otherworldly, incentive to participate (Rappaport 1999). As such, religious concepts appear to be a necessary component for the prosocial effects we see in religious groups (Chapter 6).

Returning to the interrelationship between religion, mating, and fertility, Bulbulia et al. (2015) examined predictions derived from signaling models of mate choice. These models posit that men and women use religious expressions to indicate their fidelity and overall mate quality, and likewise, potential mates assess these signals accordingly. Analyzing data from the longitudinal New Zealand Attitudes and Values Study, these researchers found that church attendance was linked to higher social prestige. Moreover, church attendance and fertility exhibited the bimodal relationship anticipated by religious studies scholar Jason Slone (2008); religious men and women without children attended church frequently, presumably signaling their mate quality, and church attendance was positively correlated with fertility among those who had children.

Supernatural Punishment in Context

As Murray and Moore (2009) note, many religious contexts levy third-party sanctions against behaviors deemed religiously unacceptable. When violations of sacred taboos are directly punished by a community, there may be little need for costly rites that overcome the problems of cooperation (Sosis 2005a). Supernatural agents may serve this function in specific contexts. As discussed in Chapters 1 and 6, an evolutionary account of how selection favored commitments to moralistic gods, known as the "Supernatural Punishment Hypothesis," predicts that engaging supernatural agent concepts minimizes antisocial behavior and/or promotes prosocial behavior (Bering and Johnson 2005; Johnson and Bering 2006; Lang et al. 2019; Schloss and Murray 2011).

In a number of important studies, researchers have found priming of religion-associated concepts increases prosocial behavior. For example, Shariff and Norenzayan (2007) found that implicit priming of religious concepts positively affected generosity in economic games (though secular authority primes had a similar effect, which suggests a common causal mechanism in reputation monitoring; see Ge et al. 2019). Moreover, Bering et al. (2005) found that individuals were less likely to cheat in an experiment when primed with a ghost story, while Johnson (2005) found a

---

Box 8.1 Religious signaling

Researchers studying religious signaling often identify a costly religious behavior and reflexively apply Zahavi's handicap argument to explain its emergence and persistence. But as Barker et al. note:

> this "cost-first" approach contrasts with how signals are studied in behavioral ecology, which can be thought of as a "content-first" approach. Researchers start by identifying a putative signal and then construct hypotheses about what factors have shaped it, for example, what the benefits are of signaling versus not signaling or what (if any) costs signaling may entail.
>
> (Barker et al. 2019: 87–90)

Signaling models focus on behavior that has been designed for its strategic value as a form of communication that influences the response patterns of receivers. But all behavior has the potential to provide information to observers, making the array of possible signals overwhelming and bewildering. Therefore, a framework for identifying and analyzing signals is vital for advancing the evolutionary study of signaling. Barker et al. (2019) developed such a generalized framework in which they urge researchers to clarify the content, context, and costs of the signals under examination. Fundamentally, religious signaling concerns how an audience assesses attributes through religious behaviors, badges, and bans, the costs of which ensure the reliability of the content of these signals in defined contexts (Sosis 2022).

---

significant correlation between moralizing high gods and indices of cooperation in a massive cross-cultural sample. In a meta-analysis, Hartberg et al. (2016) show that supernatural enforcement plays a critical role in the management of collective resources in many societies. While Norenzayan and Shariff (2008) suggest that the cooperative effects of religion attract interest and lead people to commit to them, Bering and Johnson (2005) argue that religion is an adaptation that reduces self-regarding behavior and offloads costly punishments for selfishness onto supernatural agents.

But like the communicative value of ritual signals (Box 8.1), the effectiveness of supernatural punishment, too, is enriched by an appreciation for context and specific knowledge of *what* gods punish. For example, over the years, researchers have found again and again—using much of the same data or data coding schemes—that the complexity of state societies correlates with moralistic high gods (Johnson 2005; Lahti 2009; Sanderson

2008b; Stark 2001; Swanson 1960; Wallace 1966). As noted in Chapter 4, however, there are many examples of non-state societies with moralistic supernatural agents. The Nuer, for instance, believe in an omniscient moralizing god similar to the Abrahamic deity (Evans-Pritchard 1956); the Ju/'Hoansi of the Kalahari believe their ancestors' spirits know when they misbehave and make them sick if they do (Lee 2003); and spirits among the Netsilik (Inuit) make people sick for violating taboos (Balikci 1970: 226).

However, many reports suggest that, in a variety of other contexts, some supernatural agents do not explicitly care about morality and do not necessarily punish people. For example, among the Christian Maisin in Papua New Guinea, "With the somewhat ambiguous exception of the Christian god, spiritual entities are ultimately amoral. They can aid, harm, or ignore the living as they please" (Barker 2008: 122). As discussed in Chapter 3, Tyvan spirit masters in Inner Asia are particularly concerned about ritual behavior and resource preservation rather than about human morality, at least explicitly (although Tyvans do claim spirit-masters are interested in morality when directly asked; Purzycki 2010, 2011). The people of Ifaluk believe in malevolent and benevolent spirits, but divine wrath is explained by virtue of the spirits' malevolence, not necessarily by human misconduct. In fact, human misconduct is explained by spirit possession. On Ifaluk, residents direct individual aggression toward culturally sanctioned targets (Spiro 1952). In such cases, there seems to be little to no supernatural response to human immorality.

However, this does not necessarily mean religions do not contribute to the cooperative, "moral" behaviors in such communities. Even where religions are not explicitly moralistic—that is, where they lack explicit instructions concerning how to behave towards others—they may still be *functionally* moralistic (Teehan and Shults 2019). One of the underappreciated and therefore underexploited values of this ethnographic research is that it suggests that not only do religious content and forms change to accommodate new socioecological contexts, but that the specific functions of traditions may actually shift under new ecological conditions and challenges (Chapter 10; Rossano 2006, 2007, 2009). In other words, as conditions change, successful religions will change to maintain their *functional* relevance to moral behavior. As noted above, increasing anonymity in densely populated state societies might have rendered the monitoring of ritual performance difficult; thus, moralistic supernatural agents developed to overcome the new challenges to cooperation. This system was probably modified from one of stimulating and rationalizing (i.e., explaining costly behaviors with appeals to unverifiable agents) religious ritual—as found in traditional societies—to one of a transcendent monitoring system which has indeed been shown to affect prosocial behavior (Chapter 4). However, more specifically, we find considerable variation around the world in (a) the form of supernatural agents (e.g., human-like, animal-like, etc.), (b) the objects of supernatural agents' concerns, (c) the breadth of knowledge, (d) how this variation informs religious behavior, and (e) how these religious complexes make sense in their socioecological contexts. In other words, we need to look beyond the human mind for evidence of religion's contributions to our sociality.

Religion beyond Mind

As discussed in Chapter 1, religions comprise niches into which we are born. We are all part of interconnected and interpenetrating niche-systems, whether they are economic, academic, religious, or political. Yet, these niche-systems, including religious systems, are analytically isolatable and tractable. Our shared representations and behaviors actually forge a context within which we navigate our social lives. Alcorta and Sosis (2005: 325) argue that "religion may best be understood as an evolved complex of traits incorporating cognitive, affective, behavioral, and developmental elements selected to solve an adaptive problem." These traits make the essential elements of religion possible, but also inform each other and therefore co-evolve (see Buskell et al. 2019).

As Chomsky rightly notes:

> Organs do not evolve independently, of course, and a viable organism has to hang together in complicated ways; breeders know how to breed bigger horses, but it won't help if size increases without highly intricate corresponding changes in the brain, the circulatory system, and much more.
>
> (Chomsky 1996: 16)

Like horse breeding, the constituent elements of religious systems can change through the deliberate efforts of religious leaders. However, religious traditions also change outside of conscious decisions of individual agents in response to systemic changes and perturbations in the social ecology. Communities share religious concepts, and how this sharedness affects behavior is of utmost significance in understanding how religion adaptively changes as a dynamic system.

Even outside of state societies' correlation with moralistic high gods (see Skoggard et al. 2020; Snarey 1996; Swanson 1960; Wallace 1966), we find that the content and form of religious expression changes through time and space in similar and predictable ways in non-state traditions as well; religious traditions show striking cross-cultural similarities given the socioecological context in which they operate. For example, there appears to be a worldwide association between herding communities and ritualized cairn practices devoted to local spirits (Sierksma 1963); populations with more exposure to war have rituals with more intense requirements (Sosis, Kress, and Boster 2007); horticulturalists from disparate continents engage in garden magic and ritualized appeals to garden spirits (Bonnemaison 1991; Brown and Van Bolt 1980). These examples suggest that at the very least, belief-practice complexes will correspond to economies in important ways (see Chapter 10).

Moreover, there is significant evidence to suggest that specific religious traditions function to regulate resource use by virtue of emergent properties which are largely invisible to individual constituents (e.g., Atran et al. 2002; Lansing 2007; Lansing and Kramer 1993). In other words, properties which exist at the level of the population may indeed affect individuals' fitness. Native scholars have consistently emphasized the inextricable relationship between a people, their religious beliefs, and natural resources (Battiste and Henderson 2002: 97–116; Deloria 1992). In fact, local indigenous populations have globally appealed to their respective religious traditions to resist ecological overexploitation and development (Klubnikin et al. 2000; LaDuke 2005). How do these relationships develop?

Religious systems regularly converge around very practical concerns ranging from life history events (Reynolds and Tanner 1995) and the coordination of access to valuable resources (Atran et al. 2002; Lansing 2007; Lansing and Kremer 1993) to motivating people to organize against a colonial power (Carroll 1975; Wallace 1956) and fostering in-group cooperation (Sosis and Bressler 2003). Religion is—at least in traditional societies—inextricably linked to much of social life and may become of heightened significance during times of organizational need, such as war (Finkel et al. 2010; Henrich et al. 2019). Not only does the complex adaptive systems perspective reemphasize the importance of the "secular utility" of religion (Durkheim 2001 [1912]; Wilson 2002), but it also hints at the possibility of a devoted study of the phylogeny of religion based on ecological context that is not reducible to sociological or non-religious categories alone (see Matthews et al. 2013; Watts et al. 2015, 2017). In other words, measurable

elements of religions—such as beliefs, costs, location, and timing of rituals—converge independently in part because they successfully achieve
some material end. We examine this further in Chapter 10.

Through time, religious systems often acclimate in order to solve particular socioecological problems for their constituents. Individual actors
in these systems are not necessarily conscious of these changes but may
nevertheless reap the benefits from participation. This also suggests that
there are properties of religion that emerge beyond the awareness of
individual constituents and exist only at the level of a collectivity. The
challenge for future researchers will be to systematically investigate if the
specific contents of the defining components of religion—commitment
to supernatural agents and ritual behaviors—respond to socioecological
changes in predictable ways.

Conclusion

As many have argued, the evolutionary emphasis on how ecological factors
shape response patterns illustrates why the nature-nurture dichotomy is
a false one; genotypes do not occur in a vacuum but rather are expressed
as phenotypes through ontogenetic processes that are sensitive to environmental conditions (Barkow et al. 1992; Pinker 2003; Ridley 2004). While
the search for a "religious gene" or "religion module" is probably futile,
there is good reason to ask about the heritability of religious psychological
propensities. It has been demonstrated in twin studies, albeit consistently
ignored in the social scientific literature, that religiosity (but not religious
affiliation) is partly heritable (Bouchard 2004; Bouchard and McGue 2003).
Moreover, there is evidence that carriers of genetic expressions for social
sensitivity are variously benefitted psychologically in particular cultural
contexts (Sasaki and Kim 2021; Sasaki et al. 2011). As with the significant
heritability of political attitudes, the direct as well as indirect action of the
genes in question probably gives rise to *predispositions* for religious commitment which the environment mediates. However, these facts about
religious commitment may be used in other contexts as well; byproduct
accounts may demand evidence that these genes are exclusively *for* religious commitment rather than ideological or political commitment generally (see Kirkpatrick 2006). As discussed above, though, adaptationist
accounts do not require such exclusivity. Again, while the quest for finding any essential mechanisms that specifically evolved for religion will

probably fail, chalking up religion to an exclusively learned phenomenon misrepresents what we now know about human cognition.

The cognitive science of religion raises important new questions about the nature of religious concepts and processing, but its experimental work heavily relies on Western populations. This renders *a priori* generalizations from empirical work difficult (Henrich et al. 2010; Sears 1986). Throughout this volume we have begun to map out the space of variation in the expression of religious systems, as this will provide clues about the interdependencies among its elements. This is where a dynamic systems approach will shed more light on all of the components of religion, but also how the content of these components will change in accordance with how people interact with their socioecological environments. Moreover, while there are notable exceptions in the theoretical literature (McCauley and Lawson 2002; Whitehouse 2004), the cognitive sciences of religion have focused primarily on how we represent and process religious concepts and propositions (see Barrett and Keil 1996; Boyer and Ramble 2001). While these approaches shed light on the nature of the religious mind, the conclusion that religion is a byproduct does not follow from the idea that religion is possible by virtue of otherwise mundane cognitive mechanisms. Just the fact that religious concepts correlate with ritual and these rituals may have effects on individual fitness indicates that more is at work than byproduct accounts suggest.

A dynamic systems approach to religion encompasses both religious mind and behavior and treats them as inextricably linked components of an ever-changing social system. Only by giving equal attention to the nature of the human mind, the natural and social environments, history, and all of the forces that exert influence upon them and their relationships will we be able to come to terms with explaining why humans do the things they do. More specifically, we need to understand these dynamic relationships in order to understand why humans are religious. These dynamics inform why *particular* traditions are the way they are and shed light on the natural laws that have forged their paths.

Chapter 9

Approaching Religion as a Complex Adaptive System

For more than a decade, we have advocated with our colleagues Candace Alcorta (Alcorta and Sosis 2005, 2006; Sosis and Alcorta 2003, 2004), John Shaver (Shaver, Purzycki, and Sosis 2016; Sosis and Shaver 2015), Jordan Kiper (Kiper and Sosis 2014, 2016, 2020; Sosis and Kiper 2014a, 2014b, 2018), and Connor Wood (Wood and Sosis 2019) that religion may best be understood as an adaptive complex of traits incorporating cognitive, neurological, affective, behavioral, and developmental elements. We have argued that these traits derive from pre-human ritual systems and were selected for in early hominin populations because they contributed to the ability of individuals to overcome ever-present ecological challenges. By fostering cooperation and extending the communication and coordination of social relations across time and space, these traits served to maximize the potential resource base for early human populations, thereby increasing individual fitness. The religious system is an exquisite, complex adaptation that serves to support extensive human cooperation and coordination and social life as we know it.

Bringing together the mechanical elements from the previous chapters, this chapter describes the religious system, or, specifically, how religion can be understood as a complex adaptive system more globally. We will begin by describing the building blocks of religious systems. Then we will outline the feedback processes that constitute the integrated religious system. This will be followed by a discussion of some implications of this systemic approach and why the religious system is best understood as a complex adaptive system.

We have asserted that religions are systems, but we are not alone in making such a claim. Two of the most influential anthropologists to study religion in the last 50 years, Clifford Geertz and Roy Rappaport, both approached religion as a system, although they did so in very different ways. One of Geertz's most celebrated articles, "Religion as a Cultural System" (Geertz 1973 [1966]), embeds the study of religion in the nexus of a hermeneutic approach to culture, whereas Rappaport's magnum opus, *Ritual and Religion in the Making of Humanity* (1999), describes religion as a cybernetic system.

Despite the unabated influence of both Geertz and Rappaport's work, the academic study of religion has not taken a systemic turn. There are a few exceptions, however. For example, William Green and colleagues have recently begun to analyze the Abrahamic religions as complex adaptive systems (De Sondy, Martinez, and Green 2020; Green 2014). Others have offered theoretical advances. István Czachesz (2014), for instance, developed a formal network model to explore the evolutionary dynamics of religious systems. His model relies on the interrelationship between religious beliefs, such as toward a god or spirit, and religious artifacts, including texts and ritual objects. Francisca Cho and Richard Squier (2013) cautiously explore the methodological merits of recognizing religions as complex systems, most notably the facilitation of cross-cultural comparisons. They are at least partially motivated by concerns of reductionism in the scientific study of religion (Cho and Squier 2008).

Indeed, the primary approach of most cognitive and evolutionary researchers of religion is to break religion down and scrutinize its elements. For example, scientists who study ritual maintain that we need to isolate (in experimental labs or fieldwork) the various common components that constitute ritual, such as body movement, synchrony, singing, and attire (e.g., Whitehouse and Lanman 2014). This strategy is vital to advancing our understanding of religion and it has already shown remarkable progress. Much of our own experimental work, together and independently, employs this reductionist strategy. But reductionism is just a first step in any analysis of complex phenomena. Ultimately, the pieces must be put back together; drawing conclusions about religious systems from the results of analyses that focus on only one corner of the system can therefore be misleading. Even more problematic for a purely reductionist methodology, however, is the strong possibility that religious systems exhibit emergent properties (Sosis 2016, 2017). If so, then religion cannot simply be broken down and studied in isolated fragments if we wish to gain insight into the workings of the whole system (see Chapter 8; Sosis 2009a; Sosis and Kiper 2014b).

Despite efforts to advance a theoretical foundation for a systemic approach (e.g., Sørensen 2004), most religious studies scholars remain highly suspicious of attempts to generalize "religion" as a system. Nonetheless, advances in the study of complexity over the past several decades suggest that religion not only possesses systemic features, but it can be characterized specifically as a *complex adaptive system*.[1] It is worth clarifying how we have understood this term in our studies of religion, and how the term has entered anthropological discourse (Lansing 2003), since transdisciplinary terms can suffer shifts in meaning as they cross disciplinary boundaries. This is particularly true in the case of complexity studies; one of the few unanimities in the "field" appears to be that it is not (yet), in fact, a unified field at all (Mitchell 2009).

Systems, whether economic, political, or digestive, can be described as a set of interacting or interdependent elements that form an integrated whole (Von Bertalanffy 1972). "Complex" is also a term that carries colloquial meaning, but it holds a specific meaning in the context of complex adaptive systems. Miller and Page (2007: 9) explain that "[c]omplexity arises when the dependencies among the elements become important. In such a system, removing one such element destroys system behavior to

---

1. Commenting on standard modeling procedures, Miller and Page (2007) quip that "[t]he ability to collect and pin to a board all of the insects that live in the garden does little to lend insight into the ecosystem contained therein" (10). Likewise, detailing the essential organs of the religious system will ultimately shed little light on the internal dynamics and co-dependencies of that system and how it interacts with external constraints and influences. Rather, emphasizing the *interactions* between the components of the religious system and the individuals participating in them suggest that the whole is indeed greater than the sum of its parts. There may be emergent properties of these components that are wholly unrecognized by most current approaches to understanding religion (for further discussion see Holland 1995; Miller and Page 2007: 44–53).

Trends in computational modeling, typically employed in artificial intelligence and economics, focus on understanding the laws governing complex adaptive systems. Religion is a complex adaptive system *par excellence* because:

> (*i*) It consists of a network of interacting agents (processes, elements); (*ii*) it exhibits a dynamic, aggregate behavior that emerges from the individual activities of the agents; and (*iii*) its aggregate behavior can be described without a detailed knowledge of the behavior of the individual agents. An agent in such a system is *adaptive* if it satisfies an additional pair of criteria: the actions of the agent in its environment can be assigned a value (performance, payoff, fitness, or the like); and the agent behaves so as to increase this value over time. A complex adaptive system, then, is a complex system containing adaptive agents, networked so that the environment of each adaptive agent includes other agents in the system.
>
> (Holland and Miller 1991: 365)

an extent that goes well beyond what is embodied by the particular element that is removed ... Complicated worlds are reducible, whereas complex ones are not." Lastly, complex adaptive systems are "adaptive" in the sense that they are flexible and they respond successfully—in terms of the system's survival—to local social and ecological conditions.

Yet trying to explain what complex adaptive systems are by defining the words that constitute the taxonomic label is not sufficient. In fact, it highlights a key characteristic of actual complex adaptive systems: they are more than the sum of their parts (Holland 1998; Kauffman 1995). Below, we describe a number of defining features of complex adaptive systems in general and discuss how they are manifest within religious systems in particular. First, however, we explore how religious systems are "built."

The Building Blocks of Religious Systems

Holland (1995) lists "building blocks" as one of the seven basic characteristics that are common to all complex adaptive systems. As Holland explains, the component parts of any complex adaptive system are not arbitrary. Rather, complex adaptive systems consist of categories of elements that combine to create the system. The building block mechanism, that is, the combining of elements to create a system, can generate astonishing variation. Holland illustrates this variation by considering the construction of faces. The building blocks of faces are features such as noses, ears, mouths, eyes, hair, cheeks, foreheads, and chins. Within each of these building block categories there is variation, such as size, shape, and color: large oval green eyes, long wavy blonde hair, broad angular brown chin, and so forth. Using this variation an almost limitless number of unique faces can be built simply by combining facial building blocks.

Religious systems also exemplify remarkable diversity, yet underlying all of this diversity is a set of recurring core features. Namely, religious systems typically maintain eight building blocks: authority, meaning, moral obligation, myth, ritual, the sacred, supernatural agents, and taboo. Each of these building blocks is most usefully conceived of as a unique category that may have an independent phylogenetic history, but within religious systems they are inherently interconnected to the other building blocks within the system. As we discuss below, other features of religion are common, such as music, spirit possession, afterlife beliefs, prophecy, superstition, and pilgrimage, but they are not *essential* to the working of the religious system; rather, they are better understood as secondary forms of one of the essential building blocks identified above. Here we describe the religious system's building block categories.

- *Ritual.* Rappaport (1999: 24) defines ritual as "the performance of more or less invariant sequences of formal acts and utterances not entirely encoded by the performers." One of the most obvious aspects of ritual is that it requires human bodies; it is a physical action (Rappaport 1979). This banal observation turns out to be critically important, as will be evident below. Without performance there is no ritual by definition; unlike myth, for example, rituals are dead if they only exist in books or memories. Rappaport's definition, like most definitions of ritual (e.g., Smith 1979; Turner 1969; cf. Bell 1997), recognizes the formality of ritual in the sense that rituals are typically stylized, repetitive, and stereotyped. This formality distinguishes ritual from ordinary behaviors. Norms surrounding ritual generally define the appropriate times and places of performance. And rituals, of course, vary considerably in their intensity and pageantry (Whitehouse 2004); singing from the psalter on a Sunday morning and diving into a partially frozen lake to retrieve a cross at Epiphany are both religious rituals. As we will discuss below, rituals are the central building block of religious systems.
- *Taboo.* Taboos are often conceived of as anti-rituals. That is, whereas rituals must be performed, taboos restrict behaviors. Religions maintain taboos on countless activities, including the consumption of food and drink, social relationships, sex, smoking, gambling, wearing jewelry, exposing certain body parts, types of work, and so on. Some taboos are always in effect, such as Mormon prohibitions on smoking or Muslim bans on pork, but many taboos are temporally regulated, such as Catholic meat consumption during Lent. Taboos are effective at creating boundaries between populations, often limiting the types of social engagements that are possible (Douglas 1966).
- *Authority.* Religious systems generally have leaders, experts, or authority figures who possess particular power and influence within a community (see Chapter 7). These authorities include priests, prophets, gurus, magicians, shamans, imams, rabbis, ministers, seers, sorcerers, and witches. It is worth emphasizing

that, as the plethora of different titles suggests, religious authorities have distinct, widely varying roles and functions in different
societies. Yet they invariably gain and maintain their authority through access to specialized knowledge and/or specialized
access to supernatural beings and the worlds these beings inhabit.
Personal charisma and oratory skills often aid rise to prominence
(Weber 1947). In summary, these figures function as organizational mechanisms for constituents. While some religious leaders,
such as the pope, command considerable authority, others, such as
a synagogue president, lead primarily by following the will of the
community.

- *Myth.* Myths within religious systems serve to provide a contextual narrative for many of the other building blocks of religious
systems. For example, myths often describe the origins and deeds
of the gods, the reasons for certain rituals and taboos, and how
religious leaders have been granted their authority. Myths also
serve as explanations for religious beliefs such as the sanctity of
certain hills, rivers, and cities, accounts of the creation and history of a people, and justifications for specific moral obligations.
However, myths do not offer logical, or what might be described as
scientific, explanations (Levi-Strauss 1994 [1964]). Myths are lived
explanations. They are better understood as one of the fundamental forms of religious discourse, if not the fundamental form.
Indeed, communities often define themselves by the myths they
share, and divergences in narratives often demarcate the fissure
point between related religious groups. For example, incompatible
narratives about Jesus distinguish the different Abrahamic religions from one another, despite their shared Hebraic roots. Myths
do more than inform group boundaries and identity, though. They
also entertain, whether by frightening and alarming listeners or
by evoking laughter—or both at once, as in many trickster tales
(Radin 1972 [1956]). For many, religious myths provide a window
into what it means to be human.

- *Sacred.* Durkheim (2001 [1912]) famously distinguished between
the sacred (that which is set apart) and the profane (that which is
mundane). As many anthropologists have remarked (Alcorta and
Sosis 2005; Rappaport 1999), sanctity is not discovered through
encounter but rather created through ritual. Since ritual can sanctify just about anything, the range of sacred things is quite varied,

including food items, books, land, clothing, weapons, animals, plants, people, ideas, symbols, words, and discourse. In the context of religious systems, to say that something is sacred is to suggest that it has particular emotional valence for individuals living within that system.

- *Supernatural agent.* Throughout this volume, we have conceptualized supernatural agents as beings that exist and operate outside of physical reality, although they typically have impacts on the physical world. They are agents in the sense that they are ascribed actions and motives for those actions (Purzycki et al. 2012). The term "supernatural" itself is contested in the religious studies literature because many cultures do not perceive their gods, spirits, ghosts, demons, angels and assorted beings as supernatural at all. Rather, these beings are perceived as a natural part of their social and physical landscape (Guthrie 2016; Klass 1995; Saler 1977). The concept of the supernatural, these scholars correctly argue, is a western concept. When we impose it on non-western cultures, we fail to understand how non-westerners experience their religious worlds. Westerners often relate to their supernatural agents through what is described as "belief" or "faith." Such a relationship to supernatural agents, though, is quite foreign to many of the small indigenous populations that anthropologists have studied, as well as many historical populations (Kugel 2017; Smith 1998). For example, as Keller notes regarding relations with ancestral spirits in the Malagasy communities she worked with (discussed in Chapter 7), "one doesn't 'believe' in one's ancestors, as one does not 'believe' in elders" (Keller 2005: 178). Nonetheless, while we appreciate that individuals within such populations might not conceive of particular beings as supernatural, we employ the term supernatural agents to describe a building block category because it offers a useful analytic position—an etic perspective—that distinguishes these agents from living beings (humans and animals), as well as fictional characters that populate contemporary entertainment genres.
- *Moral obligation.* Anthropologists have long pointed out that religious systems and moral systems that are concerned with social ethics are generally distinct in traditional societies. It is only after the rise of domestication, intensive agriculture, and the associated sedentary lifestyle that an indelible link between religious systems

and social ethics emerges. Nonetheless, even in traditional foraging societies in which moral prohibitions such as sexual infidelity,
theft, and murder are not supported through religious sanctions
(that is, they are immoral behaviors but there are no priests or holy
books that give such prohibitions authority), moral obligation is
often established through religious systems, particularly through
ritual (Kiper and Sosis 2014). Rappaport (1999: 132) suggests that
breach of obligation may be "one of the few, if not, indeed, the only
act that is always and everywhere held to be immoral." In short,
Rappaport argues that ritual performances establish obligations
to behave according to the moral values explicitly or implicitly
encoded in the rituals.

• *Meaning.* Religious systems not only offer explanations for the
existence of humanity and the existence of particular communities; they offer a purpose for this existence. The comprehensive-
ness of religious systems—their ability to inform every aspect of
an individual's life—enables them to generate meaning for individuals. Religious systems work to keep nihilism at bay, enabling
adherents to make sense of their lives and give it purpose. Religious
meanings range from fixing society through social justice to seeking individual salvation to preparing the world for the messiah.
When religious systems are functioning optimally, religious meanings powerfully organize lives and establish order within communities (e.g., Levine 2003).

Why have these eight features served as building blocks for religious systems? To adequately answer this question, we would need a phylogenetic
account of the emergence of the religious system, and unfortunately our
understanding of religion as a complex adaptive system is not yet developed enough to pursue such an analysis. Nonetheless, we do know enough
to recognize that, as in all complex adaptive systems (Miller and Page
2007), the elimination of one of the religious system's building blocks
would result in either a collapse or transformation of the system into
something else. Remove one of the building blocks, and the adaptive functionality of the religious system will be compromised. A religious system
that lacks organization (authority), fails to impart significance (meaning), forsakes ceremonial activity (ritual), maintains no limits on activity
(taboo), is unable to sanctify anything (sacred), offers no beings capable of
transcending the natural world (supernatural agents), does not establish

social commitments (moral obligation), or provides no narratives that can link all of these elements together into an explanatory framework (myth) will ultimately falter or transform into some other kind of social institution. Notably, religious systems are impressively resistant to the elimination of one of their core building blocks, as the persistence of supernatural elements within Buddhist cultures and Jewish Reconstructionist congregations attest.

Holland (2012) distinguishes between two types of building blocks: generators and conglomerates. Generators do not change over their life course and they behave consistently in similar contexts. Over the course of their existence they fit together with other generators in the same way, following the same set of fixed rules in their reaction with other generators. Conglomerates, on the other hand, are building blocks that do change over their lifespan, sometimes dividing to produce other building blocks or adjusting to compensate for the loss of another building block. For example, the brain's ability to self-repair through rewiring or taking over the functions of damaged areas suggests that the brain is built on conglomerate building blocks (Holland 2012: 112). The imperviousness and essentialness of the religious system's building blocks suggest that they are generators. It is possible that some of the religious system's building blocks should be conceived as conglomerates, but this is an area that needs further investigation. In social environments where governments seek to eliminate specific building blocks of religious systems, the conditions might provide a natural experiment in which this possibility could be explored.

A few further comments concerning the religious system's building blocks are necessary. First, the building blocks identified above are probably universal across religious systems, but they are not building blocks because of their universality; there are other universal features of religions that are not core building blocks (e.g., symbolization, the creation of alternative worlds, etc.). Rather, the eight features we have described are building blocks because they each appear to play a *distinct* and *integrative* role within religious systems. Second, and related to the first point, the identification of these eight core features is based on our understanding of how religious systems work. In other words, religious systems appear to function in particular ways and exhibit specific structural features, as we will describe below. Third and relatedly, while some common features of religion, such as pilgrimage, altered states of consciousness, spirit possession, and so forth, are best depicted as subsumed under one of the eight building block categories (e.g., altered states of consciousness are achieved through ritual), some religious systems may develop such that secondary features become building blocks. For example, the centrality of the peyote hunt among the Huichol Indians of northern Mexico (Myerhoff 1974), may suggest that pilgrimage is a building block of this particular religious system; without the pilgrimage for peyote, the system would probably collapse. The characterization of religious systems that we describe below depicts how most religious systems generally function, but as just noted, there are undoubtedly exceptions to these generalizations.

Our understanding of how the religious system's building blocks are put together is rudimentary, but we can make a few observations with some confidence. First, the adhesive holding the building blocks together is language. Indeed, the religious system is inconceivable without language; discourse serves to indicate the moral obligations conveyed in ritual performance, describe unseen supernatural agents, articulate prohibited behaviors, reveal myths, and so on.

Second, the building blocks interrelate through inherent patterns. These patterns probably constitute a grammar (Bulbulia 2012) and it is the ongoing task of evolutionary and cognitive researchers studying religion to uncover these grammatical rules. This task, however, is genuinely challenging because of the nonlinear nature of the interactions between the building blocks. As Holland (2012) points out, standard statistical observations will not suffice to uncover the rules interconnecting building blocks for any complex adaptive system.

Nonetheless, evolutionary and cognitive researchers have offered various theories that provide insights into the possible rules regulating relations between religion's building blocks. For example, the Modes Theory of Religion provides a useful framework for understanding the mechanisms that enable rituals to create meaning, and significantly, how variation in the frequency of ritual performance is related to variation in the formation of meaning (Whitehouse 2004). Likewise, Cronk's (1994) theory of signal manipulation provides a powerful explanation of how religious authorities employ ritual for means of exploitation (also see Watts et al. 2017). Sacred values research (Ginges et al. 2007; Tetlock 2003), offering another example, highlights the relationship between the sacred-profane distinction and taboo. Other theories we have discussed throughout this book, such as supernatural punishment theory (Johnson 2016; Schloss and Murray 2011), signaling theory (Irons 2001; Bulbulia and Sosis 2011), MCI theory (Purzycki and Willard 2016), hazard precaution system theory

(Liénard and Boyer 2006), and ritual form theory (McCauley and Lawson 2002), offer further insights about how all the building blocks within religious systems interrelate.

The Structure of Religious Systems

We are now in a position to provide a general outline of the structure of religious systems and what we currently know about how they work. Figure 9.1 depicts a general illustration of the structure of religious systems. Religious systems begin with a group of socially engaged individuals. Individuals are agents of the model, and they can enter as well as depart from the group. Like all communities, the group is influenced by external factors, including the social, political, economic, ecological, and religious environment in which the group is situated. Notably, however, religious groups are not simply influenced by their external conditions; they actively shape them (Bulbulia 2012; Chapter 1). These external factors, as well as the internal social dynamics of the group, motivate human action in the form of ritual behavior. Like all systems, religious systems require energy and information to function. Ritual performance introduces social information about the state of performers (Rappaport 1999), as well as energy in the form of calories diverted away from individual metabolism or other needs, into the religious system. All systems transform energy and information; likewise, the religious system transforms the energy and information of human ritual behaviors into human cooperative and coordinated behaviors.

Since ritual is a physical performance, it may be self-evident that it utilizes and transforms energy; however, the information contained by ritual is less obvious. Ritual, as Rappaport (1999) explains, carries two types of information: indexical and canonical. Indexical information refers to messages that reveal the current state of the performer. For example, consider prayer. How loudly one prays or how vigorously one gesticulates can indicate the enthusiasm of the reciter, whereas one who prays with a scowl or teenage eye-roll on their face, or mumbles through their prayers, suggests a less enthusiastic endorsement of Sunday morning in the pews. Rituals also contain information about the past and future; indeed, performers often perceive rituals to have enduring or even eternal referents. This information is known as canonical, and it is often (but not always) contained in the verbal part of the ritual (Rappaport's "utterances" from the definition above). Continuing the example of prayer, the actual words being recited in prayer are canonical information. Moral codes are typically embedded, implicitly or explicitly, in ritual's canonical information.

How does human action in the form of ritual behaviors emerge from social groups? The proximate motivations are likely to be diverse, varying by socioecological context. Fortunately, to appreciate how religious systems operate we do not have to fully apprehend this process, although this is an important area for future work. We do know that rituals spontaneously emerge when communities are under threat. The ethnographic literature on cargo cults (e.g., Whitehouse 1995; Worsley 1957) offers abundant examples, while ethnographers have also detailed ritual practices that have emerged during times of war, such as psalm recitation in response to the Second Intifada (Sosis 2007) and the 2006 Lebanon War (Sosis and Handwerker 2011). But it is clear that "community threat" is just one avenue through which ritual behaviors arise; new technologies, social movements, ecological changes, and demographic factors are among the many potential avenues that need to be further explored.

While we await future work that examines these external forces, it is important to recognize that the structures of rituals themselves play a role in their emergence. Specifically, successful ritual behaviors—that is, those that are performed and passed on to future generations—require cognitive support. Humans have implicit understandings of how rituals are supposed to work (Barrett and Lawson 2001; Legare and Souza 2012; Liénard, Feeny, and Sørensen 2006; McCauley and Lawson 2002) and it is likely that rituals that are successfully motivated (i.e., brought to life) are those that are consistent with these implicit understandings. Put simply, some rituals are more compelling than others; those rituals that take a form that is congruent with cognitive expectations are likely to be more compelling than rituals that are more difficult to mentally process.

It is useful to distinguish between proximate motivations that can explain the emergence of ritual behaviors within a group from proximate motivations for continuing ritual behaviors that have previously stabilized within a community. Rituals generally emerge within groups in response to varying socioecological conditions and are motivated by cognitive and physiological mechanisms that can detect and respond to these changing conditions. Mechanisms for the continuance of ritual behaviors, on the other hand, include social learning (Henrich 2009), social pressure (Sosis 2003), rationalizations about the efficacy of the ritual behaviors (Sosis and

Handwerker 2011), and intuitive cognitive processes.[2] Significantly, there appear to be critical developmental windows that facilitate the generational transmission of ritual knowledge (Alcorta and Sosis 2005; Finkel, Swartwout, and Sosis 2010).

It is somewhat misleading to describe energy "entering" religious systems in the form of ritual behavior, because in fact ritual only manifests its full character through its interactions with other elements within the system. More accurately, human intentions and motivations enter the system and are transformed into ritual action through their interactions with other elements of the system. Subsequent inputs into the system take the form of the behavior transformed into religious ritual. Once energy enters the religious system through ritual behaviors, the elements that constitute the system interact with ritual behavior in feedback loops. Within religious systems, for example, ritual behaviors become associated with supernatural agents. Supernatural agents can take on various roles in ritual performance, such as the recipient of sacrificed food or the target of petitionary prayers. But whether supernatural agents are seen as receivers, creators, or enforcers of a ritual performance, once such agents become linked to a ritual, desires to please or appease the agents can proximally motivate the ritual performance. Indeed, the human action that emerges from the social group in which the religious system is grounded will be transformed into what we recognize as religious ritual once it interacts and incorporates the other elements of the system.

The interaction of the religious system's core building blocks results in five primary individual-level effects: physiological, emotional, cognitive, neurological, and technological effects. The first four are internal responses of ritual performers. These responses span the entire gamut of human experience and are likely to vary significantly depending on whether the base rituals are, for example, dysphoric, such as Hindu fire walking (Power 2017a), or euphoric, such as Sufi dancing (Trimingham 1971). In addition to these internal effects on individuals, the religious system also produces a primary external effect, or what can be considered

---

2. Specifically, believing in the adequacy and/or effectiveness of ritual practices is associated with a host of deeper inferential processes. For instance, there appear to be optimal levels of repetitiveness and numbers of formalized, ordered steps that harness causal cognition. Rituals' associations with spiritual agents also contributes to belief in ritual efficacy (see Legare and Souza 2012) as do their interaction with the kinds of goals rituals are thought to accomplish (see Liénard, Feeny, and Sørensen 2006).

an extended phenotype (see Purzycki and Sosis 2013; Chapter 1), in the form of ritual objects. These artifacts include masks, mats, beads, pipes, attire, and countless other items fashioned by individuals immersed in their religious system.

These primary individual-level effects yield various group-level effects. Specifically, group-level effects include shared cognitive schemata, ethos, symbolic meanings, material culture, historical memories, and group identities. Group-level effects are an emergent property of the religious system and they can powerfully shape individual lives. Indeed, group-level effects produce societal order by creating structured and stable social worlds—often fantastically imaginative—that individuals inhabit and navigate. They are also generally the most salient features of religious systems and why religions are typically characterized as a collective phenomenon. They provide the basis for sustained communal engagement.

The Emergence of Social Norms in Religious Systems

What emerges from these group-level effects are social norms; specifically, expectations and patterns of behavior that characterize communities. This is no small matter. Humans are able to conceive of alternative ways of engaging, understanding, and organizing life. Consequently, our social norms—that is, the way we pattern our lives—are always at risk of modification (Seligman and Weller 2012). Rappaport (1999) argues that this potential instability is minimized because our social norms become internalized and naturalized (Chapter 1). One of the extraordinary features of human experience is that individuals view the norms in which they are entwined as a natural part of their existence (Berger 1967). Indeed, norms typically only become noticeable as non-natural or contingent when behavior is in tension with them, such as when one stands facing the back of an elevator or reaches out to shake hands with one's left hand,

Rappaport (1999) suggests that ritual plays a key role in the emergence of social norms from religious systems. Let's consider his argument. Rappaport observes that ritual's inherent structure is binary; one either performs a ritual or not. He maintains that while ritual behaviors appear to be shrouded in mystery, they are deliberate and their message to others is clear: participation in a ritual performance indexically signals acceptance of (and not necessarily belief in) the moral values encoded in the ritual. Participation, therefore, always carries obligations, and participants can

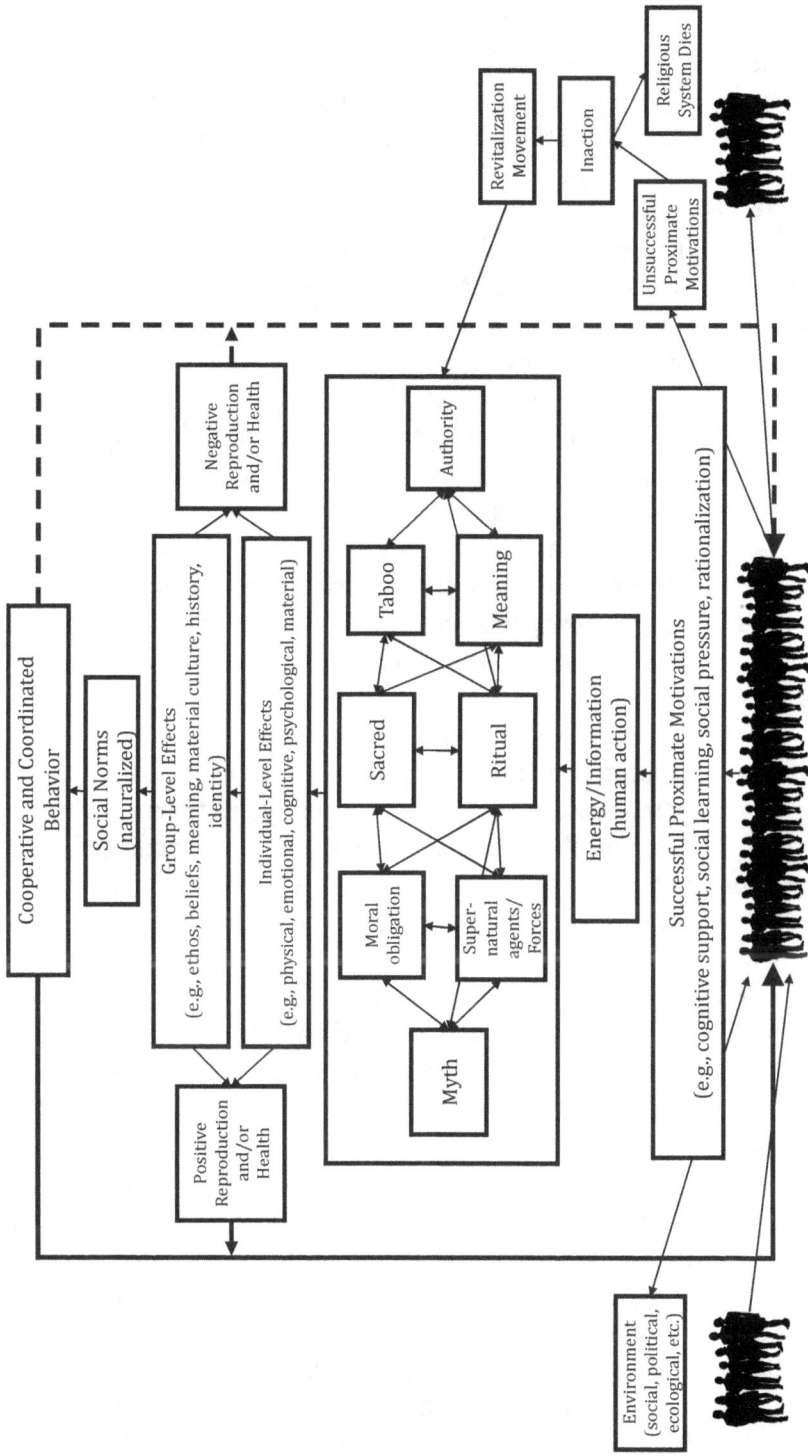

Figure 9.1 Religious system. Solid lines are positive inputs and dashed lines are negative inputs.

be held accountable if these obligations are compromised. Lovers can be unfaithful to one another at any time, but they can only commit *adultery* after the marriage ceremony. Notably, flipping the correspondence theory of truth on its head, when the world does not conform to the moral order encoded in rituals, it is not the ritual that is wrong, but rather the world that needs to be adjusted.

As many anthropologists, including Rappaport, have emphasized, the sacred is not discovered, but rather it is created through ritual. This process occurs via at least two pathways. First, some rituals can evoke numinous experiences. The power of these experiences, which are undeniable to those who experience them (e.g., D'Aquili et al. 1979), make the discursive aspects of ritual unquestionable—that is, sacred. Second, rituals consist of behavioral and discursive components. Rappaport (1999) describes the latter as invariant. Again, consider prayer, which consists of bodily movements—at minimum, moving one's mouth—as well as words. While the intensity of bodily movements, including how loudly prayers are recited, can vary across performers, what is recited (i.e., the canonical messages) is largely invariant within any given tradition. Canonical messages are not encoded by the performer (those sitting in the pews did not write the Psalms) and all performers utter the same words. This verbal aspect of ritual therefore does not transmit any information, since information formally requires signals with a probability less than 100 percent (such as 0 or 1 in binary code, each of which has a 50% probability of being selected for any bit) (e.g., Bloch 1974). But, it is argued, the meaning of the "informationlessness" that emerges from canonical invariance is certainty, which is understood to be unquestionable and true (Wallace 1966). Consequently, the moral messages carried by ritual seem correct, the arbitrariness of norms is transformed to necessity, and these norms seem natural and continuous with the physical world (Rappaport 1999).

While rituals create and support religious systems, they also produce other social constructions such as governments, kin networks, sports teams, and libraries. In other words, rituals spawn many systems; our focus here specifically on religious systems should not obscure the role that these other systems play in the manifestation of social life.

Ritual, sometimes within religious systems and sometimes in other systems, thus provides the stable grounding of social institutions. While not all institutions or their products, such as collective norms, are directly associated with ritual performance, social institutions are interlocking (e.g., consider how libraries systems are connected to monetary, educational, governmental, and other systems) and it appears that all foundational institutions (e.g., governments, legal systems) engender and sustain rituals. Indeed, this may be one of ritual's defining features. It is plausible that rituals inevitably emerge in such institutions because these physical acts provide the sanctity and grounding for our abstract construction of social reality, even outside of "religious" contexts. Rappaport (1999: 137) consequently sees ritual as the "basic social act." Ritual provides the source for the naturalization of social norms; thus, he maintains, social life would not be possible without ritual performance. Ritual, as Seligman and Weller (2012) note, does not eliminate the ambiguities of social life, but it does enable us to live with this ambiguity.

Generating Cooperation and Coordination

While religious systems generate diverse social norms through ritual, the norms that sustain religious systems involve community-level cooperation and coordination. The cooperative and coordinated behaviors that are produced via these norms are, in evolutionary terms, the ultimate goals of religious systems. The success of religious systems in motivating cooperative and coordinated behaviors goes a long way toward explaining their emergence and perdurance.

The energetic output of religious systems, therefore, is cooperative and coordinated behavior. It is worth bearing in mind that the religious system is a stunningly convoluted way to produce such behavioral responses. Other social organisms have devised ways of achieving collective goals that are less complicated and mysterious. Selection, however, operates on available traits and the religious system was built on the existing cognitive and behavioral foundation of prehuman hominids. Also, human language has necessitated complex solutions for sustaining cooperation and coordination. As Rappaport (1999) observes, the symbolic nature of language means there is always the possibility of deceit and lying, since the relationships between signs and their significata are arbitrary. Thus, ultimately, actions (i.e., rituals) speak louder than words (Barker et al. 2019).

The religious system is cybernetic in the sense that feedback is inherent to its structure. Successful cooperation and coordination support the group through the acquisition of energy (for example, through collaborative actions that increase farm output or hunting success). The energy then feeds back into the system. Unsuccessful cooperation and coordination also feed back into the group via decreased energetic input, which informs the group of failure and warns them about impending resource challenges. In addition to these energetic feedbacks, information (usually implicit) about health, mating, and reproductive effects also feed back into the group, informing them about group vitality and offering proximate cues about the value of continuing to engage in ritual behavior.

This information about health, mating, and reproduction emerges from individual and group-level effects. The individual and group-level effects that impact health can potentially be positive, as numerous studies on the health benefits of religion attest (Koenig, King, and Carlson 2012). But they can also be negative, as many rituals are dangerous, including subincision and scarification ceremonies in unhygienic environments (Hogbin 1970), ritual club fights (Hill and Hurtado 1996), and fire walking (Power 2017a). And some religious beliefs can lead to mental instability (e.g., Luhrmann 2012). Moreover, both individual and group-level effects can impact mating and reproduction, again both positively and negatively. Religions are associated with some of the highest fertility rates in the world (Kaufmann 2010; Shaver 2017), as well as the lowest (e.g., celibate monks, Shakers, etc.).

Ritual performance, within religious systems, can be understood as a barometer for the health of the community. When the balance of feedback is positive, individuals perform ritual behaviors, which feed the system with the necessary energy it needs to be sustained. However, when the balance of feedback is negative, proximate factors will tend not to motivate ritual behavior, driving the system down one of two possible pathways. If conditions warrant, the group will undergo a religious revitalization (Heimola 2012; Wallace 1966). This will generally require an individual (or group of individuals) who emerges as an inspirational authority to reinvigorate the group and motivate ritual action. Without the emergence of such a figure, the religious system is likely to die, which has been the fate of the majority of religious systems that have existed in human history. Obviously most religious systems spend much of their existence fluctuating between periods of success, stasis, failure, and revitalization. But ultimately, religious systems either die or transform beyond the recognition of the old system.

Adaptability of Religious Systems

Religion's ability to change, that is, its ability to adapt, turns out to be one of its most extraordinary, and most misunderstood, features. Religious claims are rarely stagnant, nor do they offer permanent truths about the world; they are flexible, responding (sometimes effectively, sometimes not) to changing socioeconomic and ecological conditions (Alcorta and Sosis 2005; Sosis 2009a, 2011; Chapter 7). Religions are adaptive systems that are not only responsive to changing conditions, but they are often instrumental in facilitating social change, as exemplified by the Ghost Dances among the Sioux (Mooney 1965) and Pawnee (Lesser 1978), and Black Churches in the Civil Rights Movement (Billingsley 1999). In these cases, marginalized and oppressed people rekindled identities and collective action against dominating forces within the United States.

If religions are responsive to changing circumstances, why do religions often appear to be so resistant to change? Why is religion often viewed as a conservative social force? One of the remarkable features of religion is its ability to adapt to local environmental conditions while adherents experience partaking in an eternally consistent and changeless tradition. Rappaport (1999) argues that religion achieves this through a hierarchy of religious discourse, for there is an inverse relationship between the material specificity of a religious claim and the durability of the claim. Religious ideas are hierarchically organized within communities, and at the apex of a community's conceptual hierarchy is what Rappaport refers to as ultimate sacred postulates, such as the *Shahada, Shema*, or *Vandana Ti-sarana* for Muslim, Jewish, and Buddhist communities respectively. These ultimate sacred postulates lack material specificity and are highly resistant to change. However, below ultimate sacred postulates in the hierarchy of religious discourse are various cosmological axioms, ritual proscriptions, commandments, directives, social rules, and other religious assertions that do experience varying levels of change, depending on their material specificity.

While the rules of religions change through time, those who experience such adjustments consider them as an intensification of their own religious acceptance (Rappaport 1999). Religions rarely invalidate the old completely: change occurs by adding to and elaborating upon some previous practices and beliefs, while other beliefs and practices slip away unnoticed. Once sacralization is internalized, it is indeed very difficult to convince adherents that something consecrated is no longer holy. Hence, when undergoing change, religions often retain the most sacralized elements and augment them. For example, Jewish prayers were retained in early Christianity, becoming part of the Catholic Mass. Similarly, when proselytizing to indigenous populations, missionaries often retain the dates of indigenous ritual celebrations and tolerate the continued commitment to indigenous ancestral spirits (e.g., Shaver 2015). Change for adherents therefore is not experienced as something radically new. It is rather experienced as an increased acceptance of eternal and personally relevant truths that, for the practitioners, have always been part of their religious tradition.

It is important to appreciate that sacred texts such as the Bible, Koran, or Bhagavad-Gita do not impede the ability of religions to adapt. Intuitively, it may seem that once sacred texts become an essential part of a religious system, as they are in contemporary world religions, the permanence of these texts would make religions more inflexible. In fact, it is a testament (forgive the pun) to the adaptability of religious systems that textual resources often *facilitate* change.

Religious texts that endure do so because they are open to multiple literary interpretations. They tend to make use of metaphor and poetry that engage subconscious processes of personal significance and create contextual meaning. As a result, each new generation reinterprets religious texts in relation to their own meaningful experiences, thereby keeping them living, relevant, and fresh. Past interpretations are not necessarily rejected per se, but are instead transformed or ignored by the community. They nonetheless remain available should cultural change make their message relevant again. Indeed, the sacred writings of contemporary religious traditions are vast repositories that leaders draw upon, emphasizing aspects that are socially and politically expedient, and disregarding those that are not. Though religious radicals often revive past interpretations to justify their radicalization and violence (Sosis, Phillips, and Alcorta 2012; cf. Teehan 2010), use of these latent textual resources is not always so contrived and manipulative. For example, the writings of twelfth-century condemned heretic, Peter Abelard, were largely forgotten until his ecumenical voice was "rediscovered" in the nineteenth century, when his writings received a more welcome reception than they did during his lifetime (Armstrong 1993; Carroll 2001).

While religious texts do not inherently impede the ability of religion to adapt, religions are at risk of over-sanctifying texts and other discourse. When religions sanctify—that is, make unquestionable—discourse that is materially specific it renders the religious system maladaptive. If low-level materially specific discourse, such as social rules about homosexual marriage or the driving of cars by women, are highly sanctified, it limits the religious system's ability to respond adaptively to changing socioecological conditions. These points resonate well with the observations of complexity theorists that complex adaptive systems exist on the edge of chaos (Kauffman 1995). Complex adaptive systems that are too ordered become inflexible, like fundamentalist religions. On the other hand, complex adaptive systems that are too chaotic are unable to gain traction within an environment. Likewise, religious systems without rules and expectations will not endure because the boundaries of such communities will remain undefined.

One last point is worth emphasizing about the adaptability of religious systems: adaptation is local. This is a source of confusion when discussing religions because we use labels such as Hinduism, Islam, Catholicism and so forth to describe what we imagine are particular religions. But religious systems are local affairs, and therefore the taxonomic labels that we ascribe to religions actually consist of multiple and often diverse religious systems. Religious systems that fall under the same taxonomic label are linked in the minds and even actions of those who identify with the label. These linked systems, in other words, are part of the environmental input that impacts individuals within a system. Interestingly, complexity scientists recognize that taxonomic labels can influence system dynamics (Holland 1992, 2012). Religious taxonomic labels are often contested, with significant implications for human welfare and lives, especially since the rise of nation-states (e.g., Seeman 2010). The important point here is that the broad taxonomic labels, particularly of major world religions, should not be confused with religious systems; religious systems are locally defined and they adapt locally. World religions consist, then, of many varied localized religious systems. This hierarchical structure is what complexity theorists would anticipate. Holland (2012: 110), for instance, comments that in "most complex adaptive systems, building blocks at one level of complexity are combined to get building blocks for structures at a higher level of complexity."

Features of Religions as Complex Adaptive Systems

Primary Features of Complex Adaptive Systems

In addition to building block mechanisms, complexity scholars have delineated many features that are deemed essential to all complex adaptive systems. Here we list some of these features and briefly discuss how they are manifest in religious systems.

Emergence

Emergence is a debated topic, sometimes heatedly so, among complexity scientists (see Corning 2002; Deacon 2010; Holland 1998). As is often the case, competing definitions have inflamed debate and complicated rather than clarified matters. Nonetheless, most scholars would agree that emergence is exhibited where properties result from the interactions of a system's components that are not in evidence among the components themselves. Emergence implies that phenomena cannot be explained from linear interactions among the system's components.

Religious systems exhibit emergent properties, including group identities, shared symbolic meanings, and other group-level features discussed above. When the core features of religious systems coalesce, social phenomena are created, specifically group-level properties, which are not in evidence independently among religion's core elements. For example, a child's belief that ghosts reside in her closet does not produce shared symbolic meanings, but belief in ghosts embedded within an animist religious system, such as Sosis encountered during ethnographic fieldwork in Micronesia (Sosis 2005b; Spiro 1952), will generate many group-level effects.

The emergent nature of religious systems has significant implications for how we understand religious beliefs. The complex systems approach to understanding religion emphasizes that religious beliefs are not independent propositional claims about the world (Sosis and Kiper 2014a). Religious beliefs emerge from within a cultural system and they must be understood within that system. In other words, religious belief, as an element of a larger religious system, cannot be analyzed independently of the system in which it is embedded. To do so is like evaluating a symphony when you can hear only one instrument.

Interestingly, the emergent nature of religious beliefs, especially in relation to myth, is a point of potential agreement between some atheists and theologians. Atheist philosopher Daniel Dennett, for instance, argues that telling stories is fundamental to humanity. Notably, he writes "Our tales are spun, but for the most part we don't spin them; they spin us. Our human consciousness, and our narrative selfhood, is their product, not their source" (Dennett 1991: 418). Protestant theologian Paul Tillich would probably agree. For him, religions employ myth "because symbolic expression alone is able to express the ultimate" (Tillich 1957: 41). Myths are not history—and Tillich warns that mistaking myth for history is idolatrous—but myths remain powerful because they are able to transcend themselves and express group values and identity (Mecklenburger 2012), a point with which Dennett would probably be in agreement.

One final point concerning emergence: because religions exhibit emergent properties, studying their building blocks independently as though they are not embedded within a religious system can result in misleading conclusions about religions. Since religions are the complex results of nonlinear interactions between building blocks, they simply cannot be broken down and easily reassembled. It is the interaction between components of the system that must be understood (Sosis 2009a). We will return to this issue below.

Self-organization

Complex adaptive systems spontaneously self-organize, that is, they do not require top-down or bottom-up orchestration to develop; they emerge inherently from the interactions of the system's components. One of the fascinating characteristics of religious systems is that they seem to arise naturally wherever humans live as a community. And as countless commentators of communist China and Russia have remarked, they even arise in the face of social and political forces that are designed to prevent their emergence. Equally intriguing, secular groups who distance themselves from religious dogma nonetheless often adopt the features of religious systems, and some might be considered quasi-religious. Greek fraternities at U.S. universities, for instance, often generate unverifiable mythic narratives, intense ritual routines, and unfalsifiable ideologies concerning "brotherhood" (Shaver et al. 2018; Sosis and Bressler 2003). Likewise, successful secular terrorists, similar to their religious counterparts, employ features of religion such as emotionally evocative symbols, rituals, and myths (Sosis, Phillips, and Alcorta 2012).

Self-organization does not imply a lack of hierarchical structure. While some complex adaptive systems, such as bird flocks, lack central organization, others, such as the nervous system, develop central controls. Religious systems appear to require hierarchical organization—notably, religious leaders emerge in the form of priests, shamans, healers, gurus, prophets, and so forth—despite countless attempts to build perfectly egalitarian religious communities.

Unconsciousness

Constituent entities within complex adaptive systems are unconscious of the process of self-organization. The design of complex adaptive systems such as biological cells can appear to observers to be ingenious, but the constituent entities—in this case, ribosomes, lysosomes, Golgi apparatus, and so forth—need not themselves be intelligent or even aware of the larger systems in which they participate. Their information is limited to their local environment.

Like most complex adaptive systems, religious systems self-organize without top-down or bottom-up orchestration, and the agents (i.e., humans) lack complete information about the workings of the systems they enliven. Their interactions are generally not consciously aimed at creating religious systems. Indeed, one of the successful regulatory mechanisms of religious systems appears to be the ability to cognitively shelter agents (i.e., adherents) from explicit understanding of the functioning and goals of the system itself. Accurate insight into the workings of religious systems might actually be a destabilizing force; mythic narratives and supernatural rewards and punishments, reinforced through ritual routines, tend to be better motivators of obligatory behavior than transparent knowledge and instrumental incentives.

Decentralization

Complex adaptive systems typically lack central control. However, this does not mean that all constituent entities play an equal role in the emergence and functioning of a complex adaptive system. Indeed, as noted above, complex adaptive systems are often hierarchically organized, and this seems to be the case for most if not all religious systems. Importantly, complex adaptive systems that exhibit hierarchical organization maintain their structure despite the constant flow of agents through the system. Cells within the human body are ephemeral, firms succeed and fail within economic markets, and in the Catholic Church popes are chosen only to eventually resign or pass away, while the hierarchical structure of these respective systems endures.

Regulatory Mechanisms

Complex adaptive systems require regulatory mechanisms that enable them to respond adaptively to changing environmental conditions. Our discussion of the hierarchy of religious discourse, above, describes one of the regulatory mechanisms that enable religious systems to adapt to changes in the environment. Moreover, the nature of the feedback loops in religious systems is such that, when a system is not producing cooperative and coordinated behavior or when group members experience negative health or reproductive impacts on average, the performance of ritual behaviors declines. Accordingly, the system itself will adjust by possibly revising rules, weaving new motivational myths, or even imagining novel supernatural worlds; otherwise the system will die.

Open

Complex adaptive systems are open systems; that is, they have fuzzy (i.e., not well-defined) and porous (i.e., easily crossed) boundaries. Religious groups of course vary in how open or closed they are (Wilson et al. 2017). Some religions proselytize and seek outside members, such as most forms of Christianity, whereas other religions, such as Judaism, discourage new members from joining. Further, individual mobility varies significantly across religious landscapes. For example, in the U.S., where religions are experienced as free market commodities, there are much higher levels of denominational switching than in European countries where state-supported religious monopolies exist (Putnam and Campbell 2010). There are also considerable differences between world and indigenous religions in their openness; major world religions tend to be much more open. In many indigenous communities, the only way to join the religious community is to participate in the local initiation ritual; there are no anonymous members in distant lands (Whitehouse 2004).

Amplification of Random Fluctuations

Positive feedback loops direct complex adaptive systems toward divergent evolutionary pathways. In other words, because interactions among agents are nonlinear, small random changes or fluctuations that are not necessarily adaptive responses to environmental conditions can result in substantial differences across systems. This observation of course has significant consequences for understanding religious systems. For example, Jewish communities that Sosis has visited in North America, South America, Europe, Africa, the Middle East, and India exhibit extraordinary religious diversity. Their differences in food preferences, dress, greetings, language, styles of prayer, and so forth are a product of the local sociocultural environment. But how and why communities initially settled in a particular area is often the result of the fortuitous decision of a religious leader, a ship simply landing where the winds took it, myths of golden streets, or any of countless other random factors that are not adaptive responses to environmental conditions. Yet these factors result in astonishing differences between communities over time. Or consider religious holidays that mark a historical event. Jews, for instance, observe four minor fast days to commemorate tragedies in their history, or in one case a tragedy narrowly averted, but the dates themselves are the incidental consequence of history. Yet, once the fast days were canonized as part of the Jewish calendar, the shape and rhythm of the Jewish year and the lived experiences of Jews were altered. The amplification of random fluctuations suggests that researchers must be cautious not to over-interpret the adaptive nature of religious systems; adaptive responses are often built on random fluctuations.

History

One implication of the amplification of random fluctuations for complex adaptive systems is that historical contingency is always partially responsible for present behavior. This means that historical analyses will play an important role in understanding any complex adaptive system, and religious systems are no exception. Indeed, it would be impossible to understand why any religion takes the form it does without understanding the historical factors that shaped the religion accordingly.

Unpredictability of Agents

It is generally difficult to predict the behavior of specific agents in a complex adaptive system. Even when group-level behavioral patterns appear to stabilize, it is very difficult, if not impossible, to predict individuals' actions or life paths. For example, we can confidently anticipate a gathering of parishioners at a local church on Sunday morning, but even regular worshippers will fail to attend occasionally due to illness, travel, or mood—factors we are unlikely to foresee.

Disequilibrium

One of the most interesting and significant features of complex adaptive systems is that they do not operate at equilibria conditions. This does not mean that they do not experience moments of stasis, but their responsiveness to changing environments keeps complex adaptive systems in nearly constant flux. The reason that this feature of religious systems is so important is because it implies that they are continuously evolving. This claim will strike some as extraordinary and even outlandish. But as discussed above, while religious systems give the impression to adherents and outsiders that they are eternal and stable, real religious systems are in fact constantly adjusting to local socioecological conditions. As Bulbulia (2009a) has astutely noted, a historical glance at any religion will reveal both surprising stability (e.g., the Lord's Prayer) as well as extensive change (e.g., the language in which it is recited).

Four Additional Features of Complex Adaptive Systems

One of the world's leading complexity theorists, computer scientist John Holland (1992), offers four additional features of complex adaptive systems. First, agents interact by sending signals that interact simultaneously, a process he terms parallelism. Second, agents are characterized by conditional action in that they respond to signals as if-then statements. Third, the regulatory mechanisms of complex adaptive systems are modular in the sense that groups of rules combine to form what we might think of as subroutines. These subroutines enable complex adaptive systems to deal with novel conditions. Fourth, not only do complex adaptive systems themselves adapt and evolve, but agents and constituent elements within these systems adapt and evolve as well.

There are several points to emphasize when considering how these features relate to religious systems. First, signaling theory offers a robust collection of models that have been rigorously applied to religion by economists, sociologists, biologists, psychologists, and anthropologists (see Bulbulia and Sosis 2011; Chapters 1, 7, and 8). However, this work has not yet recognized that religious signals lie at the core of the communication structure that enables religious systems to operate. Second, what Holland in the language of computer science refers to as subroutines are particularly important for understanding religious systems. Many of the predictable relationships between building blocks of religious systems, such as those identified in Modes Theory and Supernatural Punishment Theory, are subroutines in Holland's terms. Moreover, the linkage of rules also occurs at the level of agent-agent interactions, because religious rules are regularly tied together. Religious communities expect adherents who follow one rule to obey the other rules as well. The Muslim who habitually prays five times each day but enjoys a ham sandwich after evening prayers will be eyed with suspicion, and notably, the prayers themselves, even if heartfelt, will no longer serve as effective signals of his or her commitment to the community. Third, not only do religious systems adapt, but individual adherents change along with the systems' core elements. It is indeed likely that the building blocks of religious systems have been transformed over time, lending weight to anthropologists' recurrent warning not to generalize across categories of religions, such as tribal, chiefdom, and contemporary world religions (Evans-Pritchard 1965). Religious meaning differs considerably across these categories, and as Whitehouse (2004) observes, this is probably a function of variation in the frequency of ritual performance.

Discussion

Viewing religions as complex adaptive systems is a powerful framework for analyzing the unwieldy phenomenon of religion, but scholars have yet to fully explore its potential. Part of its promise as a framework lies in the fact that the analysis of complex adaptive systems is a transdisciplinary enterprise. Much work, not surprisingly, has been advanced by mathematicians and computer scientists. But complexity theory has also received attention in the social sciences, most notably in economics, sociology, political science, and linguistics, as well as the natural sciences, including physics, geology, and evolutionary and systems biology (Mitchell 2009). This consilience across disciplines will enable the study of religion to benefit from rich methodological and analytical techniques from across the sciences, as well as from the modeling sophistication of these fields.

For example, Wood and Sosis (2019) recently developed a system dynamics model to assess the validity of the complex adaptive systems approach to religion. In their experimental simulations, they found that stable societies tended to have higher legitimacy—that is, agents perceived institutions as credible—than unstable ones, and that higher legitimacy leads to greater cooperativeness. Simulated communities maximized their population growth by overexploiting their resource base, but this in turn led to a collapse of the community. Certain communities, however, showed greater longevity when they had strong potential for charismatic leadership that could challenge structural authority in the event of declining system legitimacy (specifically, a parameter characterizing charismatic authority was maximized). As Wood and Sosis note, religious charisma in the simulated social systems postponed community collapse, but crashes did eventually occur, and they were often more extreme than community crashes that lacked the intervention of a revived, charismatic religious authority.

In addition to the systemic approach's natural links to the sciences, it can also provide a connection to the humanities (Sosis 2020a, 2020b). As noted above, complex adaptive systems, including religions, exhibit nonlinearity, amplification of random fluctuations, and historical contingency. The systemic approach, in other words, not only recognizes the significance of history for understanding religion, it suggests that historical work is indispensable to explaining the evolution of religion. Indeed, it would be impossible to understand why any religion takes the form it does without understanding the historical factors that shaped the religion accordingly. Such considerations are also important for defining the appropriate parameters of adaptive analyses. While many religious beliefs and practices confer adaptive benefits (e.g., Shaver et al. 2019), the specific details of many religious acts, such as why one religious garment is worn instead of another, are simply the result of arbitrary circumstances. Why medieval Jews, for instance, adopted European rather than Chinese demons has little to do with the relative adaptive qualities of beliefs about these respective demons (Sosis 2020b); rather, it is a consequence of historically contingent factors. As others have noted (Buskell et al. 2019; Lang and Kundt 2020), the necessity of historical analyses for the systemic approach suggests it has the potential to offer that elusive bridge from the sciences to the humanities.

One reason that historical contingency is important for understanding religious systems is that religious systems are clearly organic. The coalescence of various cognitive, neurological, behavioral, affective, and developmental aspects of humanity has resulted in self-sustaining and cross-culturally recurring systems to which individuals, interacting through signaling mechanisms, bring life. One of the most important lessons of the complex adaptive approach to religion is that altering one part of a complex adaptive system has significant effects on other parts. Those effects, notably, are difficult to predict even for those most familiar with religious systems, including scholars and religious leaders. For example, sociologists Rodney Stark and Roger Finke (2000) have argued that when the Second Vatican Council in 1962 repealed many of the Catholic Church's prohibitions and reduced the level of strictness in the church, it had unforeseeable consequences. Vatican II was, among other things, an attempt to regain the commitments of wavering Catholics, but it inadvertently initiated a decline in church attendance among American Catholics and reduced the overall enrollments in seminaries. In the late 1950s almost 75 percent of American Catholics were attending Mass weekly, but since Vatican II there has been a steady decline to the current rate of less than 35 percent (D'Antonio et al. 2007; Hadaway and Marler 2005). A similar reduction in commitment is associated with the purging of ritual obligations in Reform Judaism as well (Iannaccone 1994; Lazerwitz and Harrison 1979). Though many other instances could be referenced, what these two examples illustrate is that religions grow organically; thus, naïve tampering with them can result in unexpected changes, even stunted growth or collapse.

Most contemporary discussions of religion involve concerns about the rising, seemingly uncontrollable geopolitical influence of religion today. The merit of any theory lies in its ability to explain current trends, and by that measure the complex adaptive systems approach fares comparatively well. Understanding religions as complex adaptive systems underscores how external pressures that aim to change religions can sometimes result in dangerous consequences. For instance, religious radicalization, such as the emergence of the Muslim Brotherhood in Egypt, Turkey, and elsewhere, appears to have been a response to aggressive secular campaigns (Armstrong 2000; Ruthven 2004). Minimizing religious extremism in the future thus requires secularists to countenance religious traditions and design policies accordingly. This will not be easy, for even externally imposed changes that are intended to benefit religious communities can have long-term negative consequences. For example, on March 3, 1948, during a period of civil war prior to the Israeli War of Independence, Ben-Gurion established a military exemption for yeshiva students. He presumably felt he was saving a cultural remnant of European Jewry that was otherwise headed toward extinction with the birth of the secular Israeli state (Efron 2003). As the yeshiva population has grown exponentially because of the extraordinary birth rates of Israeli Ultra-Orthodox Jews, not serving in the military has emerged as a costly signal of one's commitment to the community. For Jewish Israelis, not serving in the military is a stigma with consequences in the labor market. But this stigma serves as a gatekeeper within the religious community: one way of demonstrating one's commitment is staying in yeshiva not just until the possibility of being drafted has passed due to age, but even several years after one is eligible for the draft (Berman 2000). As a result, yeshiva students and their families are exceedingly poor, because under the terms of their military exemption they are only permitted minimal employment. Due to their failure to recognize that the military exemption has been transformed into a religious commitment signal, the government has attempted to alleviate the financial plight of these yeshiva students by increasing their subsidies, but this has only exacerbated the problem (Berman 2009). By increasing payments to yeshiva students, the government has increased the amount of time yeshiva students must remain in the yeshiva to serve as an effective signal of commitment. In short, the government subsidies have effectively had the opposite of the intended effect.

Complexity theorists acknowledge that because of the nonlinear dynamics of complex adaptive systems it will be a challenge to develop a general theory of complex adaptive systems that will generate reliable predictions. However, these theorists also argue that such a pursuit is not hopeless. They emphasize, for example, that all complex adaptive systems exhibit lever points (Holland 1995). These are points in the system where small changes can have predictable system-wide effects. One obvious lever point in religious systems is ritual performance. As Atkinson and Whitehouse (2011) have shown, changes in a ritual's frequency and intensity have predictable consequences for the hierarchical structure of the ritual community as well as cognitive impacts on individual perceptions of local versus universal communities. Of course, likewise, eliminating a ritual entirely can have profound effects on a community. Tuzin (1997), for example, ethnographically documents how social dynamics among the Ilahita Arapesh were transformed following the demise of the central ritual cult known as the Tambaran, as described in Chapter 3. The secret male cult was eliminated when a revivalist movement overtook the Ilahita villages where Tuzin was conducting fieldwork. Fathers lost the respect and control of their sons, which had previously been secured by the brutal initiation rites of the Tambaran. Wives, who were left out of the Tambaran, now had social power that enabled them to dominate their husbands. Beyond social relations, work itself also completely changed. Garden work, especially yam cultivation, lost its meaning for Ilahita men; what was once an activity motivated by the possibility of pleasing the spirits and contributing to Tambaran feasts now became drudgery for these men.

While ritual performance is clearly a lever point in religious systems, the examples discussed throughout this chapter suggest that our ability to anticipate changes at this lever point are limited. Like other systems in nature, religions are dynamic, emergent, and difficult to predict. Our understanding of them is incomplete. By recognizing religions as complex adaptive systems, it is hoped that students, scholars, and policymakers appreciate that if there are compelling reasons to control or reform religions, we currently have limited understanding of how to do so, and naïve policies seeking change are likely to have unintended consequences. This does not mean that societies are simply at the mercy of religious exigencies, but it does suggest that effective engagements with religions will require an appreciation that they are dynamic complex systems, along with all that this implies.

Conclusion

Debate within any academic field is healthy and usually productive. But current debates within the scientific study of religion are focused on the narrow details of specific isolated elements within religious systems, without attention to the context in which these elements are situated. To be clear, breaking down complex systems into manageable units is essential to scientific advancement. However, the instinctive reductionism that currently dominates the scientific study of religion is directing us away from urgent questions about how the elements of religious systems interrelate, the selective pressures that have favored the coalescence of these elements across time and space, and the implications of this coalescence for the perdurance of religious thought and expression in our world today. The framework presented here not only raises these questions, but its connection to broader work in complexity theory points to the tools—phylogenetic, historical, cross-cultural, ethnographic, experimental, and modeling techniques—that can be employed to answer these questions and advance a more holistic and accurate study of religion. We now turn to one of these tools, which has been at the heart of anthropology since the field's inception.

Chapter 10

Prospects for an Evolutionary Ethnography of Religion

If we begin from the simplest, theoretical definition of religion—practices done to engage with and alter the states and attitudes of spiritual agents (Chapter 1)—and proceed to examine the variation in those practices and their associated beliefs (e.g., the objective costs, timing, and spatio-temporal distribution of ritual, or beliefs about what angers the gods), it becomes clear that religions are universal (Chapter 3). That is, all societies have complexes of ritual and belief that refer to supernatural beings, although their forms and content may vary tremendously along a wide range of dimensions. Moreover, their features somehow evolve in ways that conform to the socioecological conditions of communities (Chapter 4). In this chapter, we frame these socioecological conditions more formally as cooperative dilemmas.

Observing these patterns, many cultural anthropologists have appreciated that each of these elements interrelate in a kind of systemic cultural logic of meaning (Chapter 6; Geertz 1973 [1966]; Rappaport 1999; Spiro 1987). Throughout this volume, we have treated religions as systems of both information *and* energy, positing that their content and structure flexibly adjust to novel conditions. In order for religious systems to function adaptively and alleviate the stresses of living, their elements must inform and respond to each other. By re-routing the allocation of resources into collective and other ritual acts with signaling functions, religions inhibit the kinds of selfishness that otherwise plague social life.

This view diverges from one major claim in the cognitive science of religion and complements another. It diverges from the view that religions are merely byproducts of human cognition; we have argued that the form, variation, and fitness returns that religions offer indicate a far more significant role in human evolution than mere epiphenomena of other adaptations would normally be expected to play (Chapters 1 and 2). Accepting this possibility entails expanding our conception of behavioral adaptations beyond the functionally isolated cognitive systems in which the cognitive science of religion and evolutionary psychology are largely interested. Instead, we see adaptations—even those cognitive systems themselves—as constellations of other sub-components (Chapter 8). Complementing non-*tabula rasa* views of the mind, on the other hand, a complete view of religion as a functional adaptation nevertheless *requires* us to pay attention to the cognitive mechanisms underlying the retention of, energy expenditure for, and motivation to transmit beliefs, values, and the practices they encode, as biocultural scientists of religion advocate (Chapters 4–6).

While we hold sharedness and cultural transmission as critical features of the evolution of religious systems (Chapters 6 and 7), we do not limit our investigation or explanations to the mechanisms of social learning, nor do we think social learning is a satisfactory explanation of religion on its own or with cognition in consideration. Of course people learn these traditions; we take that as a given (see D'Andrade 1981) and cognitive processes underlie the management and processing of that cultural information. Rather, we seek to understand why people are transmitting their particular traditions, and if and why those traditions make sense within their particular socioecological environments (Chapter 4). As such, our view also stresses the importance of ethnographic inquiry.

If there is a correspondence between religions and social ecologies, we should expect the cultural evolution of religious traditions to be in certain respects dissimilar to that of, say, linguistic accents, fashion trends, or ice cream preferences. In such cases, historical contingency, social learning processes, and evolved cognition might explain the bulk of the variation. Instead, the evolution of religion is more likely to resemble other cultural adaptations such as foraging strategies and domicile constructions, where historical contingency and social learning may explain some variance, but phenotypic design in fact largely corresponds functionally to particular socioecological conditions (Chapter 2). We see this in terms of local situational context harnessing particular cognitive faculties. More specifically, cognitive mechanisms such as agency detection and corollary moral cognition (Chapter 5) are triggered in particular religious contexts. And as we have stressed throughout, sharedness is critical to this view; we teach each other *when* and *where* to engage these systems through religious thought and practice. Many of the important features of any social system, however, are also things that are not explicitly transmitted socially, such as the emergent properties of such systems' interacting components (Chapter 9).

In this chapter, we refine this view, apply it to some examples, and discuss how we might use it to enrich further empirical ethnographic studies. The next section introduces aspects of the religious systems found among the Martu of Australia, the water temples of Bali, and the animistic system of Tyvans of southern Siberia. We then construe some of these case studies in terms of game-theoretical social dilemmas, pointing to how religious beliefs and practices may offset the payoffs of these elementary games. After this, we turn to some brief examples of recent changes in the content and form of religious systems, discussing them in light of this framework. We conclude with prospects for future directions in the evolutionary, biocultural, and cognitive sciences of religion.

Gods, Games, and Socioecologies

Martu Field Burning

The indigenous Martu of Western Australian burn fields in a controlled manner. This practice has the effect of reducing the sizes of natural and less controllable fires, such as from lightning strikes. It also enriches the soils, aiding the growth of seed-producing plants upon which smaller animals feed and so increasing species diversity. These animals are prey for monitor lizards which, in turn, the Martu hunt. In this system, then, controlled burning increases the availability of resources for people over the long term. Behavioral ecologist Rebecca Bliege Bird and colleagues (Bliege Bird et al. 2013) modelled this system (illustrated in Figure 10.1) and subsequently found that hunting is more successful in places where Martu burn than where they do not. Note that each arrow in the figure represents a tractable relationship that is empirically testable. Here, then, we have a system of niche construction and foraging behaviors that co-vary with measurable gains.

What about the role of beliefs? What makes Martu field burning qualify as "religious" in our view is that the Martu justify this practice with appeals to "the dreaming" and the will of ancestors. According to the authors, such beliefs "are the institutionalization of...histories of ecological practice" (Bliege Bird et al. 2013: 6), thus implying that these practices are maintained in part by religious appeals. In other words, the Martu

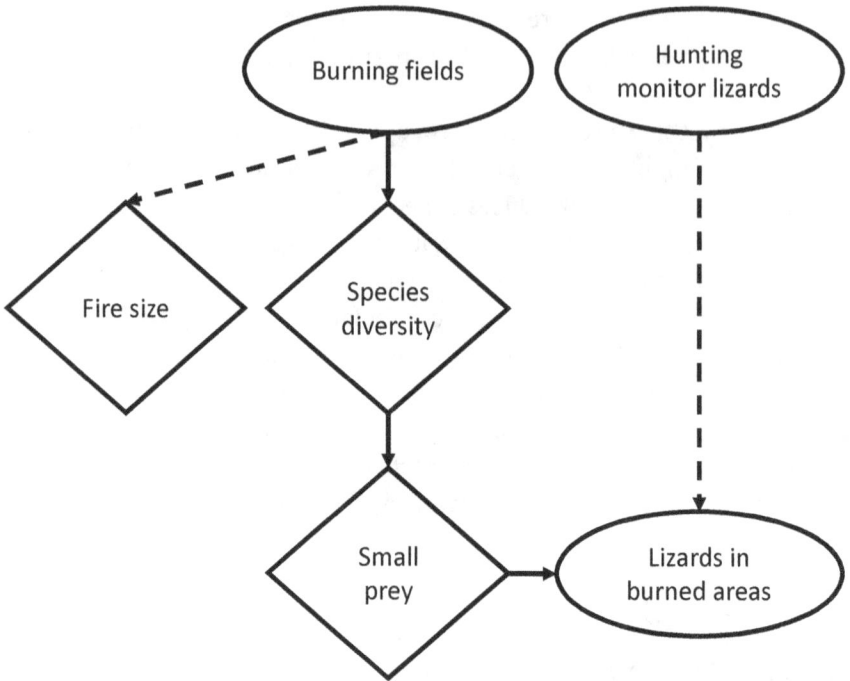

Figure 10.1 Martu field burning system. Solid lines are positive inputs and dashed lines are negative inputs. Adapted from Bliege Bird et al. (2013).

imbue these practices with religious meaning, reducing energetic and informational uncertainty and thereby increasing efficiency (see Box 6.2). Further bolstering the significance and predictability of burning, some Martu hold that the stakes are quite high:

> Critical to the perpetuation of life is the proper adherence to the Law …
> [that] frames the importance of hunting and sharing within the notion
> that "country must be used and appropriately burned" if life is to con-
> tinue. As one elder put it, to stop using up resources, to stop hunting and
> burning, would mean "the end of the world."
>
> (Bird et al. 2016: S71)

And finally, successful hunting means successful sharing: "hunting is always embedded in a context of social exchange … the goal is not to eat more but to share more to other members" of the group (ibid.: S73). Successful hunting affords some status to the hunter, but it also facilitates the development of an individual's cooperative network through trusting relationships (Bliege Bird and Power 2015). Burning fields to maintain the Law and the wills of ancestors clearly provides caloric gains for individuals and their communities. The collapse of this system, ceteris paribus, might very well entail the cessation of the Martu's social ecology.

There are two things to note here. First, even though the ethnographic descriptions of Bliege Bird and colleagues (also see Tonkinson 1991) suggest that field burning is religiously inspired and maintained, the role of beliefs in this system remains unclear and unmeasured. But if we could toggle the presence or absence of beliefs among the Martu, what would happen to field burning practices over time? Would the lack of divinely inspired motivations make the system appear impractical or unproductive (see Johnson 2005)? The collapse of the Tambaran cult among the Ilahita Arapesh (see Chapters 3 and 9), for example, transformed garden work, which had provided subsistence for the Arapesh as well as their ancestors, from a "meaningful endeavor into unredeemed drudgery" (Tuzin 1997: 34), resulting in reduced work efforts and productivity. Would the Martu system suffer a similar fate if religious beliefs were altered or eliminated?

Imagining such scenarios raises an obvious question: Why not instead make secular appeals—that is, appeals that do not point to a transcendent order—to maintain the Martu field burning system? Would it disintegrate sooner because secular rationales are easier to manipulate and alter, or because the authority of gods is generally perceived to be more powerful than human authority (Rappaport 1999; Rossano and Leblanc 2017; Sosis and Bressler 2003)? While ethnographers characterize Martu cosmological beliefs about field burning as institutionalized, which implies sharedness, researchers have not examined why the Martu have not institutionalized this system in a secular way (e.g., "we have always done this to get more lizards").

The second thing to note is that while this system functions to extract more energy from the environment, and increasing resources might fuel more cooperation among individuals embedded in this system, Bliege Bird et al.'s model does not address the potential social dilemma(s) implicated in this process. However, we might analyze the task of getting people to collectively participate in field burning as a coordination problem. Table 10.1 frames the payoffs involved in getting people to collectively burn as a "stag hunt" dilemma (see Rousseau 2016 [1755]; Skyrms 2004). In this dilemma, one has to choose between a smaller but more reliable payoff and a larger but less reliable one. More specifically, since it is costly to hunt, and bigger game (i.e., the stag) can only be captured with the assistance of a partner, it is better to hunt for big game only when your partner does. In other words, it pays to look for smaller game (e.g., a rabbit) on your own when others won't contribute to hunting larger game, even when hunting larger game would yield higher per capita net benefits.

In the present case of the Martu, individuals in the model can choose to participate in collective burning or not. In this two-person game, the benefits of burning collectively, *b*, include the aforementioned lizards. Hypothetically, if a Martu chooses to burn without help, she is unable to control the fire and captures nothing. If she chooses to not burn, she accrues the benefits of slacking, *s*. What makes this a dilemma for individuals is the assumption that $b > s$; the individual net payoffs for collectively burning fields outweigh the individual net payoffs when fields are not burned. How can people work together to reap the larger benefits that require coordination? Does the threat of "the end of the world" motivate individuals to coordinate their actions? Beliefs about such costs might increase the likelihood of choosing to join in with field burning activities. In other words, collective pressure and religious appeals might motivate individuals to opt for the riskier—but more profitable—coordination strategy.

Our next case study, in contrast to our putative model of Martu field burning, has been explicitly modeled as a social dilemma by ethnographers. The religious "solution" in the system we describe is an institutional mechanism that efficiently motivates and generates coordination between individuals.

Table 10.1 Payoff matrix for coordination in Martu field burning. Payoffs are for player on left side of table.

	Burn	Don't burn
Burn	*b*	0
Don't burn	*s*	*s*

Water Temples of Bali

In Chapter 2 we briefly described the Balinese water temple ecosystem extensively studied by J. Stephen Lansing (1987, 1991, 2006). Here we examine this system further, focusing on the inherent coordination problem faced by Balinese farmers. Table 10.2 represents this problem in the form of a payoff matrix that details the conflicts of interest between two farmers (or farming groups). One lives upstream and one lives down-stream. They can choose between two different times to plant their rice. Water comes down the mountain, ensuring that the upstream farmer can use the stream first, depleting it by factor d. Therefore, if both farmers plant their rice at the same time, there will be a loss for the downstream farmer since the water will be depleted. Lansing and Miller (2005) assume the threat of pests is reduced if both farmers plant simultaneously because pests can simply migrate from fallow to nearby planted fields. By contrast, if all the fields in a given area are fallow at the same time, pests will have nowhere to opportunistically migrate to and will die off. So, if farmers plant in a staggered, step-wise fashion, both of their yields are reduced by r, the pest-consumption factor. Therefore, it is always in the upstream famer's best interests to plant simultaneously with the down-stream farmer. However, it is only in the best interests of the downstream farmer to coordinate planting when $r > d$; if the costs of water depletion are worse than those associated with pests, then it makes sense to accept the costs of pests and not coordinate.

Table 10.2 Payoff matrix for Balinese coordination problem. First payoff in each cell is the payoff for the player on the left side of the table (the upstream player), second is for the player on the top of the table (the downstream player).

	Simultaneous	Staggered
Simultaneous	$1, 1-d$	$1-r, 1-r$
Staggered	$1-r, 1-r$	$1, 1-d$

Source: adapted from Lansing and Miller (2005)

The practical question of how to maximize *everyone's* yield, then, is this: *how can we get upstream farmers to give up some water so that the downstream farmers' crops improve to the point that they are willing to coordinate to reduce pests?* The answer, according to Lansing, is water temples: they function as structured, spiritually sanctioned forums for coordination and forging pacts sealed with the kinds of ritual-induced bonds we have discussed throughout this book. Balinese farmers meet at temples with the desire to honor various deities, receiving small ceremonial distributions of "holy water" (not irrigation water) in return. As these temples exist in a much wider temple network, they have the capacity to maintain a remarkably complex coordination system over vast areas, timing and synchronizing planting on the basis of ritual performance and holy water distribution. Each temple coordinates the planting and harvesting cycles of the farms in its area, called a "subak."

Lansing (2006: 87) "wonders whether institutions like water temples exist elsewhere in the world, and if so, what form they might take. Perhaps, like the water temples, they are regarded as religious institutions that can be safely ignored by planners and engineers." We might add evolutionary and cognitive scientists of religion to this list of professionals who have largely ignored this possibility. Indeed, like the Martu, the Balinese alter their physical landscape in coordinated ways to reap the benefits of collective action and mobilization. As we have suggested throughout this book, we suspect similar religious institutions do exist. In fact, the opportunity to explore such a possibility brought one of us to the field. We now turn to this example.

Tyvan Spirit-Masters

As discussed in Chapter 3, spirit-masters in the Tyva Republic care about rituals and the preservation of natural resources such as game and water (Purzycki 2011b, 2016). The rituals that they care about take place on territorial borders, at mineral springs, and lakes (Purzycki 2013b). Tyvans encourage each other to keep these areas clean. Additionally, hunting is strictly forbidden in some regions considered to be the hunting territories of spirit-masters (Donahoe 2006: 120). In other words, behaviors associated with spirits and their behavioral corollaries are largely distributed near markers of negotiated territory and at other discrete exploitable resources. We illustrate these scenarios in Figure 10.2.

In this illustration, there are two yurt encampments (1 and 2). By necessity, both are located by water sources. In addition to a river, one camp stands by a natural spring, marked with C. These two camps recognize their established territories, marked by a devotional cairn at B. One "territory" is the spirits' land (marked by A) where hunting is forbidden. This illustration is a condensation and simplification of real, observed scenarios:[1] many Tyvans and other Inner Asian ethnic groups are bound by a common, ancient religious system that entertains the possibility that "spirit-masters" inhabit the landscape. Specific places and regions are

---

1. Purzycki has directly observed and reported on Scenarios B and C, while Scenario A comes from stories, by implication, and reports by Donahoe (2006).

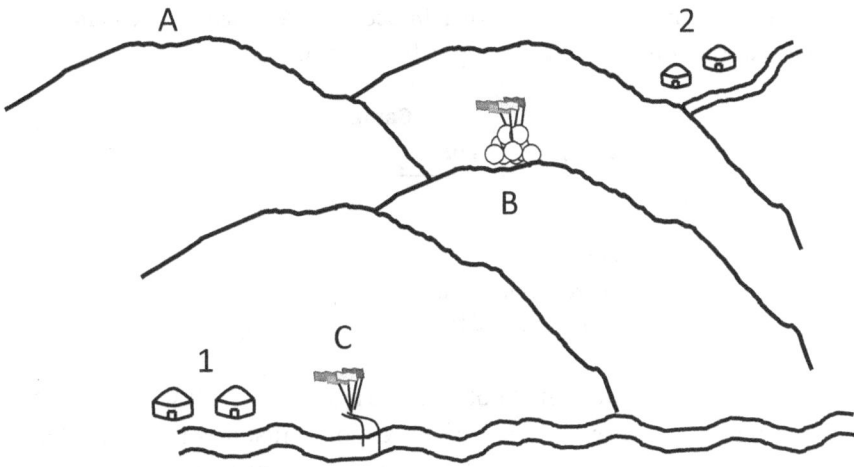

Figure 10.2 Three scenarios on the relationship between spirit-masters, ritual, and resource in Tyva.

especially associated with spirits. Those who fail to pay respect to the spirits in the locally appropriate manner risk misfortune. In other words, cognition about the moral interests (Chapter 5) and potential punishments (Chapters 2 and 4) of supernatural agents (Chapters 1 and 4) is contextually triggered, spatially distributed, and grounded in local rituals and resources. Indeed, we can model each of these scenarios as corresponding to a different social game, much like that detailed in the previous sections.

We model Scenario A as a dilemma that revolves around overexploitation, where it is tempting to hunt deer. In this territory, hunting is off limits because this is the "spirits' land," but it is in individuals' interests to hunt there anyway, especially considering the difficulty of monitoring others' behavior (or of determining where gunshots are coming from, if they're audible at all). Hardin's (1968) "tragedy of the commons" famously offered a dismal portrait of how such self-interested behavior can lead to the destruction of common-pool resources when top-down governance is absent (cf. Ostrom 2015).

We use the prisoner's dilemma to model this problem (Table 10.3). Players can either hunt or forgo hunting. One person could easily defect and continue killing deer, only to effectively wipe out the population.[2] Without restraint, two people hunting would wipe out the deer population

_____

2. Formal models often include discount parameters that adjust the value of subsequent interactions, or some time constraint parameter that toggles the likelihood of interactions

Table 10.3 Payoff matrix for Camp 1 in Scenario A: tragedy of commons as modelled as the prisoner's dilemma. Payoffs are for Camp 1.

	Camp 2	
Camp 1	Forgo	Hunt
Forgo	3	1
Hunt	4	2

Source: from Romagny, Lobry, and Canalis-Durand (1997)

even more quickly. However, if both people agree to not hunt there—possibly motivated by a territorial spirit's threat of punishment—the land may ultimately have more reliable returns in the future (since deer migrate too). In other words, spiritual punishments can alter the payoff structure so that hunting appears to be more costly than forgoing the hunt.

Scenario B concerns territorializing land, which has long been recognized as an effective solution for reducing costly conflict between individuals or groups who have a clear interest in expansion (Dyson-Hudson and Smith 1978). In this scenario, it is in both parties' best interests to expand their territory. Properly functioning borders can prevent or limit expansion, but keeping territorial borders requires maintenance. A rich literature suggests that landmarks can reduce costs associated with border maintenance. That is, physical—but non-obstructive—indices of borders can function as a reminder of territorial ownership and reduce the likelihood of aggressive conflict (Heap, Byrne, and Stuart-Fox 2012). In the context of human territories where borders are not always easy to monitor and therefore maintain, localizing the presence of a powerful deity through ritual acts can be a strategic way of maintaining borders in the absence of effective secular punishment.

As detailed in Table 10.4, territorial conflict can be modeled using the hawk–dove game (Maynard Smith 1982: 147–166; cf. Hare, Reeve, and Blossey 2016). Here, two agents compete over a resource with a specific value, v. Camps 1 and 2 could both fight, incurring the costs of fighting, c, but with only a 50 percent chance of winning. One who relents to an aggressor acquires nothing, and the aggressor gets everything. If both camps choose to relent, they divide the land by half. In this scenario, the

---

changing through time (Axelrod 1984). Depending on one's questions, the availability of a game might be represented with one of these parameters.

Table 10.4 Payoff matrix for Camp 1 in Scenario B: territory as hawk–dove game. Payoffs are for Camp 1.

	Camp 2	
Camp 1	Relent	Fight
Relent	$v/2$	0
Fight	v	$(v-c)/2$

only conditions in which Relenters can outcompete Fighters is when the costs of fighting outweigh the value of the resources ($v < c$). In the case of Tyva, placing a spiritual marker on a territorial border might reduce the temptation to engage in risky territorial expansion, turning potential Fighters into Relenters (at least proximately and psychologically). When Tyvans are directly asked, spirit-masters are treated as knowledgeable, punitive, and interested in both the ritual and general moral behavior of individuals in their vicinity (Purzycki 2011b, 2013a). Supernatural punishment may increase the perceived costs of aggressive expansion (which entails violating the sacred boundary cairn rites) and therefore facilitate the proliferation of Relenters. Tyvans perceive ritual participants to be more broadly trustworthy than those who don't participate (Purzycki and Arakchaa 2013). If disrespecting the spirits is tantamount to disrespecting communities and their rules, it would make sense to convey and adopt the idea that such disrespect would bring misfortune. Indeed, Tyvans believe that bad luck strikes travelers who fail to stop and leave a token when they encounter cairns.

The related scenario C echoes any system where outsiders are expected to pay their respects to spirits before extracting *others'* renewable resources (see the Ainu example from Chapter 6). In this scenario, Camp 2's water supply is temporarily depleted, so water must be acquired from elsewhere. When local rivers get dirty, people might collect water at neighboring mineral springs. Thus, Camp 2 must travel to someone else's territory to get water. Prior to extracting the water, Camp 2 will perform rites at the mineral spring to pay their respects to the spirit-master of the spring. Camp 2 must convey that they do not have exploitative or aggressive intentions and that they are in Camp 1, where they should not be, simply for water. Conveying deference to spirits implies the likelihood of deference to other local rules, and thus there is no reason for hostilities, especially since water is readily available in Camp 1. In this way, a small gesture of respect to the local spirits may decrease the chances of inflaming social tensions between humans.

Spirit-master concepts, evident in all three of these scenarios, are bundled together with corollary processes such as mentalizing (Chapters 1, 4, and 6), punishment (Chapter 4), and moralizing (Chapter 5). In Tyva, strategically distributed indices trigger these bundles, as well as behavioral expressions of commitment. In other words, the coupling of religious beliefs and practices (Chapter 1) systemically conforms to particular social dilemmas. With the expertise and inspiration of shamans (Chapter 7), communities collectively and ritualistically sanctify and re-sanctify these indices regularly and therefore reinforce the relationships between cognition, cultural beliefs, motivations, and behaviors, and the relative harmony offered by sustained cooperation (Chapter 8). As we have discussed throughout this book, considerable work suggests that a variety of mechanisms, such as supernatural punishment and ritual, can induce the cooperative options in these dilemmas, contribute to their proliferation, and increase the chances that individuals transmit and retain the kinds of information required to profitably engage in social institutions.

Such mechanisms are manifest in Tyva. With respect to Scenarios B and C, there is evidence that Tyvan beliefs and practices co-vary with social behavior; rituals have been shown to convey trustworthiness to observers (Purzycki and Arakchaa 2013), and the more people claim spirit-masters know, the more they exhibit honest behavior toward local community members (Purzycki and Kulundary 2018). However, it remains to be seen whether or not Scenario A, where individuals might forgo hunting because of spiritual sanctions, is adequately accounted for by spiritual sanctions. Indeed, a longstanding debate continues to rage about the so-called "ecologically noble savage" and whether or not traditional religions somehow contribute to the preservation of nature (see Hames 1991, 2007; Smith and Wishnie 2000). Yet, there is considerable experimental research showing that religiosity is related to self-restraint and self-control (see Morgan 2019; Sasaki and Kim 2021; Sosis and Ruffle 2003; Tian et al. 2018). This suggests that it is plausible that Tyvans are more likely to forgo hunting when the injunction against it is associated with spirit-masters. Unfortunately, we have no data beyond anecdotes.[3] Nevertheless, there

---

3. Some anecdotes suggest that while the relationship between spiritual punishment and overhunting is explicit, beliefs and their underlying motivations variably moderate behavior. For example, one elderly man laments that "Taiga gives to you and taiga takes it

are general proscriptions against hunting in particular areas. Whether or not these proscriptions actually encourage hunters to restrain themselves and whether or not this affects the deer populations in any systematic way remains to be established with more sophisticated methods and theoretical models. In summary, there are many reasons both direct and implied to suspect religious taboos would decrease overexploitation, but subsequent work is required to more rigorously assess this possibility.

Religious Systems Evolving

These three ethnographic examples—Martu field burning, Bali water temples, and Tyvan cairns—strongly suggest, at the very least, that religious beliefs and practices correspond to social dilemmas. But, as we have argued throughout this book, religions can restructure the payoffs of these social dilemmas, thereby minimizing incentives for selfishness. Specifically, religions can increase the chances of opting for cooperative choices and decrease the chances of opting for selfish choices by triggering cognition associated with supernatural: (a) punishment, (b) monitoring, and (c) interest in our moral lives. This bundle of religious system components can increase the perceived costs of selfish strategies (e.g., bad luck). Moreover, it can provide the currency (e.g., lizards) and context (e.g., territory) to harness the trust-enhancing capabilities of ritual obligations. As we have stressed throughout this volume, humans possess a unique ability to flexibly acclimate and overcome diverse obstacles posed by the interactions between our natural and social worlds. If a cultural technology, such as religious ritual, functions to help overcome such obstacles, its presence will co-vary with them.

We saw in the case of the Martu that associating field burning with the spirits and the cosmic order may motivate field burning and, in turn, reciprocal commitments. Among the Balinese, both theory and evidence suggest that religious institutions function to coordinate people in ways that resolve individually costly conflicts of interest. In Tyva, we see

---

away. I am blind now, it's my fault. I often hunted, sometimes too much, a passion seized me. I took a lot from taiga, now I have been paying for my bad attitude to taiga. The female master punished me for this" (Arakchaa 2009: 50). Though it's left to the imagination what would have happened in the absence of this taboo against hunting too much, the taboo did not appear to work very well in this individual's case.

that various dilemmas attract religious solutions. Together, the Martu, Balinese, and Tyvan examples show that religious traditions can evolve in ways that are not satisfactorily reducible to individual cognition or transmission processes (Chapter 8). More general models that formally ignore behavioral payoffs miss the factors that maintain systems both synchronically and diachronically. Simple game-theoretic models nicely frame and clarify how religion might nudge individual adherents' strategies toward cooperation. But different societies present their members with different cooperative games, some of which emerge from persistent ecological problems associated with the way people acquire resources. While focusing on the transmission of religious concepts and practices without attending to these contextual relations has heuristic value (see the studies discussed in Chapter 6), doing so may overlook essential—but more complicated—factors involved in the persistence and evolution of religion.

If our general approach has merit, the elements of the religious system detailed in Chapter 9 will respond to changes in the payoff structure of extant problems, as well as the payoffs of new socioecological problems that arise. In Figure 10.3, religious beliefs and behaviors are dynamically related to the specific kinds of social dilemmas and conflicts communities endure. Such social dilemmas are likely to elicit the use of religious technologies that can facilitate their resolution (Bendixen and Purzycki 2020, 2021). The model in Figure 10.3 is a crude if not oversimplified depiction of how deeper individual-level mental processes co-inform individual beliefs and behaviors, which in turn contribute to shared (group) beliefs and behaviors that then feed back into individual-level cognitive processes once more. Here, while individuals' deeper cognitive processes might generate, constrain, and modify beliefs and behaviors, beliefs and behaviors can all feed back to cognition as well. As we discussed in Chapter 8, much of the cognitive science of religion over-emphasizes the bottom-up pathways from cognition to beliefs and behaviors while minimizing or denying the top-down influence from social groups or social ecologies.

One general prediction of our models is that the cost of social engagement, often experienced as risk of exploitation, affects the content of religious beliefs. As the costs of being exploited increase, we anticipate an increase in religious appeals—that is, appeals to powerful spiritual agents—in a strategic attempt to raise the perceived costs of selfishness. We similarly expect a proliferation or intensification of religious appeals when communities face novel environmental threats. Accordingly, natural experiments across varying socioecological contexts show an

Game 1

Camp 1	Camp 2	
	Forego	Hunt
Forego	3	1
Hunt	4	2

Game 2

Camp 1	Camp 2	
	Relent	Fight
Relent	$v/2$	0
Fight	v	$(v-c)/2$

Game 3

Camp 1	Camp 2	
	Refuse	Drink
Refuse	0	-1
Drink	1	2

Behaviors

Religious Appeals

Cognition

Cognition

Individual/Camp 1

Individual/Camp 2

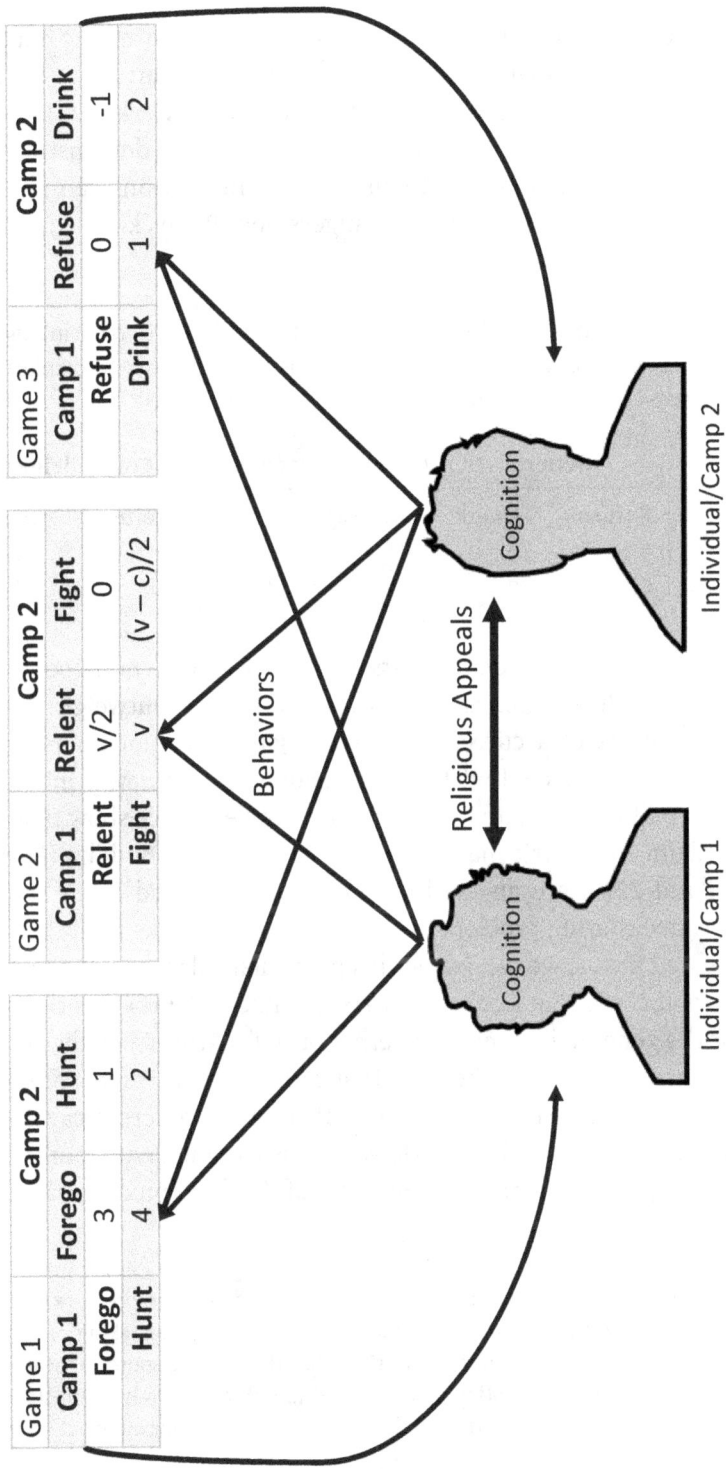

Figure 10.3 Religion evolving with feedback from social ecology, represented here by payoff matrices.

increase in religious expression and commitment—often among relatively non-religious individuals—during times of stress (Henrich et al. 2019; Sibley and Bulbulia 2012; Sosis 2007; Sosis and Handwerker 2011; Vardy and Atkinson 2009). Moreover, controlled experiments demonstrate that breaches in mutually beneficial trust-reliant interactions can alter the content of believers' models of what angers God (Purzycki, Stagnaro, and Sasaki 2020).

Table 10.5 Payoff matrices for perceived costs and benefits of drinking. Left matrix is perceived payoffs of drinking; right is shifting costs to drinking and drinking socially.[4] Payoffs are for Camp 1.

	General		Peer pressure		Costly drinking	
Camp 1	Refuse	Drink	Refuse	Drink	Refuse	Drink
Refuse	a	b	0	−1	0	−1
Drink	c	d	1	2	−1	−3

We also expect that when the costs of interacting with non-cooperators in newly introduced games (i.e., novel conditions) outweigh the corresponding costs of a currently "played" game, religious appeals will increasingly include content that corresponds to the newly introduced problem. To illustrate, ethnographic and survey evidence show that some Tyvans claim that spirit-masters (Purzycki 2016) and Buddha (Purzycki and Holland 2019) are angered by the alcohol use and abuse that has become a devastating problem in the Tyva Republic. Like the other cases we discussed above, we can frame this particular dilemma in terms of its benefits and costs. The leftmost matrix in Table 10.5 provides the payoff cells for the general dilemma of whether or not to drink socially. Refusing to drink entails a loss of the benefits that come with the respect of a drinking companion, so $d > c > a > b$. An example of more concrete payoffs is in the middle matrix of Table 10.5. However, associating divine punishment with drinking behavior renders the costs of drinking much greater than

---

4. See Medicine's discussion of drinking behavior among Lakota (Sioux) males where refusing to drink implies femininity and there is abundant peer pressure to imbibe (Medicine 2007: 53–76). See, too, Shermer (2008) for a similar take on taking performance enhancing drugs in athletic competitions. Note that the Koranic source appealed to in discussions of alcohol consumption and gambling (Surah Al-Baqarah 2:219) states that "There is a great harm in both, although they have some benefit for men; but their harm is far greater than their benefit."

the social costs of not drinking. Here, then, $d < c = b < a$ (rightmost matrix in Table 10.5).

Simply learning that a god will punish you for alcoholism is unlikely to curtail consumption. Rather, changing the incentive structure and ensuring the presence of effective institutional and social support with access to resources are more likely to help. Religious appeals can certainly change the perception of the payoffs, then, but we anticipate that fully fledged religious *institutions* will be more effective in expediting and strengthening the kind of social support that contributes to abstinence and recovery.

Religions also adapt, adjusting their perceived payoffs, to further meaningful ideologies. Take, for example, the Taiwanese goddess of the sea, Mazu, who became the patron saint of the anti-nuclear energy movement among a group of activists (Shih 2012). Having found little support among the political parties in power, and alienated by a system that failed to address a problem that was salient to these activists, activists consulted an oracle who "predicted" that if it was Mazu's will, the development of another nuclear power plant would be halted. It was, and thus the activists were emboldened to adopt Mazu as their patron saint. Here, then, an already salient problem existed, a secular institution failed to address it, and through the oracular powers of a specialist, a deity was subsequently transformed into a patron saint of a contemporary movement. Believing that one's actions will prevent environmental collapse is probably appreciated as an inequality between resistance and catastrophe. Commitment to the idea that a deity supports one's efforts should offset the perceived costs of engaging and resisting industry and the state.

A related example of religious evolution is the real and perceived expanding association between environmental preservation and the Abrahamic faiths (see Taylor, Wieren, and Zaleha 2016; White 1967). More specifically, while the Pope's encyclical *Laudato si* probably increased Catholic perception that environmental conservation is God's will, it is much less likely that such beliefs would have been adopted if so many Catholics were not already aware and concerned about the environment. In other words, religious change is not random. Had the Pope or the Mazu oracle instead expressed concern about bunny-rabbit invaders from Mars, participation in these religious institutions would probably decline.

While content-biased transmission (see Chapter 1) might account for the dispersion of religious ideas, such transmission does not obviously happen without extant, pressing, and perceived *costs* already present; religious systems draw attention to threats that already have a prior precedence in a community (Bendixen and Purzycki 2020, 2021). But the spread of beliefs is not enough to make changes in behavior, of course (D'Andrade and Strauss 1992).[5] Instead, beliefs must trigger, ontogenetically habituate, and naturalize (Chapter 1) the motivation to behave in locally contingent, self-restrained ways that facilitate cooperation. To the extent that these mechanisms contribute to survival and reproduction, we can construe such systems as adaptive. While the long-term evolution of any social system often escapes precise description, and different evolutionary processes could have been behind the convergent phenomena social scientists study (see issues of equifinality discussed in Barrett 2019; Kandler and Powell 2018; von Bertalanffy 1968), we expect that actively assessing such systems—rather than declaring that they don't exist—will only enrich the study of religion.

Future Work

Upon getting a better sense for these questions—and they are questions to be addressed—what can we do? First, we anticipate that methodologically rich ethnography will take us quite far (Purzycki and Watts 2018). Field researchers can: (a) tabulate what gods care about (Chapter 4); (b) investigate the patterns of behaviors those concerns point to; (c) examine those behaviors *in situ*; and (d) document observable variation in those behaviors. Of course, there are many ways to model religious systems that can generate testable predictions. Thankfully, many talented and well-organized modelers are coming to terms with the complexity of religious systems in valuable ways (e.g., Diallo et al. 2019).

There is also a growing commitment to fieldwork among younger generations of researchers in the biocultural study of religion. Accompanying this recent shift is a reconsideration of the cognitive anthropological tradition that the cognitive science of religion largely bypassed. Much of this work focuses on cultural schemas and models, and it employs a suite of ethnographic methods designed to make sense of the content, structure, and distribution of cultural information. Importantly, many researchers are also linking religious cognition to behavior as well, thus not limiting their inquiries to mental phenomena alone. Examples

---

5. See Moya, Peniche, Kline, and Smaldino (2020) for a cultural evolutionarily minded discussion of the challenges of changing behavior in response to COVID-19.

include ritual postures in Mauritius (Kundtová Klocová 2017); views of the Catholic Church among the Irish in relation to declining church involvement (Turpin 2018); tabooed animals among shamans and their perceived trustworthiness in Indonesia (Singh et al. 2021); views of vodou in New Orleans (Ward 2019); cross-cultural models of rewards and punishment in the afterlife and how they predict cooperation (Willard et al. 2020); and the degree to which beliefs in Buddha correspond to cooperation among Mongolians (Berniūnas et al. 2020). Next-generation researchers are also keen to examine the relationship between social ecology and religion (e.g., Caluori et al. 2020). This increased interest in linking facets of what we have been calling the "adaptive religious system" to both greater social context and the distribution of energy within that context gives us considerable hope for the future of our field.

Conclusion

We have argued that a systemic view can help us make better sense of the religious variation we see in the world. And, while systematic, rigorous, and directly comparable ethnography is essential (see Hewlett 2016; Purzycki and Watts 2018), it should be engaged directly and dialogically with multiple models (see Page 2018). Fortunately, there has been a recent influx of work, both formal (e.g., Buskell, Enquist, and Jansson 2019; Teehan and Shults 2019; Wood and Sosis 2019) and informal (e.g., Diallo et al. 2019; Hinde 2009; Lang and Kundt 2020; Lanman and Turpin 2022; Nielbo, Braxton, and Upal 2012; Sosis 2020a, 2020b), that explicitly embraces complexity, utilizes formal modelling, and speaks directly to evolutionary approaches to religion. Empirical research along the lines we have detailed in Chapter 10 await future investment.

To summarize the predictions generated in this book, we expect that:

- Religious cognition, culture, and behavior dynamically interact with social dilemmas.
  - What gods care about will point individuals toward behaviors that can minimize costs and/or increase benefits that contribute to cooperation in locally specific ways.
  - Gods and spiritual sanctions will either motivate/justify judicious acquisition and exploitation of resources (i.e., energy) to fuel cooperative relations or directly address social dilemmas.
  - Gods' knowledge breadth and moral scope will conform to the breadth of the *problem's* coverage, intensity, and/or relevance.
- Engaging in religious behavior feeds back into individual's ideational commitments and signals compliance with more general social mores.
- Important, measurable features of religious behaviors (e.g., timing and costs of rituals, taboos or restrictions on certain resources,

etc.) will co-evolve with the particular cost-benefit regimes of social life. Places and times where the temptation to act selfishly is higher will be associated with correspondingly more conspicuously placed and timed religious practices to bolster self-restraint.

Throughout this book we have argued for the merits of conceiving religion as a system, specifically a complex adaptive system. The advantages of this understanding of religion are manifold. First, the systemic approach offers a holistic model of religion, unifying the narrow research foci typically—with a few exceptions (e.g., Bulbulia 2009a; Czachesz 2014; Geertz 2010; Sørensen 2004)—pursued by evolutionary and cognitive scientists of religion. Notably, it avoids the reductionism regularly decried by religious studies scholars (see Proudfoot 1985). To be clear, we do not agree that reductionism is unilaterally problematic, or necessarily problematic at all (see Wildman et al. 2011); rather, we see reductionist analyses as only a first step in a more comprehensive investigation of religion. Second, the systemic approach offers a more contextual model of religion than current alternatives in the cognitive sciences of religion. Significantly, in contrast to these alternatives, it emphasizes the importance of ecology in explaining the design of religious systems. Third, and relatedly, systemic models highlight the flexibility and adaptability of religious systems. Religions' ability to respond to local ecologies—social, political, environmental, and economic factors—at least partially explains their extraordinary prevalence and endurance throughout human history. Fourth, our systemic model provides a viable functional explanation of religion; that is, it explains—solely in evolutionary terms—what religion is for. This explanation effectively and efficiently links social norms, resource acquisition, and fitness in a tightly organized feedback relationship. Specifically, it clarifies how individuals' health and reproduction are tied to social coordination and cooperation challenges in local energy production, and the role of religious systems in resolving, or at least navigating, those challenges.

In addition, the systemic approach has direct implications for the academic study of religion. First, it offers possible resolutions to various debates within the evolutionary and cognitive sciences of religion concerning the naturalness of religion (Sosis and Kiper 2018), the transmission of religious ideas (Sosis 2020b), and byproduct versus adaptationist models (Chapter 8). Second, we believe the systemic approach can provide that elusive bridge from the sciences to the humanities, especially with its focus on history and path-dependence (Buskell et al. 2019; Lang and Kundt

2020; Sosis 2020a). Third, as noted above, the systemic approach points to the value of new and powerful methodologies, ranging from the quantitative ethnography discussed in Chapter 10 to phylogenetic analyses (Watts et al. 2015, 2017) and computer simulations (Diallo 2019; Wildman et al. 2017, 2020).

These advantages of the systemic approach all highlight its value for scholars of religion. However, equally if not more important is its value for public understandings of religion. This is an academic book, intended for our colleagues, and unlikely to reach lay audiences. Yet it is hoped that our work will inspire other researchers to explore the systemic approach to religion and insights from this collective work will find their way into the public discourse. Indeed, we believe it is not only the responsibility of scholars to inform the public about their research findings, but also to explain the implications and meanings of those findings. With the extraordinary reach of social media and our seemingly ever-expanding social networks, this seems more critical now than ever. The public discourse on religion is remarkably shallow, and sadly, neither the religious nor non-religious have a monopoly on the superficiality of this discourse. Moreover, we are witnessing the rise of an unparalleled distrust in science and a widening divide between secular and religious worldviews.

Despite the secularizing trends that scholars have long acknowledged (Norris and Inglehart 2012), religion remains a potent force in the public sphere. Failure to appreciate the dynamics of religious change can have substantial social and economic consequences, as we discussed in Chapter 9. It is hoped the systemic approach we offer here will provide a more accurate assessment of religion that can inform policymakers, government officials, religious leaders, and others who aim to influence religions' impact within the public sphere. Moreover, if these ideas find their way into public discourse, it is hoped that the systemic approach can help non-religious people better understand their religious neighbors and vice versa. The systemic approach is certainly not a panacea for all of society's ills, or even those problems related to religion. But we do contend that a better appreciation of religion, how it changes and how it influences human lives, will facilitate many of the vital dialogues that are needed to heal the deep divisions in our world, many of which are related to religion. The approach offered here, we believe, is the first step in that process.

References

Ahmed, Ali M. and Osvaldo Salas. 2011. "Implicit Influences of Christian Religious Representations on Dictator and Prisoner's Dilemma Dame Decisions." *Journal of Socio-economics* 40: 242–246.

Alcorta, Candace S. and Richard Sosis. 2005. "Ritual, Emotion, and Sacred Symbols: The Evolution of Religion as an Adaptive Complex." *Human Nature* 16(4): 323–359.

Alcorta, Candace S. and Richard Sosis. 2006. "Why Ritual Works: A Rejection of the By-Product Hypothesis." *Behavioral and Brain Sciences* 29: 613–614.

Alcorta, Candace S. and Richard Sosis. 2020. "Adolescent Religious Rites of Passage: An Anthropological Perspective." In *Encyclopedia of Adolescent Development: History, Theory, and Culture*, vol. 1, edited by Stephen Hupp and Jeremy D. Jewell. New York: John Wiley & Sons Publishers.

Alexander, Richard D. 1987. *The Biology of Moral Systems.* New Brunswick, NJ: Aldine Transaction.

Amin, Shahina and Imam Alam. 2008. "Women's Employment Decisions in Malaysia: Does Religion Matter?" *Journal of Socio-economics* 37: 2368–2379.

Anderies, John M. 1998. "Culture and Human Agro-ecosystem Dynamics: the Tsembaga of New Guinea." *Journal of Theoretical Biology* 192(4): 515–530.

Andersen, Marc. 2019. "Predictive Coding in Agency Detection" *Religion, Brain and Behavior* 9(1): 65–84. https://doi.org/10.1080/2153599X.2017.1387170.

Anderson, John R. 2007. *How Can the Human Mind Occur in the Physical Universe?* New York: Oxford University Press.

Apicella, Coren Lee. 2018. "High Levels of Rule-Bending in a Minimally Religious and Largely Egalitarian Forager Population." *Religion, Brain and Behavior* 8(2): 133–148. https://doi.org/10.1080/2153599X.2016.1267034.

Arakchaa, Tayana. 2009. *Household and Property Relations in Tuva.* Doctoral dissertation: Boise State University. Accessible at: https://scholarworks.boisestate.edu/td/38.

Armstrong, Karen. 1993. *A History of God.* New York: Ballantine Books.

Armstrong, Karen. 2000. *The Battle for God.* New York: Random House.

Atkins, David C., Donald H. Baucomand, and Neil Jacobson. 2001. "Understanding

Infidelity: Correlates in a National Random Sample." *Journal of Family Psychology* 15: 735–749.

Atkinson, Quentin D. and Pierrick Bourrat. 2011. "Beliefs About God, the Afterlife and Morality Support the Role of Supernatural Policing in Human Cooperation." *Evolution and Human Behavior* 32(1): 41–49. https://doi.org/10.1016/j.evolhumbehav.2010.07.008.

Atkinson, Q. D. and H. Whitehouse. 2011. "The Cultural Morphospace of Ritual Form: Examining Modes of Religiosity Cross-culturally." *Evolution and Human Behavior* 32: 50–62.

Atkinson, Richard C. and Richard M. Shiffrin. 1968. "Human Memory: A Proposed System and its Control Processes." In *The Psychology of Learning and Motivation*, edited by Kenneth W. Spence and Janet T. Spence, 89–195. New York: Academic Press.

Atran, Scott. 1989. "Basic Conceptual Domains." *Mind and Language* 4: 7–16.

Atran, Scott. 2002. *In Gods We Trust: The Evolutionary Landscape of Religion.* New York: Oxford University Press.

Atran, Scott, Doug L. Medin, Norbert Ross, Elizabeth B. Lynch, Valentina Vapnarsky, Edilberto Ucan Ek', John D. Coley, Christopher Timura, and Michael Baran. 2002. "Folkecology, Cultural Epidemiology, and the Spirit of the Commons: A Garden Experiment in the Maya Lowlands 1991–2001." *Cultural Anthropology* 43(3): 421–450.

Atran, Scott and Ara Norenzayan. 2004. "Religion's Evolutionary Landscape: Counterintuition, Commitment, Compassion, Communion." *Behavioral and Brain Sciences* 27(6): 713–770.

Axelrod, Robert. 1984. *The Evolution of Cooperation.* New York: Basic Books.

Bacon, Margaret K., Irvin L. Child, and Herbert Barry. 1963. "A Cross-cultural-study of Correlates of Crime." *Journal of Abnormal Psychology* 66: 291–300.

Bakan, Joel. 2004. *The Corporation: The Pathological Pursuit of Profit and Power.* New York: Free Press.

Bakhtin, Mikhail Mikhaĭlovich. 1984. *Rabelais and His World.* Bloomington, IN: Indiana University Press.

Balikci, Asen. 1970. *The Netsilik Eskimo.* Prospect Heights, IL: Waveland Press.

Barber, Nigel. 2011. "A Cross-national Test of the Uncertainty Hypothesis of Religious Belief." *Cross-Cultural Research* 45(3): 318–333. https://doi.org/10.1177/1069397111402465.

Barker, John. 2008. *Ancestral Lines: The Maisin of Papua New Guinea and the Fate of the Rainforest.* Tonawanda: University of Toronto Press.

Barker, Jessica L., Eleanor A. Power, Stephen Heap, Mikael Puurtinen, and Richard Sosis. 2019. "Content, Cost, and Context: A Framework for Understanding Human Signaling Systems." *Evolutionary Anthropology: Issues, News, and Reviews* 28(2): 86–99. https://doi.org/10.1002/evan.21768.

Barkow, Jerome, Leda Cosmides, and John Tooby. 1992. *The Adapted Mind:*

Evolutionary Psychology and the Generation of Culture. New York: Oxford University Press.

Baron-Cohen, Simon. 1995. *Mindblindness: An Essay on Autism and Theory of Mind.* Cambridge, MA: MIT Press.

Barrett, Brendan J. 2019. "Equifinality in Empirical Studies of Cultural Transmission." *Behavioural Processes* 161: 129–138. https://doi.org/10.1016/j.beproc.2018.01.011.

Barrett, H. Clark and Robert Kurzban. 2006. "Modularity in Cognition: Framing the Debate." *Psychological Review* 113: 628–647.

Barrett, Justin L. 1998. "Cognitive Constraints on Hindu Concepts of the Divine." *Journal for the Scientific Study of Religion* 37: 608–619.

Barrett, Justin L. 1999. "Theological Correctness: Cognitive Constraint and the Study of Religion." *Method and Theory in the Study of Religion* 11: 325–339.

Barrett, Justin L. 2002 "Dumb Gods, Petitionary Prayer, and the Cognitive Science of Religion." In *Current Approaches in the Cognitive Science of Religion*, edited by Ilkka Pyysiäinen and Veikko Anttonen. New York: Continuum.

Barrett, Justin L. 2004. *Why Would Anyone Believe in God?* New York: AltaMira Press.

Barrett, Justin L. 2007a. "Cognitive Science of Religion: What Is It and Why Is It?" *Religion Compass* 1(6): 768–786. https://doi.org/10.1111/j.1749-8171.2007.00042.x.

Barrett, Justin L. 2008a. "Coding and Quantifying Counterintuitiveness in Religious Concepts: Theoretical and Methodological Reflections." *Method and Theory in the Study of Religion* 20(4): 308–338.

Barrett, Justin L. 2008b. "Why Santa Claus is not a God." *Journal of Cognition and Culture* 8(1–2): 149–161.

Barrett, Justin L. 2012. *Born Believers: The Science of Children's Religious Belief.* New York: Free Press.

Barrett, Justin L. 2021. *Oxford Handbook for the Cognitive Science of Religion.* Oxford: Oxford University Press.

Barrett, Justin L. and Frank C. Keil. 1996. "Conceptualizing a Nonnatural Entity: Anthropomorphism in God Concepts." *Cognitive Psychology* 313: 219–247.

Barrett, Justin L. and E. Thomas Lawson. 2001. "Ritual Intuitions: Cognitive Contributions to Judgments of Ritual Efficacy." *Journal of Cognition and Culture* 1(2): 183–201.

Battiste, Marie and James Y. Henderson. 2000. *Protecting Indigenous Knowledge and Heritage: A Global Challenge.* Saskatoon: Purich Publishing.

Bechtel, William and Adele A. Abrahamsen. 2002. *Connectionism and the Mind: Parallel Processing, Dynamics, and Evolution in Network*, 2nd edition. Malden, MA: Blackwell Publishing.

Beck, Scott H., Bettie S. Cole, and Judith A. Hammond. 1991. "Religious Heritage and Premarital Sex: Evidence from a National Sample of Young Adults." *Journal for the Scientific Study of Religion* 30: 173–80.

Becker, Ernest. 1973. *The Denial of Death.* New York: Simon and Schuster.

Beebe, James R. and Leigh Duffy. 2020. "The Memorability of Supernatural Concepts: Effects of Minimal Counterintuitiveness, Moral Valence, and Existential Anxiety on Recall." *The International Journal for the Psychology of Religion* 30(4): 322–341

Beheim, Bret, Quentin Atkinson, Joseph Bulbulia, Will M. Gervais, Russell Gray, Joseph Henrich, Martin Lang, et al. 2021. "Treatment of missing data determines conclusions regarding moralizing gods." *Nature*, 595: E29–E34.

Beit-Hallahmi, Benjamin. 1997. "Biology, Density and Change: Women's Religiosity and Economic Development." *Journal of Institutional and Theoretical Economics* 153: 166–178.

Bell, Catherine. 1997. *Ritual: Perspectives and Dimensions*. New York: Oxford University Press.

Bell, Chris M. and Emily Sternberg. 2001. "Emotional Selection in Memes: The Case of Urban Legends." *Journal of Personality and Social Psychology* 81: 1028–1041.

Bendixen, Theiss and Benjamin Grant Purzycki. 2020. "Peering into the Minds of Gods: What Cross-cultural Variation in Gods' Concerns Tell Us about the Evolution of Religion." *Journal for the Cognitive Science of Religion* 5: 142–165.

Bendixen, Theiss and Benjamin Grant Purzycki. 2021. "Competing Forces Account for the Stability and Evolution of Religious Beliefs." *International Journal for the Psychology of Religion* 31(4): 307–312.

Berger, Peter L. 1967. *The Sacred Canopy*. New York: Anchor Books.

Bering, Jesse M. 2002. "The Existential Theory of Mind." *Review of General Psychology* 6(1): 3–24.

Bering, Jesse M. 2004. "Natural Selection is Non-denominational: Why Evolutionary Models of Religion Should be More Concerned with Behavior than Concepts." *Evolution and Cognition* 10: 126–137.

Bering, Jesse. 2011. *The Belief Instinct: The Psychology of Souls, Destiny, and the Meaning of Life*. New York: W. W. Norton & Company.

Bering, Jesse M. and Dominic P. Johnson. 2005. "'O Lord ... You Perceive My Thoughts from afar': Recursiveness and the Evolution of Supernatural Agency." *Journal of Cognition and Culture* 5: 118–142.

Bering, Jesse M., Katrina McLeod, and Todd K. Shackelford. 2005. "Reasoning About Dead Agents Reveals Possible Adaptive Trends." *Human Nature* 16(4): 360–381.

Bering, Jesse M. and Todd K. Shackelford. 2004. "The Causal Role of Consciousness: A Conceptual Addendum to Human Evolutionary Psychology." Review of General Psychology 8(4): 227–48. https://doi.org/10.1037/1089-2680.8.4.227

Berman, Eli. 2000. "Sect, Subsidy and Sacrifice: An Economist's View of Ultra-Orthodox Jews." *Quarterly Journal of Economics* 115: 905–953.

Berman, Eli. 2009. *Radical, Religious, and Violent: The New Economics of Terrorism*. Cambridge, MA: MIT Press.

Berndt, Ronald M. 1972. "The Walmadjeri and Gugadja." In *Hunters and Gatherers Today: A Socioeconomic Study of Eleven Such Cultures in the Twentieth Century*, edited by Marco G. Bicchieri. New York: Rinehard and Winston.

Berniūnas, Renatas, Vilius Dranseika, and Delgermend Tserendamba. 2020. "Between Karma and Buddha: Prosocial Behavior among Mongolians in an Anonymous Economic Game." *The International Journal for the Psychology of Religion* 30(2): 142–160. https://doi.org/10.1080/10508619.2019.1696497.

Biale, David. 2011. *Not in the Heavens: The Tradition of Jewish Secular Thought*. Princeton, NJ: Princeton University Press.

Billingsley, Andrew. 1999. *Mighty like a River: The Black Church and Social Reform*. Oxford: Oxford University Press.

Billy, John O. G., Koray Tanfer, William R. Grady, and Daniel H. Klepinger. 1993. "The Sexual Behavior of Men in the United States." *Family Planning Perspectives* 25: 52–60.

Binford, Lewis R. 1962. "Archaeology as Anthropology." *American Antiquity* 28(2): 217–225.

Bird, Douglas W., Rebecca B. Bird, Brian F. Codding, and Nyalangka Taylor. 2016. "A Landscape Architecture of Fire: Cultural Emergence and Ecological Pyrodiversity in Australia's Western Desert." *Current Anthropology* 57(S13): S65–S79. https://doi.org/10.1086/685763.

Blackwell, Aaron D. 2009. *Life History Trade-Offs in Growth and Immune Function: The Behavioral and Immunological Ecology of the Shuar of Amazonian Ecuador, an Indigenous Population in the Midst of Rapid Economic and Ecological Change*. Doctoral dissertation. University of Oregon. Retrieved from https://scholarsbank.uoregon.edu/xmlui/handle/1794/10546.

Blanes, Roy Llera and Galina Oustinova-Stjepanovic (eds.). 2017. *Being Godless: Ethnographies of Atheism and Non-religion*. New York: Berghahn Books.

Bliege Bird, Rebecca and Eric A. Smith. 2005. "Signaling Theory, Strategic Interaction, and Symbolic Capital." *Current Anthropology* 46(2): 221–248.

Bliege Bird, Rebecca, Nyalangka Tayor, Brian F. Codding, and Douglas W. Bird. 2013. "Niche Construction and Dreaming Logic: Aboriginal Patch Mosaic Burning and Varanid Lizards (*Varanus Gouldii*) in Australia." *Proceedings of the Royal Society B: Biological Sciences* 280(1772): 20132297. https://doi.org/10.1098/rspb.2013.2297.

Bliege Bird, Rebecca and Eleanor A. Power. 2015. "Prosocial Signaling and Cooperation among Martu Hunters." *Evolution and Human Behavior* 36(5): 389–97. https://doi.org/10.1016/j.evolhumbehav.2015.02.003.

Bloch, Maurice. 1974. "Symbols, Song, Dance and Features of Articulation: Is Religion an Extreme Form of Traditional Authority?" *European Journal of Sociology* 15: 54–81.

Bloch, Maurice. 1983. *Marxism and Anthropology*. New York: Oxford University Press.

Blume, Michael. 2009. "The Reproductive Benefits of Religious Affiliation." In *The Biological Evolution of Religious Mind and Behavior*, edited by Eckart Voland and Wulf Schiefenhövel, 117–126. New York: Springer.

Blume, Michael. 2010. "Von Hayek and the Amish Fertility: How Religious Communities Manage to be Fruitful and Multiply. A Case Study." In *The Nature of God: Evolution and Religion*, edited by Ulrich Frey, 159–175. Marburg: Tectum Verlag.

Boehm, Christopher. 2008. "A Biocultural Evolutionary Exploration of Supernatural Sanctioning." In *Evolution of Religion: Studies, Theories, and Critiques*, edited by Joseph Bulbulia, Richard Sosis, Erica Harris, Russell Genet, Cheryl Genet, and Karen Wyman, 143–152. Santa Margarita, CA: Collins Foundation Press.

Bonnemaison, Joel. 1991. "Magic Gardens in Tanna." *Pacific Studies* (Laie, Hawaii) 14(4): 71–89.

Bouchard, Thomas J. 2004. "Genetic Influence on Human Psychological Traits: A Survey." *Current Directions in Psychological Science* 13: 148–151.

Bouchard, Thomas J. and Matt McGue. 2003. "Genetic and Environmental Influences on Human Psychological Differences." *Journal of Neurobiology* 54(1): 4–45.

Bourdieu, Pierre. 1977. *Outline of a Theory of Practice*. Cambridge: Cambridge University Press.

Bourke, John G. 1891. *Scatalogic Rites of All Nations*. Washington, DC: W. H. Lowdermilk & Co.

Bouton, Jacques. 1635. "Concerning The Savages Called Caribs." In *An Account of the Establishment of the French in the Year 1635 on the Island of Martinique*, translated by Marshall McKusick and Pierre Verin, published by Chez S. Cramoisy. Retrieved from https://ehrafworldcultures.yale.edu/document?id=st13-003.

Boyd, Robert. 2018. *A Different Kind of Animal: How Culture Transformed Our Species*. Princeton, NJ: Princeton University Press.

Boyd, Robert and Peter J. Richerson. 1985. *Culture and the Evolutionary Process*. Chicago, IL: University of Chicago Press.

Boyd, Robert, Peter J. Richerson, and Joseph Henrich. 2011. "The Cultural Niche: Why Social Learning Is Essential for Human Adaptation." *Proceedings of the National Academy of Sciences* 108 (Supplement 2): 10,918–10,925. https://doi.org/10.1073/pnas.1100290108.

Boyer, Pascal. 1994a. "Cognitive Constraints on Cultural Representations: Natural Ontologies and Religious Ideas." In *Mapping the Mind*, edited by Lawrence A. Hirschfeld and Susan A. Gelman, 39–67. Cambridge: Cambridge University Press.

Boyer, Pascal. 1994b. *The Naturalness of Religious Ideas: A Cognitive Theory of Religion*. Berkeley, CA: University of California Press.

Boyer, Pascal. 1996. "What Makes Anthropomorphism Natural: Intuitive Ontology and Cultural Representations." *The Journal of Royal Anthropological Institute* 2(1): 83–97.

Boyer, Pascal. 2000. "Functional Origins of Religious Concepts: Ontological and Strategic Selection in Evolved minds." *The Journal of the Royal Anthropological Institute* 6(2): 195–214.

Boyer, Pascal. 2001. *Religion Explained: The Evolutionary Origins of Religious Thought.* New York: Basic Books.

Boyer, Pascal. 2002. "Why Do Gods and Spirits Matter at All?" In *Current Approaches in the Cognitive Science of Religion*, edited by Ilkka Pyysiäinen and Veikko Anttonen, 68–92. New York: Continuum.

Boyer, Pascal. 2003. "Religious Thought and Behaviour as By-products of Brain Function." *Trends in Cognitive Sciences* 7(3): 119–124.

Boyer, Pascal. 2011. "Why Would (Otherwise Intelligent) Scholars Believe in." Pascal Boyer's blog, February 2. Retrieved from http://cognitionandculture.net/blog/pascals-blog/why-would-otherwise-intelligent-scholars-believe-in (accessed December 31, 2020).

Boyer, Pascal. 2018. *Minds Make Societies: How Cognition Explains the World Humans Create.* Yale: University Press.

Boyer, P. 2020. "Informal Religious Activity outside Hegemonic Religions: Wild Traditions and Their Relevance to Evolutionary Models." *Religion, Brain and Behavior* 10: 459–472.

Boyer, Pascal and Brian Bergstrom. 2008. "Evolutionary Perspectives on Religion." *Annual Review of Anthropology* 37: 111–130.

Boyer, Pascal and Pierre Liénard. 2006. "Why Ritualized Behavior? Precaution Systems and Action Parsing in Developmental, Pathological, and Cultural Rituals." *Behavioral and Brain Sciences* 29: 1–56.

Boyer, Pascal and Pierre Liénard. 2020. "Ingredients of 'Rituals' and their Cognitive Underpinnings." *Philosophical Transactions of the Royal Society B.* 375: 20190439.

Boyer, Pascal and Charles Ramble. 2001. "Cognitive Templates for Religious Concepts: Cross-cultural Evidence for Recall of Counter-intuitive Representations." *Cognitive Science* 25(4): 535–564.

Breton, Raymond. 1929. "An Account of the Island of Guadaloupe." Translated by Armand, Thomas de Turner. Historie Coloniale 1. https://ehrafworld cultures.yale.edu/document?id=st13-001.

Brewer, William F. 2000. "Bartlett's Concept of the Schema and Its Impact on Theories of Knowledge Representation in Contemporary Cognitive Psychology." In *Bartlett, Culture and Cognition*, edited by Akiko Saito, 69–89. Guildford: Psychology Press.

Bricker, Victoria Reifler. 1973. *Ritual Humor in Highland Chiapas.* Austin, TX: University of Texas Press.

Bromham, Lindell, Alexander Skeels, Hilde Schneemann, Russell Dinnage, and

Xia Hua. 2021. "There Is Little Evidence that Spicy Food in Hot Countries is an Adaptation to Reducing Infection Risk." *Nature Human Behaviour* 5: 878–891.

Brown, Joseph E. 1989 [1953]. *The Sacred Pipe: Black Elk's Account of the Seven Rites of the Oglala Sioux.* New York: MJF Books.

Brown, Michael F. and Margaret L. Van Bolt. 1980. "Aguaruna Jivaro Gardening Magic in the Alto Rio Mayo, Peru. *Ethnology* 19(2): 169–190.

Bulbulia, Joseph. 2004a. "Religious Costs as Adaptations that Signal Altruistic Intention." *Evolution and Cognition* 10(1): 19–38.

Bulbulia, Joseph. 2004b. "The Cognitive and Evolutionary Psychology of Religion." *Biology and Philosophy* 18: 655–686.

Bulbulia, Joseph. 2008. "Meme Infection or Religious Niche Construction?: An Adaptationist Alternative to the Cultural Maladaptationist Hypothesis." *Method and Theory in the Study of Religion* 20: 67–107.

Bulbulia, Joseph. 2009a. "Charismatic Signalling." *Journal for the Study of Religion, Nature, Culture* 3(4): 518–551.

Bulbulia, Joseph. 2009b. "Why 'Costly-Signalling' Models of Religion Require Cognitive Psychology." In *Origins of Religion, Cognition, and Culture*, edited by Armin W. Geertz. London: Equinox.

Bulbulia, Joseph. 2012. "Spreading Order: Religion, Cooperative Niche Construction, and Risky Coordination Problems." *Biology and Philosophy* 27(1): 1–27.

Bulbulia, Joseph A. and Andrew Mahoney. 2008. "Religious Solidarity: The Hand-grenade Experiment." *Journal of Cognition and Culture* 8(3–4): 295–320.

Bulbulia, Joseph, John Shaver, Lara M. Greaves, Sosis, Richard, and Chris G. Sibley. 2015. "Religion and Parental Cooperation: An Empirical Test of Slone's Sexual Signaling Model." In *The Attraction of Religion: A Sexual Selectionist Account*, edited by D. Jason Slone and James A. Van Slyke, 29–62. London: Bloomsbury.

Bulbulia, Joseph and Richard Sosis 2011. "Signaling Theory and the Evolution of Religions." *Religion* 413: 363–388.

Bulbulia, Joseph, Richard Sosis, Russell Genet, Cheryl Genet, Erica Harris, and Karen Wyman. 2008. *The Evolution of Religion: Studies, Theories, and Critiques.* Santa Margarita, CA: Collins Foundation Press.

Bushman, Brad J., Robert D. Ridge, Enny Das, Colin W. Key, and Gregory Busath. 2007. "When God Sanctions Killing: Effect of Scriptural Violence on Aggression." *Psychological Science* 18: 204–207.

Buskell, Andrew, Magnus Enquist, and Fredrik Jansson. 2019. "A Systems Approach to Cultural Evolution." *Palgrave Communications* 5(1): 1–15. https://doi.org/10.1057/s41599-019-0343-5.

Buss, David M. and David P. Schmitt. 1993. "Sexual Strategies Theory: A contextual Evolutionary Analysis of Human Mating." *Psychological Review* 100: 204–232.

Call, Josep and Michael Tomasello. 2008. "Does the Chimpanzee Have a Theory of Mind? 30 Years Later." *Trends in Cognitive Sciences* 12(5): 187–192.

Call, Vaughn R. A. and Tim B. Heaton. 1997. "Religious Influence on Marital Stability." *Journal for the Scientific Study of Religion* 36: 382–392.

Caluori, Nava, Joshua Conrad Jackson, Kurt Gray, and Michele Gelfand. 2020. "Conflict Changes How People View God." *Psychological Science* (January): 0956797619895286. https://doi.org/10.1177/0956797619895286.

Carroll, James. 2001. *Constantine's Sword*. Boston, MA: Houghton Mifflin Co.

Carroll, Michael P. 1975. "Revitalization Movements and Social Structure: Some Quantitative Tests." *American Sociological Review* 40(3): 389–401.

Chagnon, Napoleon A. 1996. *The Yanomamo*, 5th edition. Belmont, CA: Wadsworth Publishing.

Cho, Francisca and Richard K. Squier. 2008. "'He Blinded Me with Science': Science Chauvinism in the Study of Religion." *Journal of the American Academy of Religion* 76(2): 420–448.

Cho, Francisca and Richard K. Squier. 2013. "Religion as a Complex and Dynamic System." *Journal of the American Academy of Religion* 81: 357–398.

Chomsky, Noam. 1965. *Aspects of the Theory of Syntax*. Cambridge, MA: MIT Press.

Chomsky, Noam. 1980. *Rules and Representations*. New York: Columbia University Press.

Chomsky, Noam. 1996. *Powers and Prospects: Reflections on Human Nature and the Social Order*. Boston, MA: South End Press.

Cohen, Adam B. 2002. "The Importance of Spirituality in Well-being for Jews and Christians." *Journal of Happiness Studies* 3: 287–310.

Cohen, Adam B., Joel I. Siegel, and Paul Rozin. 2003. "Faith Versus Practice: Different Bases for Religiosity Judgments by Jews and Protestants." *European Journal of Social Psychology* 33(2): 287–295. https://doi.org/10.1002/ejsp.148.

Cohen, Emma. 2007. *The Mind Possessed: The Cognition of Spirit Possession in an Afro-Brazilian Religious Tradition*. New York: Oxford University Press.

Cohen, Emma, Robin Ejsmond-Frey, Nicola Knight, and Robin I.M. Dunbar. 2010. "Rowers' High: Behavioural Synchrony is Correlated with Elevated Pain Thresholds." *Biology Letters* 6: 106–108.

Collier, Jane F., Michelle Z. Rosaldo, and Sylvia Yanagisako. 1997 [1982]. "Is There a Family? New Anthropological Views." In *The Gender/Sexuality Reader: Culture, History, Political Economy*, edited by Roger N. Lancaster and Michaela D. Leonardo, 71–81. New York: Routledge.

Copeman, Jacob and Johannes Quack. 2017. "Godless People and Dead Bodies: Materiality and the Morality of Atheist Materialism." In *Being Godless: Ethnographies of Atheism and Non-Religion*, edited by Roy B. Llera and Galina Oustinova-Stjepanovic, 40–61. Oxford: Berghahn Books.

Corning, Peter A. 2002. "The Re-emergence of 'Emergence': A Venerable Concept in Search of a Theory." *Complexity* 7(6): 18–30.

Cosmides, Leda and John Tooby. 1992. "Cognitive Adaptations for Social Exchange." In *The Adapted Mind: Evolutionary Psychology and the Generation of Culture*, edited by Jerome H. Barkow, Leda Cosmides, and John Tooby, 163–228. Oxford: Oxford University Press.

Cosmides, Leda and John Tooby. 2000. "Evolutionary Psychology and the Emotions." In *Handbook of Emotions*, 2nd edition, edited by Michael Lewis and Jeannette M. Haviland-Jones, 91–115. New York: Guilford.

Cox, Michael, Sergio Villamayor-Tomas, and Yasha Hartberg. 2014. "The Role of Religion in Community-based Natural Resource Management." *World Development* 54: 46–55.

Creanza, Nicole, Laurel Fogarty, and Marcus W. Feldman. 2012. "Models of Cultural Niche Construction with Selection and Assortative Mating." *PLoS One* 7(8): e42744.

Cronk, Lee. 1994. "Evolutionary Theories of Morality and the Manipulative Use of Signals." *Zygon* 29(1): 810–101.

Cronk, Lee. 2005. "The Application of Animal Signaling Theory to Human Phenomena: Some Thoughts and Clarifications." *Social Science Information* 44(4): 603–620.

Cronk, Lee and Beth L. Leech. 2013. *Meeting at Grand Central: Understanding the Social and Evolutionary Roots of Cooperation*. Princeton, NJ: Princeton University Press.

Crumrine, N. Ross. 1969. "Čapakoba, the Mayo Easter Ceremonial Impersonator: Explanations of Ritual Clowning." *Journal for the Scientific Study of Religion* 8(1): 1–22. https://doi.org/10.2307/1385250.

Czachesz, István. 2014. "The Evolutionary Dynamics of Religious Systems: Laying the Foundations of a Network Model." In *Origin of Religion, Cognition and Culture*, edited by Armin Geertz, 98–120. New York: Routledge.

D'Andrade, Roy Goodwin. 1981. "The Cultural Part of Cognition." *Cognitive Science* 5(3): 179–195. https://doi.org/10.1016/S0364-0213(81)80012-2.

D'Andrade, Roy. 1992. "Schemas and Motivation." In *Human Motives and Cultural Models*, edited by Roy D'Andrade and Claudia Strauss, 23–44. Cambridge: Cambridge University Press.

D'Andrade, Roy. 1995. *The Development of Cognitive Anthropology*. Cambridge: Cambridge University Press.

D'Andrade, Roy and Claudia Strauss. 1992. *Human Motives and Cultural Models*. Cambridge: Cambridge University Press.

D'Antonio, William V., James Davidson, Dean R. Hoge, and Mary L. Gautier. 2007. *American Catholics Today: New Realities of their Faith and their Church*. New York: Rowman & Littlefield Publishers.

D'Aquili, Eugene G., Charles D. Laughlin, and John McManus 1979. *The Spectrum of Ritual: A Biogenetic Structural Analysis*. New York: Columbia University Press.

Darwin, Charles. 2004 [1859]. *The Origin of Species*, 6th edition. Edison: Castle Books.

Darwin, Charles. 2004 [1879]. *The Descent of Man*, 2nd edition. New York: Penguin Classics.

Dawkins, Richard. 1982. *The Extended Phenotype: The Long Reach of the Gene*. New York: Oxford University Press.

Dawkins, Richard. 1989 [1976]. *The Selfish Gene*. New York: Oxford University Press.

Dawkins, Richard. 2004. "Extended Phenotype—But Not Too Extended. A Reply to Laland, Turner and Jablonka." *Biology and Philosophy* 19: 377–396.

Dawkins, Richard. 2006. *The God Delusion*. New York: Mariner Books.

Dawkins, Richard and John R. Krebs. 1979. "Arms Races Between and Within Species." *Proceedings of the Royal Society of London, Series B. Biological Sciences* 205(1161): 489–511.

Deacon, Terrence. 2010. *Incomplete Nature*. New York: Norton.

de Bary, William Theodore. 1969. *The Buddhist Tradition in India, China and Japan*. New York: Vintage Books.

DeBono, Amber, Azim Shariff, and Mark Muraven. 2017. "Forgive Us Our Trespasses: Priming a Forgiving (But Not a Punishing) God Increases Theft." *Psychology of Religion and Spirituality* 9(Suppl 1): S1–S10. https://doi.org/10.1037/rel0000105

Deloria, Vine Jr. 1979. *The Metaphysics of Modern Existence*. New York: Harper & Row Publishers.

Deloria, Vine Jr. 1992. *God is Red: A Native View of Religion*. Golden: Fulcrum Publishing.

DeMallie, Raymond J. 1987. "Lakota Belief and Ritual in the Nineteenth Century." In *Sioux Indian Religion*, edited by Raymond J. DeMallie and Douglas R. Parks. Norman, OK: University of Oklahoma Press.

Dennett, Daniel C. 1971. "Intentional Systems." *The Journal of Philosophy* 68(4): 87–106.

Dennett, Daniel C. 1987. *The Intentional Stance*. Cambridge, MA: MIT Press.

Dennett, Daniel C. 1991. *Consciousness Explained*. Boston, MA: Little, Brown & Co.

Dennett, Daniel C. 1995. *Darwin's Dangerous Idea: Evolution and the Meanings of Life*. New York: Simon and Schuster.

Dennett, Daniel C. 2006. *Breaking the Spell: Religion as a Natural Phenomenon*. New York: Viking.

De Sondy, Amanullah, Michelle A. Gonzalez, and William S. Green. 2020. *Judaism, Christianity, and Islam: An Introduction to Monotheism*. London: Bloomsbury.

Dewey, John. 1932. *Human Nature and Conduct: An Introduction to Social Psychology*. New York: The Modern Library.

Diallo, Saikou Y. 2019. "Five Things to Know About Modeling and Simulation." *Archive for the Psychology of Religion* 41(2): 172–185.

Diallo, Saikou Y., Wesley Wildman, F. LeRon Shults, and Andreas Tolk (eds.). 2019. *Human Simulation: Perspectives, Insights, and Applications*. Berlin: Springer

International Publishing.

Donahoe, Brian. 2006. "Who Owns the Taiga? Inclusive vs. Exclusive Senses of Property among the Tozhu and Tofa of Southern Siberia." *Sibirica* 5(1): 87–116. https://doi.org/10.3167/136173606780265306.

Douglas, Mary. 1966. *Purity and Danger: An Analysis of Concepts of Pollution and Taboo.* New York: Routledge.

Dow, James. 2008. "Is Religion an Evolutionary Adaptation?" *Journal of Artificial Societies and Social Simulation* 11(2): 2.

Dunbar, Robin I. M. 2003. "The Social Brain: Mind, Language, and Society in Evolutionary Perspective." *Annual Review of Anthropology* 32: 163–181.

Dunbar, Robin I. M. and Richard Sosis. 2018. "Optimising Human Community Sizes." *Evolution and Human Behavior* 39(1): 106–111.

Dunn, Oliver and James E. Kelley Jr. 1989. *The Diario of Christopher Columbus's First Voyage to America, 1492-1493.* Norman, OK: University of Oklahoma Press.

Durkheim, Émile. 2001 [1912]. *The Elementary Forms of Religious Life.* New York. Oxford University Press.

Dyson-Hudson, Rada and Eric Alden Smith. 1978. "Human Territoriality: An Ecological Reassessment." *American Anthropologist* 80(1): 21–41. https://doi.org/10.1525/aa.1978.80.1.02a00020.

Edgell, Penny, Joseph Gerteis, and Douglas Hartmann. 2006. "Atheists as 'Other': Moral Boundaries and Cultural Membership in American Society." *American Sociological Review* 71: 211–234.

Efron, Noah J. 2003. *Real Jews: Secular vs. Ultra-Orthodox and the Struggle for Jewish Identity in Israel.* New York: Basic Books.

Elster, Jon. 1979. *Ulysses and the Sirens.* Cambridge: Cambridge University Press.

Elster, Jon. 1983. *Explaining Technical Change: A Case Study in the Philosophy of Science.* Cambridge: Cambridge University Press.

Elster, Jon. 2007. *Explaining Social Behavior: More Nuts and Bolts for the Social Sciences.* Cambridge: Cambridge University Press.

Erdoes, Richard and Alfonso Ortiz. 1999. *American Indian Trickster Tales.* London: Penguin.

Evans-Pritchard, Edward Evan. 1956. *Nuer Religion.* New York: Oxford University Press.

Evans-Pritchard, Edward Evan. 1965. *Theories of Primitive Religion.* London: Oxford University Press.

Evans-Pritchard, Edward Evan. 1976. *Witchcraft, Oracles, and Magic among the Azande* [abridged]. Oxford: Clarendon Press.

Everett, Daniel L. 2005. "Cultural Constraints on Grammar and Cognition in Pirahã Another Look at the Design Features of Human Language." *Current Anthropology* 46(4): 621–646. https://doi.org/10.1086/431525.

Everett, Daniel L. 2008. *Don't Sleep, There Are Snakes.* New York: Vintage Departures.

Everett, Daniel L. 2009. "Pirahã Culture and Grammar: A Response to Some

Criticisms." *Language* 85(2): 405–442.

Feierman, Jay R. 2009. *The Biology of Religious Behavior: The Evolutionary Origins of Faith and Religion.* Santa Barbara: Praeger.

Feraca, Stephen E. 1998. *Wakinyan: Lakota Religion in the Twentieth Century.* Lincoln, NE: University of Nebraska Press.

Fernandez, James W. 1965. "Symbolic Consensus in a Fang Reformative Cult." *American Anthropologist* 67(4): 902–929.

Fincher, Corey L. and Randy Thornhill. 2012. "Parasite-stress Promotes In-group Assortative Sociality: The Cases of Strong Family Ties and Heightened Religiosity." *Behavioral and Brain Sciences* 35(2): 61–79.

Finkel, Daniel N., Paul Swartwout, and Richard Sosis. 2010. "The Socio-Religious Brain: A Developmental Model." *Proceedings of the British Academy* 158: 283–307.

Fodor, Jerry. 1983. *The Modularity of Mind: An Essay on Faculty Psychology.* Cambridge, MA: MIT Press.

Fodor, Jerry. 1998. *In Critical Condition: Polemical Essays on Cognitive Science and the Philosophy of Mind.* Cambridge, MA: MIT Press.

Fodor, Jerry. 2000. *The Mind Doesn't Work that Way: The Scope and Limits of Computational Psychology.* Cambridge, MA: MIT Press.

Fodor, Jerry. 2005. "Reply to Steven Pinker 'So How Does the Mind Work?'" *Mind and Language* 20(1): 25–32.

Foin, Theodore C. and William G. Davis. 1984. "Ritual and Self-regulation of the Tsembaga Maring Ecosystem in the New Guinea Highlands." *Human Ecology* 12(4): 385–412.

Fortunato, Laura. 2015. "Marriage Systems, Evolution Of." In *International Encyclopedia of the Social and Behavioral Sciences* (2nd edition), edited by James D. Wright, 611–19. Oxford: Elsevier. https://doi.org/10.1016/B978-0-08-097086-8.81059-4.

Fortunato, Laura and M. Archetti. 2010. "Evolution of Monogamous Marriage by Maximization of Inclusive Fitness." *Journal of Evolutionary Biology* 23 (1): 149–156. https://doi.org/10.1111/j.1420-9101.2009.01884.x.

Frank, Robert H. 1988. *Passions within Reason: The Strategic Role of Emotions.* New York: W. W. Norton and Company.

Frazer, James G. 2006 [1890]. *The Golden Bough: A Study of Magic and Religion.* Sioux Falls, SD: NuVision Publications.

Freedman, Harry. 2014. *The Talmud: A Biography.* London: Bloomsbury.

Frejka, Tomas and Charles F. Westoff. 2008. "Religion, Religiousness and Fertility in the US and in Europe." *European Journal of Population* 24: 5–31.

Friedman, Hershey H. and Linda Weiser Friedman. 2014. *God Laughed: Sources of Jewish Humor.* New York: Routledge.

Fuentes, Agustin. 2020. *Why We Believe: Evolution and the Human Way of Being.* New Haven, CT: Yale University Press.

Gathercole, Susan E. 1997. "Models of Verbal Short-term Memory." In *Cognitive Models of Memory*, edited by Martin A. Conway, 13–44. Cambridge, MA: MIT Press.

Ge, Erhao, Yuan Chen, Jiajia Wu, and Ruth Mace. 2019. "Large-Scale Cooperation Driven by Reputation, Not Fear of Divine Punishment." *Royal Society Open Science* 6(8): 190991. https://doi.org/10.1098/rsos.190991.

Geertz, Armin W. 2010. "Brain, Body and Culture: A Biocultural Theory of Religion." *Method and Theory in the Study of Religion* 22: 304–321.

Geertz, Armin W. 2020. "How Did Ignorance Become Fact in American Religious Studies?: A Reluctant Reply to Ivan Strenski." *Studi E Materiali Di Storia Delle Religioni* 86(1): 365–403.

Geertz, Clifford. 1973 [1966]. *The Interpretation of Culture.* New York: Basic Books.

Gelman, Rochel, Frank H. Durgin, and Lisa Kaufman. 1996. "Distinguishing Between Animates and Inanimates: Not by Motion Alone." In *Causal Cognition: A Multidisciplinary Debate*, edited by Dan Sperber, David Premack, and Ann Premack. Oxford: Plenum Press.

Gervais, Will M. 2011. "Finding the Faithless: Perceived Atheist Prevalence Reduces Anti-atheist Prejudice." *Personality and Social Psychology Bulletin* 37: 543–556.

Gervais, W. M. and Joseph Henrich. 2010. "The Zeus Problem: Why Representational Content Biases Cannot Explain Faith in Gods. *Journal of Cognition and Culture* 10(3–4): 383–389.

Gervais, Will M., Azim Shariff, and Ara Norenzayan. 2011. "Do You Believe in Atheists? Trust and Anti-atheist Prejudice." *Journal of Personality and Social Psychology* 101: 1189–1206.

Gillett, William Kendall and Charles Ripley Gillett. 1892. "The Religious Motives of Christopher Columbus." *Papers of the American Society of Church History* 4: 3–26.

Gil-White, Francisco J. 2001. "Are Ethnic Groups Biological 'Species' to the Human Brain?: Essentialism in our Cognition of some Social Categories." *Current Anthropology* 42(4): 515–554.

Ginges, Jeremy, Scott Atran, Douglas Medin, and Khalil Shikaki, D. 2007. "Sacred Bounds on Rational Resolution of Violent Conflict." *Proceedings of the National Academy of Sciences* 104: 7357–7360.

Goldberg, Ilan, Michal Harel, and Rafael Malach. 2006. "When the Brain Loses Its Self: Prefrontal Inactivation during Sensorimotor Processing." *Neuron* 50: 329–339.

Gonçalves, Marco Antonio Teizeira. 1990. *Nomes e Cosmos: Onomástica Entre Os Mura-Pirahã*. Rio de Janeiro: Programma de Pós-Graduação em Antropologia Social.

Gonçalves, Marco Antonio. 2000. "Pirahã—Indigenous Peoples in Brazil." Retrieved from https://pib.socioambiental.org/en/Povo:Pirah%C3%A3#Cosmology

(accessed August 23, 2020).

Goodman, Felicitas D. 1986. "Body Posture and the Religious Altered State of Consciousness: An Experimental Investigation." *Journal of Humanistic Psychology* 26: 81–118.

Goody, Jack. 1996. "A Kernel of Doubt." *The Journal of the Royal Anthropological Institute* 2(4): 667–681.

Gouinlock, James. 1994. *The Moral Writings of John Dewey.* Amherst: Prometheus Books.

Graf, Peter and Daniel L. Schachter. 1985. "Implicit and Explicit Memory for New Associations in Normal and Amnesic Subjects." *Journal of Experimental Psychology: Learning, Memory, and Cognition* 11: 501–518.

Graham, Jesse and Jonathan Haidt. 2010. "Beyond Beliefs: Religion Binds Individuals into Moral Communities." *Personality and Social Psychology Review* 14: 140–150.

Granqvist, Pehr and Lee A. Kirkpatrick. 2008. "Attachment and Religious Representations and Behavior." In *Handbook of Attachment: Theory, Research, and Clinical Applications*, 2nd edition, edited by Jude Cassidy and Phillip R. Shaver, 906–933. New York: Guilford.

Granqvist, Pehr, Mario Mikulincer, and Phillip R. Shaver. 2010. "Religion as Attachment: Normative Processes and Individual Differences." *Personality and Social Psychology Review* 14: 49–59.

Gray, Heather M., Kurt Gray, and Daniel M. Wegner. 2007. "Dimensions of Mind Perception." *Science* 315(5812): 619–619. https://doi.org/10.1126/science.1134475.

Gray, Kurt, Liane Young, and Adam Waytz. 2012. "Mind Perception is the Essence of Morality." *Psychological Inquiry* 23(2): 101–124. https://doi.org/10.1080/1047840X.2012.651387.

Green, William S. 2014. "Judaism Evolving: An Experimental Preliminary Translation." In *A Legacy of Learning*, edited by Alan Avery-Peck, Bruce D. Chilton, William Scott Green, and Gary Porton, 110–141. Leiden, Netherlands: Brill.

Greenwald, Athony G., Debbie E. McGhee, and Jordan L. K. Schwartz. 1998. "Measuring Individual Differences in Implicit Cognition: The Implicit Association Test." *Journal of Personality and Social Psychology* 74(6): 1464–1480. https://doi.org/10.1037/0022-3514.74.6.1464.

Guenther, Mathias Georg. 1979. "Bushman Religion and the (Non)Sense of Anthropological Theory of Religion." *Sociologus* 29(2): 102–132.

Guenther, Mathias Georg. 1999. *Tricksters and Trancers: Bushman Religion and Society.* Bloomington, IN: Indiana University Press.

Guthrie, Stewart E. 1980. "A Cognitive Theory of Religion." *Current Anthropology* 21(2): 181–203. https://doi.org/10.1086/202429.

Guthrie, Stewart E. 1993. *Faces in the Clouds: A New Theory of Religion.* New York: Oxford University Press.

Guthrie, Stewart Elliott. 2016. "Religion as Anthropomorphism: A Cognitive Theory." In *The Oxford Handbook of Evolutionary Psychology and Religion*, edited by James R. Liddle and Todd K. Shackelford, 1–38. Oxford: Oxford University Press.

Hadaway, Christopher Kirk and Penny Marler. 2005. "How Many Americans Attend Worship Each Week? An Alternative Approach to Measurement." *Journal for the Scientific Study of Religion* 44: 307–322.

Haley, Kevin J. and Daniel M. T. Fessler. 2005. "Nobody's Watching? Subtle Cues Affect Generosity in an Anonymous Economic Game." *Evolution and Human Behavior* 26(3): 245–256.

Hames, Raymond. 1991. "Wildlife Conservation in Tribal Societies." In *Biodiversity: Culture, Conservation, and Ecodevelopment*, edited by Margery Oldfield and Janis Alcorn, 172–199. Denver: Westview.

Hames, Raymond. 2007. "The Ecologically Noble Savage Debate." *Annual Review of Anthropology* 36(1): 177–90. https://doi.org/10.1146/annurev.anthro.35.081705.123321.

Hardin, Garrett. 1968. "The Tragedy of the Commons." *Science* 162(3859): 1243–1248.

Hare, Darragh., H. K. Reeve, and B. Blossey. 2016. "Evolutionary Routes to Stable Ownership." *Journal of Evolutionary Biology* 29(6): 1178–1188. https://doi.org/10.1111/jeb.12859.

Harris, Marvin. 1966. "The Cultural Ecology of India's Sacred Cattle." *Current Anthropology* 7(1): 51–66.

Harris, Max. 2011. *Sacred Folly: A New History of the Feast of Fools.* Cornell University Press.

Harris, Erica and Patrick McNamara. 2008. "Is Religiousness a Biocultural Adaptation?" In *The Evolution of Religion: Studies, Theories, and Critiques*, edited by Joseph Bulbulia, Richard Sosis, Russell Genet, Cheryl Genet, Erica Harris, and Karen Wyman, 79–85. Santa Margarita, CA: Collins Foundation Press.

Hartberg, Yasha, Michael Cox, and Sergio Villamayor-Tomas. 2016. "Supernatural Monitoring and Sanctioning in Community-based Resource Management." *Religion, Brain and Behavior* 6(2): 95–111.

Hauser, Marc D. 1996. *The Evolution of Communication.* Cambridge, MA: MIT Press.

Heap, Stephen, Phillip Byrne, and Devi Stuart-Fox. 2012. "The Adoption of Landmarks for Territorial Boundaries." *Animal Behaviour* 83(4): 871–878. https://doi.org/10.1016/j.anbehav.2012.01.016.

Heath, Chip, Chris Bell, and Emily Sternberg. 2001. "Emotional Selection in Memes: The Case of Urban Legends." *Journal of Personality and Social Psychology* 81(6): 1028–1041.

Heider, Karl G. 1970. *The Dugum Dani: A Papuan Culture in the Highlands of West New Guinea.* New Brunswick, NJ: Transaction.

Heimola, Mikko. 2012. *Religious Rituals and Norms in the Making of Adaptive Systems.*

Doctoral thesis. Helsinki: University of Helsinki.

Heiphetz, Larisa, Jonathan D. Lane, Adam Waytz, and Liane L. Young. 2016. "How Children and Adults Represent God's Mind." *Cognitive Science* 40(1): 121–144. https://doi.org/10.1111/cogs.12232.

Henrich, Joseph. 2004. "Cultural Group Selection, Coevolutionary Processes and Large-scale Cooperation." *Journal of Economic Behavior and Organization* 53: 3–35.

Henrich, Joseph. 2009. "The Evolution of Costly Displays, Cooperation, and Religion: Credibility Enhancing Displays and their Implications for Cultural Evolution." *Evolution and Human Behavior* 30(4): 244–260.

Henrich, Joseph. 2016. *The Secret of Our Success: How Culture Is Driving Human Evolution, Domesticating Our Species, and Making Us Smarter.* Princeton, NJ: Princeton University Press.

Henrich, Joseph, Michal Bauer, Julie Chytilova, Alessandra Cassar, and Benjamin Grant Purzycki. 2019. "War Increases Religiosity." *Nature Human Behavior* 3(2): 129–135.

Henrich, Joseph, Robert Boyd and Peter J. Richerson. 2012. "The Puzzle of Monogamous Marriage." *Philosophical Transactions of the Royal Society B: Biological Sciences* 367(1589): 657–669.

Henrich, Joseph, Jean Ensminger, Richard McElreath, Abigail Barr, Clark Barrett, Alexander Bolyanatz, Juan Camilo Cardenas, Michael Gurven, Edwins Gwako, Natalie Henrich, Carolyn Lesorogol, Frank Marlowe, David Tracer, and John Ziker. 2010. "Markets, Religion, Community Size, and the Evolution of Fairness and Punishment." *Science* 327: 1480–1484.

Henrich, Joseph and Francisco J. Gil-White. 2001. "The Evolution of Prestige: Freely Conferred Status as a Mechanism for Enhancing the Benefits of Cultural Transmission." *Evolution and Human Behavior* 22: 165–196.

Henrich, Joseph and Natalie Henrich. 2010. "The Evolution of Cultural Adaptations: Fijian Food Taboos Protect Against Dangerous Marine Toxins." *Proceedings of the Royal Academy: Biological Sciences* 277: 3715–3724.

Henrich, Joseph and Richard McElreath. 2003. "The Evolution of Cultural Evolution." *Evolutionary Anthropology* 12: 123–135.

Hereniko, Vilsoni. 1994. "Clowning as Political Commentary: Polynesia, Then and Now." *The Contemporary Pacific* 6(1): 1–28.

Herold, Edward S. and Marilyn Shirley Goodwin. 1981. "Adamant Virgins, Potential Virgins and Nonvirgins." *The Journal of Sex Research* 17: 97–113.

Hewlett, Barry S. 2016. "Evolutionary Cultural Anthropology: Containing Ebola Outbreaks and Explaining Hunter-Gatherer Childhoods." *Current Anthropology* 57(S13): S27–S37. https://doi.org/10.1086/685497.

Hill, Kim, Michael Barton, and A. Magdalena Hurtado. 2009. "The Emergence of Human Uniqueness: Characters Underlying Behavioral Modernity." *Evolutionary Anthropology* 18(5): 187–200.

Hill, Kim and Magdalena Hurtado. 1996. *Ache Life History: The Ecology and Demography of a Foraging People.* New York: Aldine de Gruyter.

Hill, Kim R., Brian M. Wood, Jacopo Baggio, A. Magdalena Hurtado, and Robert T. Boyd. 2014. "Hunter-Gatherer Inter-Band Interaction Rates: Implications for Cumulative Culture." *PLOS ONE* 9(7): e102806. https://doi.org/10.1371/journal.pone.0102806.

Hinde, Robert A. 2009. *Why Gods Persist: A Scientific Approach to Religion.* New York: Routledge.

Hirschfeld, Lawrence A. and Susan A. Gelman.1994. *Mapping the Mind: Domain Specificity in Cognition and Culture.* Cambridge: Cambridge University Press.

Hogbin, Ian. 1970. *The Island of Menstruating Men: Religion in Wogeo, New Guinea.* London: Chandler Publishing.

Holland, John H. 1992. *Adaptation in Natural and Artificial Systems: An Introductory Analysis with Applications to Biology, Control and Artificial Intelligence.* Cambridge, MA: MIT University Press.

Holland, John H. 1995. *Hidden Order: How Adaptation Builds Complexity.* New York: Basic Books.

Holland, John H. 1998. *Emergence: From Chaos to Order.* Oxford: Oxford University Press.

Holland, John H. 2012. *Signals and Boundaries: Building Blocks for Complex Adaptive Systems.* Cambridge, MA: MIT Press.

Holland, John H. and John H. Miller. 1991. "Artificial Adaptive Agents in Economic Theory." *American Economic Association Papers and Proceedings* 81(2): 365–370.

Houser, Nathan and Christian J. W. Kloesel. 1992. *The Essential Peirce: Selected Philosophical Writings,* Volume 1 (1867–1893). Bloomington, IN: Indiana University Press.

Hugues de Saint-Victor. 1648. *Canonici Regulares Sancti Victoris.* Rouen: Ioannis Berthelin. Retrieved from https://babel.hathitrust.org/cgi/pt?id=ucm.5319449723&view=1up&seq=128&skin=2021&q1=omnimodo

Hyde, Lewis. 1998. *Trickster Makes This World: Mischief, Myth and Art.* New York: North Point Press.

Iannaccone, Laurence R. 1992. "Sacrifice and Stigma: Reducing Free-Riding in Cults, Communes, and Other Collectives." *The Journal of Political Economy* 100(2): 271–291.

Iannaccone, Laurence R. 1994. "Why Strict Churches are Strong." *American Journal of Sociology* 99:1180–1211.

Iannaccone, Laurence R. 1995. "Voodoo Economics? Reviewing the Rational Choice Approach to Religion." *Journal for the Scientific Study of Religion* 34(1): 76–88.

Inzlicht, Michael, Alexa M. Tullett, and Marie Good, M. 2011. "The Need to Believe: A Neuroscience Account of Religion as a Motivated Process." *Religion, Brain and Behavior* 1(3): 192–212. https://doi.org/10.1080/2153599X.2011.647849.

Irons, William G. 2001. "Religion as a Hard-to-fake Sign of Commitment." In *Evolution and the Capacity for Commitment*, edited by Randolph Nesse, 292–309. New York: Russell Sage Foundation.

Izquierdo, Carolina, Allen Johnson, and Glenn H. Shepard Jr. 2008. "Revenge, Envy and Sorcery in an Amazonian Society." In *Revenge in the Cultures of Lowland South America*, edited by Stephen Beckerman and Paul Valentine, 163–186. Gainesville, FL: University of Florida Press.

James, William. 1958 [1902]. *The Varieties of Religious Experience*. New York: Mentor.

Johnson, Allen. 2003. *Families of the Forest: The Matsigenka Indians of the Peruvian Amazon*. Berkeley, CA: University of California Press.

Johnson, Dominic D. P. 2005. "God's Punishment and Public Goods: A test of the Supernatural Punishment Hypothesis in 186 World Cultures." *Human Nature* 16(4): 410–446. https://doi.org/10.1007/s12110-005-1017-0.

Johnson, Dominic D. P. 2015. "Big Gods, Small Wonder: Supernatural Punishment Strikes Back." *Religion, Brain and Behavior* 5(4): 290–298. https://doi.org/10.1080/2153599X.2014.928356.

Johnson, Dominic D. P. 2016. *God is Watching You: How the Fear of God Makes Us Human*. Oxford: Oxford University Press.

Johnson, Dominic D. P. and Jesse Bering. 2006. "Hand of God, Mind of Man: Punishment and Cognition in the Evolution of Cooperation." *Evolutionary Psychology* 4: 219–233.

Johnson, Kathryn A., Morris Alan Okun, and Adam B. Cohen. 2015. "The Mind of the Lord: Measuring Authoritarian and Benevolent God Representations. *Psychology of Religion and Spirituality* 7(3): 227–238.

Jong, Jonathan, Robert Ross, Tristan Philip, Si-Hua Chang, Naomi Simons, and Jamin Halberstadt. 2018. "The Religious Correlates of Death Anxiety: A Systematic Review and Meta-analysis." *Religion, Brain and Behavior* 8(1): 4–20.

Kanazawa, Satoshi and Mary C. Still. 2000. "Why Men Commit Crimes (and Why They Desist)." *Sociological Theory* 18: 434–447.

Kandler, Anne, and Adam Powell. 2018. "Generative Inference for Cultural Evolution." *Philosophical Transactions of the Royal Society B: Biological Sciences* 373(1743): 20170056. https://doi.org/10.1098/rstb.2017.0056.

Katz, Richard. 1982. *Boiling Energy: Community Healing Among the Kalahari Kung*. Cambridge, MA: Harvard University Press.

Kauffman, Stuart. 1995. *At Home in the Universe: The Search for the Laws of Self-organization and Complexity*. Oxford: Oxford University Press.

Kaufmann, Eric. 2010. *Shall the Religious Inherit the Earth? Demography and Politics in the Twenty-First Century*. London: Profile Books.

Kavanagh, Christopher M. and Jonathan Jong. 2020. "Is Japan Religious?" *Journal for the Study of Religion, Nature and Culture* 14(1): 152–180.

Keil, Frank C. 1989. *Concepts, Kinds, and Cognitive Development*. Cambridge, MA: MIT

Press.

Keller, Eva. 2005. *The Road to Clarity: Seventh-Day Adventism in Madagascar*. New York: Palgrave Macmillan.

Kendal, Rachel L., Neeltje J. Boogert, Luke Rendell, Kevin N. Laland, Mike Webster, and Patricia L. Jones. 2018. "Social Learning Strategies: Bridge-Building between Fields." *Trends in Cognitive Sciences* 22(7): 651–665. https://doi. org/10.1016/j.tics.2018.04.003.

Kiper, Jordan. 2020. "How Dangerous Propaganda Works." In *Propaganda and International Criminal Law: From Cognition to Criminality*, edited by P. Dojčinović, 217–236. New York: Routledge.

Kiper, Jordan and Richard Sosis. 2014. "Moral Intuitions and the Religious System: An Adaptationist Account." *Philosophy, Theology, and Science* 1: 172–199.

Kiper, Jordan and Richard Sosis. 2016. "The Roots of Intergroup Conflict and the Co-option of the Religious System: An Evolutionary Perspective on Religious Terrorism." In *The Oxford Handbook of Evolutionary Perspectives and Religion*, edited by James R. Liddle and Todd K. Shackelford. Oxford: Oxford University Press.

Kiper, Jordan and Richard Sosis. 2020. "The Systemics of Violent Religious Nationalism: A Case Study of the Yugoslav Wars." *Journal for the Study of Religion, Nature and Culture* 14(1): 45–70.

Kirkpatrick, Lee A. 1999. "Toward an Evolutionary Psychology of Religion and Personality." *Journal of Personality* 67(6): 921–952.

Kirkpatrick, Lee A. 2005. *Attachment, Evolution, and the Psychology of Religion*. New York: Guilford Press.

Kirkpatrick, Lee A. 2006. "Religion is Not an Adaptation." In *Where Man and God Meet: How Brain and Evolutionary Studies Alter Our Understanding of Religion, Volume 1: Evolution, Genes, and the Religious Brain*, edited by Patrick McNamara. Westport, CT: Praeger.

Kirkpatrick, Lee A. 2008. "Religion is Not an Adaptation: Some Fundamental Issues and Arguments." In *The Evolution of Religion: Studies, Theories, and Critiques*, edited by Joseph Bulbulia, Richard Sosis, Russell Genet, Cheryl Genet, Erica Harris, and Karen Wyman. Santa Margarita, CA: Collins Foundation Press.

Klass, Morton. 1995. *Ordered Universes: Approaches to the Anthropology of Religion*. Boulder, CO: Westview Press.

Klubnikin, Kheryn, Cynthia A. Annett, Maria Cherkasova, Michail Shishin, and Irina Fotieva. 2000. "The Sacred and the Scientific: Traditional Ecological Knowledge in Siberian River Conservation." *Ecological Applications* 10(5): 1296–1306.

Koenig, Harold, Dana King, and Verna B. Carson. 2012. *Handbook of Religion and Health*. Oxford: Oxford University Press.

Koenig, Harold G., Michael E. McCullough, and David B. Larson D. 2001. *Handbook of Religion and Health*. New York: Oxford University Press.

Krátký, Jan, John J. McGraw, Dimitris Xygalatas, Panagiotis Mitkidis, and Paul Reddish. 2016. "It Depends Who Is Watching You: 3-D Agent Cues Increase Fairness." *PLOS ONE* 11(2): e0148845. https://doi.org/10.1371/journal.pone.0148845.

Kugel, James L. 2017. *The Great Shift*. New York: Houghton Mifflin Harcourt.

Kundt, Radek. 2017. *Contemporary Evolutionary Theories of Culture and the Study of Religion*. New York: Bloomsbury Publishing.

Kundtová Klocová, Eva. 2017. *Body in Ritual Space: Communication through Embodied Practices in Religious Ritual*. Doctoral Dissertation. Brno: University of Masaryk.

LaDuke, Winona. 2005. *Recovering the Sacred: The Power of Naming and Claiming*. Cambridge: South End Press.

Lahti, David C. 2009. "The Correlated History of Social Organization, Morality, and Religion." In *The Biological Evolution of Religious Mind and Behavior*, edited by Eckart Voland and Wulf Schiefenhövel, 67–88. New York: Springer.

Laidlaw, James. 2004. "Embedded Modes of Religiosity in Indic Renouncer Religions." In *Ritual and Memory: Toward a Comparative Anthropology of Religion*, edited by Harvey Whitehouse and James Laidlaw, 89–109. New York: AltaMira Press.

Laland, Kevin N. 2004. "Extending the Extended Phenotype." *Biology and Philosophy* 19(3): 313–325.

Laland, Kevin N., John Odling-Smee, and Marcus W. Feldman. 2000. "Niche Construction, Biological Evolution, and Cultural Change." *Behavioral and Brain Sciences* 23: 131–175.

Lane, Jonathan D., Henry M. Wellman, and E. Margaret Evans. 2012. "Socio-cultural Input Facilitates Children's Developing Understanding of Extraordinary Minds." *Child Development* 83(3): 1007–1021. https://doi.org/10.1111/j.1467-8624.2012.01741.x.

Lane, Jonathan D., Henry M. Wellman, and E. Margaret Evans. 2014. "Approaching an Understanding of Omniscience from the Preschool Years to Early Adulthood." *Developmental Psychology* 50(10): 2380–2392. https://doi.org/10.1037/a0037715.

Lang, Martin and Radek Kundt. 2020. "Evolutionary, Cognitive, and Contextual Approaches to the Study of Religious Systems: A Proposition of Synthesis." *Method and Theory in the Study of Religion* 32(1): 1–46. https://doi.org/10.1163/15700682-12341466.

Lang, Martin, Vladimír Bahna, John H. Shaver, Paul Reddish, and Dimitris Xygalatas. 2017. "Sync to Link: Endorphin-mediated Synchrony Effects on Cooperation." *Biological Psychology* 127: 191–197.

Lang, Martin, Benjamin G. Purzycki, Coren L. Apicella, Quentin D. Atkinson, Alexander Bolyanatz, Emma Cohen, Carla Handley, Eva Kundtová Klocová, Carolyn Lesorogol, Sarah Mathew, Rita A. McNamara, Cristina Moya, Caitlyn

D. Placek, Montserrat Soler, Thomas Vardy, Jonathan L. Weigel, Aiyana K. Willard, Dimitris Xygalatas, Ara Norenzayan, and Joseph Henrich. 2019. "Moralistic Gods, Extended Prosociality, and Religious Parochialism across 15 Societies." *Proceedings of the Royal Society B* 286(1898): 20190202.

Lanman, Jonathan and Hugh Turpin. 2022. "The Failure of Religious Systems." *Oxford Handbook of the Cognitive Science of Religion*. Oxford: Oxford University Press.

Lansing, John Stephen. 1987. "Balinese 'Water Temples' and the Management of Irrigation." *American Anthropologist* 89(2): 326–341. https://doi.org/10.1525/aa.1987.89.2.02a00030.

Lansing, John Stephen. 1991. *Priests and Programmers: Technologies of Power in the Engineered Landscape of Bali*. Princeton, NJ: Princeton University Press.

Lansing, John Stephen. 2003. "Complex Adaptive Systems." *Annual Review of Anthropology* 32(1): 183–204.

Lansing, John Stephen. 2006. *Perfect Order: Recognizing Complexity in Bali*. Princeton, NJ: Princeton University Press.

Lansing, John Stephen and James N. Kremer. 1993. "Emergent Properties of Balinese Water Temple Networks: Coadaptation on a Rugged Fitness Landscape." *American Anthropologist* (new series) 95(1): 97–114.

Lansing, John Stephen and John H. Miller. 2005. "Cooperation, Games, and Ecological Feedback: Some Insights from Bali." *Current Anthropology* 46(2): 328–334. https://doi.org/10.1086/428790.

Lazerwitz, Bernard and Michael Harrison. 1979. "American Jewish Denominations: A Social and Religious Profile." *American Sociological Review* 44: 656–666.

Lee, Richard B. 2003. *The Dobe Ju/'Hoansi (Case Studies in Cultural Anthropology)*, 3rd edition. Belmont, CA: Wadsworth Publishing.

Legare, Cristine H. and André L. Souza. 2012. "Evaluating Ritual Efficacy: Evidence from the Supernatural." *Cognition* 124: 1–15.

Lehrer, Evelyn L. 1996. "Religion as a Determinant of Marital Fertility." *Journal of Population Economics* 9: 173–196.

Lesser, Alexander. 1978. *The Pawnee Ghost Dance Hand Game: Ghost Dance Revival and Ethnic Identity*. Madison, WI: University of Wisconsin Press.

Levin, Theodore Craig and Valentina Süzükei. 2006. *Where Rivers and Mountains Sing: Sound, Music, and Nomadism in Tuva and Beyond*. Bloomington, IN: Indiana University Press.

Levine, Stephanie Wellen. 2003. *Mystics, Mavericks, and Merrymakers: An Intimate Journey among Hasidic Girls*. New York: NYU Press.

Lévi-Strauss, Claude. 1994 [1964]. *The Raw and the Cooked: Introduction to a Science of Mythology*. New York: Pimlico.

Lewis, Thomas H. 1990. *The Medicine Men: Oglala Sioux Ceremony and Healing*, 52–70. Lincoln, NE: University of Nebraska Press.

Liénard, Pierre and Pascal Boyer. 2006. "Whence Collective Rituals? A Cultural Selection Model of Ritualized Behavior." *American Anthropologist* 108(4):

814–827.

Liénard, Pierre, Chelsea Feeny, and Jesper Sørensen. 2006. "Agent and Instrument in Judgements of Ritual Efficacy." *Journal of Cognition and Culture* 6: 463–482.

Luhrmann, Tanya M. 2012. *When God Talks Back: Understanding the American Evangelical Relationship with God.* New York: Vintage.

Mails, Thomas E. 1979. *Fools Crow.* Lincoln, NE: University of Nebraska Press.

Malinowski, Bronislaw. 1944. *A Scientific Theory of Culture and Other Essays.* Chapel Hill, NC: University of North Carolina.

Malley, Brian E. 1995. "Explaining Order in Religious Systems." *Method and Theory in the Study of Religion* 7(2): 5–22.

Malley, Brian E. 1997. "Causal Holism in the Evolution of Religious Ideas." *Method and Theory in the Study of Religion* 9(4): 389–399.

Malone, Jacqui. 1996. *Steppin' on the Blues: The Visible Rhythms of African American Dance.* Chicago, IL: University of Illinois Press.

Marlowe, Frank. 2010. *The Hadza: Hunter-Gatherers of Tanzania,* 1st edition. Berkeley, CA: University of California Press.

Marshall, Lorna. 1962. "!Kung Bushman Religious Beliefs." *Africa: Journal of the International African Institute* 32(3): 221–252. https://doi.org/10.2307/1157541.

Martin, Luther H. and Donald Wiebe. 2017. *Religion Explained?: The Cognitive Science of Religion after Twenty-Five Years.* New York: Bloomsbury Publishing.

Matthews, Luke J., Jeffrey Edmonds, Wesley J. Wildman, and Charles L. Nunn. 2013. "Cultural Inheritance or Cultural Diffusion of Religious Violence? A Quantitative Case Study of the Radical Reformation." *Religion, Brain and Behavior* 3(1): 3–15.

Mattison, Siobhán M. and Rebecca Sear. 2016. "Modernizing Evolutionary Anthropology." *Human Nature* 27(4): 335–350. https://doi.org/10.1007/s12110-016-9270-y.

Maynard Smith, John. 1982. *Evolution and the Theory of Games.* Cambridge: Cambridge University Press.

McCauley, Robert N. 2011. *Why Religion is Natural and Science is Not.* New York: Oxford University Press.

McCauley, Robert N. and Ernest Thomas Lawson. 1984. "Functionalism Reconsidered." *History of Religions,* 23(4): 372–381.

McCauley, Robert N. and Ernest Thomas Lawson. 2002. *Bringing Ritual to Mind: Psychological Foundations of Cultural Forms.* Cambridge: Cambridge University Press.

McClenon, James. 2002. *Wondrous Healing: Shamanism, Human Evolution, and the Origin of Religion.* DeKalb, IL: Northern Illinois University Press.

McCullough, Michael E., Paul Swartwout, John H. Shaver, Evan C. Carter, and Richard Sosis. 2016. "Christian Religious Badges Instill Trust in Christian and non-Christian Perceivers. *Psychology of Religion and Spirituality,* 8(2):

149–163.

McKay, Ryan, Charles Efferson, Harvey Whitehouse, and Ernst Fehr. 2011. "Wrath of God: Religious Primes and Punishment." *Proceedings of the Royal Society of London B: Biological Sciences* 278(1713): 1858–1863. https://doi.org/10.1098/rspb.2010.2125.

McKay, Ryan and Harvey Whitehouse. 2015. "Religion and Morality." *Psychological Bulletin* 141(2): 447–473. https://doi.org/10.1037/a0038455.

McNamara, Rita A. and Benjamin Grant Purzycki. 2020. Minds of gods and human cognitive constraints: Socio-ecological context shapes belief. *Religion, Brain and Behavior* 10(3): 223–238.

McNeill, William Hardy. 1995. *Keeping Together in Time: Dance and Drill in Human History.* Cambridge, MA: Harvard University Press.

Mecklenburger, Ralph D. 2012. *Our Religious Brains: What Cognitive Science Reveals about Belief, Morality, Community and Our Relationship with God.* Woodstock, VT: Jewish Lights Publishing.

Medicine, Beatrice. 2007. *Drinking and Sobriety among the Lakota Sioux.* Lanham, MD: Altamira.

Meggitt, Mervyn. 1977. *Blood Is Their Argument: Warfare Among the Mae Enga Tribesmen of the New Guinea Highlands.* Palo Alto: McGraw-Hill Humanities/Social Sciences/Languages.

Miller, Geoffrey. 2009. *Spent: Sex, Evolution, and Consumer* Behavior. New York: Viking.

Miller, John H. and Scott Page. 2007. *Complex Adaptive Systems: An Introduction to Computational Models of Social Life.* Princeton, NJ: Princeton University Press.

Mitchell, Melanie. 2009. *Complexity: A Guided Tour.* Oxford: Oxford University Press.

Mochizuki, Shinko. 1999. "Pure Land Buddhism in China: A Doctrinal History. Author's Preface and Chapter One: A General Survey." Edited and translated by Richard K. Payne and Leo M. Pruden. *Pacific World Journal* 3(1): 91–103.

Mooney, James. 1965. *The Ghost-dance Religion and the Sioux Outbreak of 1890.* Chicago, IL: University of Chicago Press.

Morgan, Jonathan Ross. 2019. *Religious Engagement and Varieties of Self-Regulation: Broadening Beyond Belief and Restraint.* Doctoral dissertation. Boston, MA: Boston University. Retrieved from https://search.proquest.com/docview/2196834825/abstract/CA1EE483A9BF4A5FPQ/1.

Moya, Cristina, Patricio Cruz y Celis Peniche, Michelle A. Kline, and Paul E. Smaldino. 2020. "Dynamics of Behavior Change in the COVID World." *American Journal of Human Biology* 32(5): e23485. https://doi.org/10.1002/ajhb.23485.

Murray, Michael J. and Lyn Moore. 2009. "Costly Signaling and the Origin of Religion." *Journal of Cognition and Culture* 9(3): 225–245.

Myerhoff, Barbara G. 1974. *Peyote Hunt: The Sacred Journey of the Huichol Indians.*

Ithaca, NY: Cornell University Press.

Nairne, James S., Josefa N. S. Pandeirada, Karie J. Gregory, and Joshua E. Van Arsdall. 2009. "Adaptive Memory: Fitness-Relevance and the Hunter-Gatherer Mind." *Psychological Science* 20: 740–746.

Nevins, Andrew, David Pesetsky, and Cilene Rodrigues. 2009a. "Evidence and Argumentation: A Reply to Everett (2009)." *Language* 85(3): 671–681.

Nevins, Andrew, David Pesetsky, and Cilene Rodrigues. 2009b. "Pirahã Exceptionality: A Reassessment." *Language* 85(2): 355–404. https://doi.org/10.1353/lan.0.0107.

Nielbo, Kristoffer Laigaard, Donald M. Braxton, and Afzal Upal. 2012. "Computing Religion: A new Tool in the Multilevel Analysis of Religion." *Method and Theory in the Study of Religion* 24(3): 267–290.

Nielsen, Mark. 2018. "The Social Glue of Cumulative Culture and Ritual Behavior." *Child Development Perspectives* 12(4): 264–268.

Norenzayan, Ara. 2013. *Big Gods: How Religion Transformed Cooperation and Conflict.* Princeton, NJ: Princeton University Press.

Norenzayan, Ara, Scott Atran, Jason Faulkner, and Mark Schaller. 2006. "Memory and Mystery: The Cultural Selection of Minimally Counterintuitive Narratives." *Cognitive Science* 30 (3): 531–553.

Norenzayan, Ara, and Will M. Gervais. 2013. "The Origins of Religious Disbelief." *Trends in Cognitive Sciences* 17 (1): 20–25. https://doi.org/10.1016/j.tics.2012.11.006.

Norenzayan, Ara, Will M. Gervais, and Kali H. Trzesniewski. 2012. "Mentalizing Deficits Constrain Belief in a Personal God." *PLOS ONE* 7(5): e36880. https://doi.org/10.1371/journal.pone.0036880.

Norenzayan, Ara and Azim Shariff. 2008. "The Origin and Evolution of Religious Prosociality." *Science* 322: 58–62.

Norenzayan, Ara, Azim F. Shariff, Will M. Gervais, Aiyana K. Willard, Rita A. McNamara, Edward Slingerland, and Joseph Henrich. 2016. "The Cultural Evolution of Prosocial Religions." *Behavioral and Brain Sciences* 39. https://doi.org/10.1017/S0140525X14001356.

Norris, Pippa and Ronald Inglehart. 2012. *Sacred and Secular: Religion and Politics Worldwide*, 2nd edition. Cambridge: Cambridge University Press.

North, Douglass C. 1990. *Institutions, Institutional Change and Economic Performance.* Cambridge: Cambridge University Press.

North, Douglass C. 1991. "Institutions." *Journal of Economic Perspectives* 5 (1): 97–112. https://doi.org/10.1257/jep.5.1.97.

Northover, Stefanie B. 2017. "Effect of Artificial Surveillance Cues on Reported Moral Judgment: Experimental Failures to Replicate and Two Meta-Analyses." *Evolution and Human Behavior* 38(5): 561–571. https://doi.org/10.1016/j.evolhumbehav.2016.12.003.

Northover, Stefanie B., William C. Pedersen, Adam B. Cohen, and Paul W. Andrews.

2017. "Artificial Surveillance Cues Do Not Increase Generosity: Two Meta-Analyses." *Evolution and Human Behavior* 38(1): 144–153. https://doi.org/10.1016/j.evolhumbehav.2016.07.001.

Obeyesekere, Gananath. 1991. "Buddhism and Conscience: An Exploratory Essay." *Daedalus* 120(3): 219–39.

O'Connor, Timothy. 1994. "Emergent Properties." *American Philosophical Quarterly* 31(2): 91–104.

Odling-Smee, John F. 1996. "Niche Construction, Genetic Evolution and Cultural Change." *Behavioural Processes* 35: 195–205.

Orrù, Marco and Amy Wang. 1992. "Durkheim, Religion, and Buddhism." *Journal for the Scientific Study of Religion* 31(1): 47–61. https://doi.org/10.2307/1386831.

Orwell, George. 2003 [1949]. *Nineteen Eighty-Four*. New York: Plume.

Ostrom, Elinor. 2015. *Governing the Commons*. Cambridge University Press.

Otte, Daniel. 1974. "Effects and Functions in the Evolution of Signaling Systems." *Annual Review of Ecology and Systematics* 5(1): 385–417.

Owens, D. Alfred and Mark Wagner. 1992. *Progress in Modern Psychology: The Legacy of American Functionalism*. Westport, CT: Praeger Publishers.

Page, Scott E. 2018. *The Model Thinker: What You Need to Know to Make Data Work for You*. New York: Basic Books.

Paladino, Maria Paola, Mara Mazzurega, Francesco Pavani, and Thomas Schubert. 2010. "Synchronous Multisensory Stimulation Blurs Self-other Boundaries." *Psychol Sci* 21(9): 1202–1207. https://doi.org/10.1177/0956797610379234

Pegg, Carole. 2001. *Mongolian Music, Dance, and Oral Narrative: Performing Diverse Identities*. Seattle, WA: University of Washington Press.

Peoples, Hervey C. and Frank W. Marlowe. 2012. "Subsistence and the Evolution of Religion." *Human Nature* 23(3): 253–269. https://doi.org/10.1007/s12110-012-9148-6.

Pew Research Center, July 23, 2019, "What Americans Know About Religion." Retrieved from www.pewforum.org/wp-content/uploads/sites/7/2019/07/Religious-Knowledge-full-draft-FOR-WEB-2.pdf

Pew Research Center. 2020. "The Global God Divide." Retrieved from www.pewresearch.org/global/wp-content/uploads/sites/2/2020/07/PG_2020.07.20_Global-Religion_FINAL.pdf.

Piazza, Jared, Jesse M. Bering, and Gordon P. D. Ingram. 2011. "'Princess Alice is Watching You': Children's Belief in an Invisible Person Inhibits Cheating." *Journal of Experimental Child Psychology* 109(3): 311–320.

Pinker, Steven. 1994. *The Language Instinct*. New York: Harper Perennial.

Pinker, Steven. 2003. *The Blank Slate: The Modern Denial of Human Nature*. New York: Penguin.

Pinker, Steven. 2005a. "So How Does the Mind Work?" *Mind and Language* 21(1): 1–24.

Pinker, Steven. 2005b. "A Reply to Jerry Fodor on How the Mind Works." *Mind and*

Language 20(1): 33–38.

Pinker, Steven and Paul Bloom. 1992. "Natural Language and Natural Selection." In *The Adapted Mind: Evolutionary Psychology and the Generation of Culture*, edited by Leda Cosmides, John Tooby and Jerome Barkow, 451–493. New York: Oxford University Press.

Pittendrigh, Colin Stephenson 1958. "Adaptation, Natural Selection, and Behavior." In *Behavior and Evolution, edited by Anne Roe and George Gaylord Simpson*, 390–416. New Haven, CT: Yale University Press.

Plant, John. 1994. *Heyoka: Die Contraries und Clowns Der Plainsindianer.* Verlag für Amerikanistik.

Plant, John. 2010. *The Plains Indian Clowns, Their Contraries and Related Phenomena.* Vienna, Austria. Retrieved from www.anjol.de/documents/100802_heyoka_neu.pdf (accessed August 24, 2020).

Porubanova, Michaela and John H. Shaver. 2017. "Minimal Counterintuitiveness Revisited, Again: The Role of Emotional Valence in Memory for Conceptual Incongruity." In *Religion Explained?: The Cognitive Science of Religion After Twenty-Five Years*, edited by Luther H. Martin and Donald Wiebe. Bloomsbury Academic.

Power, Camilla. 2015. "Hadza Gender Rituals—Epeme and Maitoko—Considered as Counterparts." *Hunter Gatherer Research* 1(3): 333–358. https://doi.org/10.3828/hgr.2015.18.

Power, Camilla and Ian Watts. 1997. "The Woman with the Zebra's Penis: Gender, Mutability and Performance." *The Journal of the Royal Anthropological Institute* 3(3): 537–560. https://doi.org/10.2307/3034766.

Power, Eleanor. 2017a. "Discerning Devotion: Testing the Signaling Theory of Religion." *Evolution and Human Behavior* 38(1): 82–91.

Power, Eleanor. 2017b. Social support networks and religiosity in rural South India. *Nature Human Behaviour* 1(3): 1–6.

Powers, William K. 1975. *Oglala Religion.* Lincoln, NE: University of Nebraska Press.

Premack, David and Guy Woodruff. 1978. "Does the Chimpanzee Have a Theory of Mind?" *Behavioral and Brain Sciences* 1: 515–526.

Proudfoot, Wayne. 1985. *Religious Experience.* Berkeley, CA: University of California Press.

Purzycki, Benjamin Grant. 2006. *Myth, Humor, and Ontological Templates: A Study of the Retention and Transmission of Religious Ideas.* Master's thesis. Lincoln, NE: University of Nebraska-Lincoln.

Purzycki, Benjamin Grant. 2010. "Spirit Masters, Ritual Cairns, and the Adaptive Religious System in Tyva." *Sibirica* 9(2): 21–47.

Purzycki, Benjamin Grant. 2011a. "Humor as Violation and Deprecation: A Cognitive Anthropological Account." *Journal of Cognition and Culture* 11(1–2): 217–230.

Purzycki, Benjamin Grant. 2011b. "Tyvan *Cher Eezi* and the Socioecological

Constraints of Supernatural Agents' Minds." *Religion, Brain and Behavior* 1(1): 31–45. https://doi.org/10.1080/2153599X.2010.550723.

Purzycki, Benjamin Grant. 2012. *Finding Minds in the Natural World: Dynamics of the Religious System in the Tyva Republic.* Doctoral dissertation. Storrs, CT: University of Connecticut.

Purzycki, Benjamin Grant. 2013a. "The Minds of Gods: A Comparative Study of Supernatural Agency." *Cognition* 129(1): 163–179. https://doi.org/10.1016/j.cognition.2013.06.010.

Purzycki, Benjamin Grant. 2013b. "Toward a Cognitive Ecology of Religious Concepts: Evidence from the Tyva Republic." *Journal for the Cognitive Science of Religion* 1(1): 99–120.

Purzycki, Benjamin Grant. 2016. "The Evolution of Gods' Minds in the Tyva Republic." *Current Anthropology* 57(S13): S88–S104.

Purzycki, Benjamin Grant. 2020. "Institutions, Natural Selection(s), and Religion. *Religion, Brain and Behavior* 10(1): 77–84.

Purzycki, Benjamin Grant. 2022. "Gods: Cognition, Culture, and Ecology." In *Handbook for the Cognitive Science of Religion*, edited by Justin Barrett. Oxford: Oxford University Press.

Purzycki, Benjamin Grant, Coren Apicella, Quentin D. Atkinson, Emma Cohen, Rita Anne McNamara, Aiyana K. Willard, Dimitris Xygalatas, Ara Norenzayan, and Joseph Henrich. 2016a. "Cross-Cultural Dataset for the Evolution of Religion and Morality Project." *Scientific Data* 3(160099). https://doi.org/10.1038/sdata.2016.99.

Purzycki, Benjamin Grant, Coren Apicella, Quentin D. Atkinson, Emma Cohen, Rita Anne McNamara, Aiyana K. Willard, Dimitris Xygalatas, Ara Norenzayan, and Joseph Henrich. 2016b. "Moralistic Gods, Supernatural Punishment and the Expansion of Human Sociality." *Nature* 530(7590): 327–330. https://doi.org/10.1038/nature16980.

Purzycki, Benjamin Grant and Tayana Arakchaa. 2013. "Ritual Behavior and Trust in the Tyva Republic." *Current Anthropology* 54(3): 381–388.

Purzycki, B. G., and Baimel, A. 2016. "Examining the Minds of Gods." In *Mental Religion*, edited by Niki Kasumi Clements, 45–60. Farmington Hills, MI: Macmillan.

Purzycki, Benjamin Grant, Daniel N Finkel, John Shaver, Nathan Wales, Adam B Cohen, and Richard Sosis. 2012. "What does God Know? Supernatural Agents' Access to Socially Strategic and Non-strategic Information." *Cognitive Science* 36(5): 846–869. https://doi.org/10.1111/j.1551-6709.2012.01242.x.

Purzycki, Benjamin Grant and Edward C. Holland. 2019. "Buddha as a God: An Empirical Assessment." *Method and Theory in the Study of Religion* 31(4–5): 347–375. https://doi.org/10.1163/15700682-12341453.

Purzycki, Benjamin Grant and Valeria Kulundary. 2018. "Buddhism, Identity, and

Class: Fairness and Favoritism in the Tyva Republic." *Religion, Brain and Behavior* 8(2): 205–226. https://doi.org/10.1080/2153599X.2016.1267031.

Purzycki, Benjamin Grant and Martin Lang. 2019. "Identity Fusion, Outgroups, and Sacrifice: A Cross-cultural Test. *Cognition* 186: 1–6.

Purzycki, Benjamin Grant and Rita Anne McNamara. 2016. "An Ecological Theory of Gods' Minds." In *Cognitive Science of Religion and its Philosophical Implications*, edited by Helen De Cruz and Ryan Nichols, 143–167. New York: Continuum.

Purzycki, Benjamin Grant, Anne C. Pisor, Coren Apicella, Quentin Atkinson, Emma Cohen, Joseph Henrich, Richard McElreath, Rita A McNamara, Ara Norenzayan, Aiyana K. Willard, and Dimitris Xygalatas. 2018. "The Cognitive and Cultural Foundations of Moral Behavior." *Evolution and Human Behavior* 39(5): 490–501. https://doi.org/10.1016/j.evolhumbehav.2018.04.004.

Purzycki, Benjamin Grant and Richard Sosis. 2009. "The Religious System as Adaptive: Cognitive Flexibility, Public Displays, and Acceptance." In *The Biological Evolution of Religious Mind and Behavior*, edited by Eckart Voland and Wulf Schiefenhövel, 243–256. New York: Springer-Verlag.

Purzycki, Benjamin Grant and Richard Sosis. 2010. "Religious Concepts as Necessary Components of the Adaptive Religious System." In *The Nature of God: Evolution and Religion*, edited by Ulrich Frey, 37–59. Marburg: Tectum Verlag.

Purzycki, Benjamin Grant and Richard Sosis. 2011. "Our Gods: Variation in Supernatural Minds." In *Essential Building Blocks of Human Nature*, edited by Ulrich J. Frey, Charlotte Störmer and Kai P. Willführ, 77–93. Berlin: Springer .

Purzycki, Benjamin Grant and Richard Sosis. 2013. "The Extended Religious Phenotype and the Adaptive Coupling of Ritual and Belief." *Israel Journal of Ecology and Evolution* 59(2): 99–108. https://doi.org/10.1080/15659801. 2013.825433.

Purzycki, Benjamin Grant, Richard Sosis, and Omar S. Haque. 2014. "Extending Evolutionary Accounts of Religion beyond the Mind: Religions as Adaptive Systems." In *The Evolution of Religion: Critical Perspectives and New Directions*, edited by Fraser Watts and Léon Turner, 74–91. New York: Oxford University Press.

Purzycki, Benjamin Grant, Michael N. Stagnaro, and Joni Sasaki. 2020. "Breaches of Trust Change the Content and Structure of Religious Appeals." *Journal for the Study of Religion, Nature and Culture* 14(1): 71–94.

Purzycki, Benjamin Grant and Joseph Watts. 2018. "Reinvigorating the Comparative, Cooperative Ethnographic Sciences of Religion." *Free Inquiry* 38(3): 26–29.

Purzycki, Benjamin G. and Aiyana K. Willard. 2016. "MCI Theory: A Critical Discussion." *Religion, Brain and Behavior* 6(3): 207–248.

Purzycki, Benjamin Grant, Aiyana K. Willard, Eva Kundtová Klocová, Coren Apicella,

Quentin Atkinson, Alexander Bolyanatz, Emma Cohen, Carla Handley, Joseph Henrich, Martin Lang, Carolyn Lesorogol, Sarah Mathew, Rita A. McNamara, Cristina Moya, Ara Norenzayan, Caitlyn Placek, Montserrat Soler, Jonathan Weigel, Dimitris Xygalatas, and Cody T. Ross. 2022. "The Moralization Bias of Gods' Minds: A Cross-Cultural Test." *Religion, Brain and Behavior.*

Putnam, Robert D. and David E. Campbell. 2010. *American Grace: How Religion Divides and Unites Us.* New York: Simon and Schuster.

Pyysiäinen, Ilkka. 2003. "Buddhism, Religion, and the Concept of 'God.'" *Numen* 50(2): 147–171.

Pyysiäinen, Ilkka. 2004. *Magic, Miracles, and Religion: A Scientist's Perspective.* Walnut Creek, CA: AltaMira Press.

Pyysiäinen, Ilkka and Marc D Hauser. 2010. "The Origins of Religion: Evolved Adaptation or By-product?" *Trends in Cognitive Sciences* 14(3): 104–109.

Radcliffe-Brown, Alfred Reginald. 1965. *Structure and Function in Primitive Society: Essays and Addresses.* New York: Free Press.

Radin, Paul. 1972 [1956]. *The Trickster: A Study in American Indian Mythology.* New York: Schocken.

Rahula, Walpola. 1974. *What the Buddha Taught,* revised edition. New York: Grove Press.

Randolph-Seng, Brandon and Michael E. Nielsen. 2007. "Honesty: One Effect of Primed Religious Representations." *The International Journal for the Psychology of Religion* 17: 303–315.

Rappaport, Roy A. 1979. *Ecology, Meaning, and Religion.* Berkeley, CA: North Atlantic Books.

Rappaport, Roy A. 1984 [1968]. *Pigs for the Ancestors: Ritual in the Ecology of a New Guinea People.* New Haven, CT: Yale University Press.

Rappaport, Roy A. 1999. *Ritual and Religion in the Making of Humanity.* Cambridge: Cambridge University Press.

Reddish, Paul, Penny Tok, and Radek Kundt. 2016. "Religious Cognition and Behaviour in Autism: The Role of Mentalizing." *International Journal for the Psychology of Religion* 26(2): 95–112. https://doi.org/10.1080/10508619.2014.1003518.

Reiss, Ira L., Ronald E. Anderson, and G. C. Sponaugle. 1980. "A Multivariate Model of the Determinants of Extramarital Sexual Permissiveness." *Journal of Marriage and the Family* 42: 395–411.

Resnick, Irven M. 2016. "'Risus Monasticus'. Laughter and Medieval Monastic Culture." *Revue Bénédictine* 97(1–2): 90–100. https://doi.org/10.1484/J.RB.4.01173.

Reynolds, Vernon and R. E. S. Tanner. 1995. *The Social Ecology of Religion.* Oxford: Oxford University Press.

Richerson, Peter, Ryan Baldini, Adrian V. Bell, Kathryn Demps, Karl Frost,

Vicken Hillis, Sarah Mathew et al. 2016. "Cultural Group Selection Plays an Essential Role in Explaining Human Cooperation: A Sketch of the Evidence." *Behavioral and Brain Sciences* 39: e30.

Richerson, Peter J. and Robert Boyd. 2005. *Not by Genes Alone: How Culture Transformed Human Evolution.* Chicago, IL: University of Chicago Press.

Richerson, Peter J. and Lesley Newson. 2008. "Is Religion Adaptive? Yes, No, Neutral, but Mostly, We Don't Know." In *The Evolution of Religion: Studies, Theories, and Critiques*, edited by Joseph Bulbulia, Richard Sosis, Russell Genet, Cheryl Genet, Erica Harris, and Karen Wyman. Santa Margarita CA: Collins Foundation Press.

Ridley, Matt. 2004. *The Agile Gene: How Nature Turns on Nurture.* New York: Harper Perennial.

Roes, Frans L. and Michel Raymond. 2003. "Belief in Moralizing Gods." *Evolution and Human Behavior* 24(2): 126–135. https://doi.org/10.1016/S1090-5138 (02)00134-4.

Romagny, Bruno, Claude Lobry, and Mireille Canalis-Durand. 1997. "Tragedy of the Commons and Prisoner's Dilemma." Universite Aix-Marseille III. Retrieved from https://ideas.repec.org/p/fth/aixmeq/97a20.html.

Romney, A. Kimball, Susan C. Weller, and William H. Batchelder. 1986. "Culture as Consensus: A Theory of Cultural and Informant Accuracy." *American Anthropologist* 88(2): 313–338.

Rossano, Matt J. 2006. "The Religious Mind and the Evolution of Religion." *Review of General Psychology* 10: 346–364.

Rossano, Matt J. 2007. "Supernaturalizing Social Life: Religion and the Evolution of Human Cooperation." *Human Nature* 18: 272–294.

Rossano, Matt J. 2009. "Ritual Behaviour and the Origins of Modern Cognition." *Cambridge Archaeological Journal* 19: 243–256.

Rossano, Matt J. and Adam LeBlanc. 2017. "Why Add the Supernatural?" *Religion, Brain and Behavior* 7(4): 375–377. https://doi.org/10.1080/2153599X.2016. 1249932

Rousseau, Jean-Jacques. 2016 [1755]. *A Discourse on Inequality.* New York: Open Road.

Ruffle, Bradley J. and Richard Sosis. 2007. "Does it Pay to Pray? Costly Ritual and Cooperation." *The B.E. Journal of Economic Analysis and Policy* 7: 1–35.

Ruffle, Bradley and Richard Sosis. 2020. "Do Religious Contexts Elicit More Trust and Altruism? Evidence from Decision-making Scenario Experiments." *Journal of Religion in Economics and Management* 1(1): 1–25. https://doi. org/10.1142/S2737436X20500028

Russell, Bertrand. 1961. *The Basic Writings of Bertrand Russell.* New York: Simon & Schuster.

Ruthven, Malise. 2004. *Fundamentalism: The Search for Meaning.* Oxford: Oxford University Press.

Ryan, Richard M., Scott Rigby, and Kristi King. 1993. "Two Types of Religious Internalization and Their Relations to Religious Orientations and Mental Health." *Journal of Personality and Social Psychology* 65(3): 586–596.

Saler, Benson. 1977. "Supernatural as a Western Category." *Ethos* 5(1): 31–53.

Samuels, Michael L. 1982. "POPREG I: A Simulation of Population Regulation among the Maring of New Guinea." *Human Ecology* 10(1): 1–45.

Sanders, Barry. 1995. *Sudden Glory: Laughter as Subversive History.* Boston, MA: Beacon Press.

Sanderson, Stephen K. 2008a. "Adaptation, Evolution, and Religion." *Religion* 38(2): 141–156.

Sanderson, Stephen K. 2008b. "Religious Attachment Theory and the Biosocial Evolution of the Major World Religions." In *The Evolution of Religion: Studies, Theories, and Critiques,* edited by Joseph Bulbulia, Richard Sosis, Russell Genet, Cheryl Genet, Erica Harris and Karen Wyman. Santa Margarita CA: Collins Foundation Press.

Sasaki, Joni Y., and Heejung S. Kim. 2021. "The Ego Dampening Influence of Religion: Evidence from Behavioral Genetics and Psychology. *Current Opinion in Psychology,* 40: 24-28

Sasaki, Joni Y., and Heejung S. Kim. 2020. "The Ego Dampening Influence of Religion: Evidence from Behavioral Genetics and Psychology." *Current Opinion in Psychology.*

Sasaki, Joni Y., Heejung S. Kim, and Jun Xu. 2011. "Religion and Well-Being: The Moderating Role of Culture and the Oxytocin Receptor (OXTR) Gene." *Journal of Cross-Cultural Psychology* 42 (8): 1394–1405. https://doi.org/10.1177/0022022111412526.

Schjoedt, Uffe, Hans Stødkilde-Jørgensen, Armin W. Geertz, and Andreas Roepstorff. 2009. "Highly Religious Participants Recruit Areas of Social Cognition in Personal Prayer." *Social Cognitive and Affective Neuroscience* 4(2): 199–207. https://doi.org/10.1093/scan/nsn050.

Schlieter, Jens. 2014. "'... For They Know Not What They Do'? Religion, Religions and Ethics as Conceptualized in Ara Norenzayan's *Big Gods: How Religion Transformed Cooperation and Conflict* (2013)." *Religion* 44(4): 649–657. https://doi.org/10.1080/0048721X.2014.937064.

Schloss, Jeffrey P. 2008. "He Who Laughs Best: Involuntary Religious Affect as a Solution to Recursive Cooperative Defection." In *The Evolution of Religion: Studies, Theories, and Critiques,* edited by Joseph Bulbulia, Richard Sosis, Russell Genet, Cheryl Genet, Erica Harris, and Karen Wyman. Santa Margarita, CA: Collins Foundation Press.

Schloss, Jeffrey P. and Michael J. Murray. 2011. "Evolutionary Accounts of Belief in Supernatural Punishment: A Critical Review." *Religion, Brain and Behavior* 1(1): 46–99. https://doi.org/10.1080/2153599X.2011.558707.

Searcy, William A. and Stephen Nowicki. 2005. *The Evolution of Animal Communication:*

Reliability and Deception in Signaling Systems. Princeton, NJ: Princeton University Press.

Searle, John R. 1997. *The Construction of Social Reality.* New York: Free Press.

Sears, David O. 1986. "College Sophomores in the Laboratory: Influences of a Narrow Data Base on Social Psychology's View of Human Nature." *Journal of Personality and Social Psychology* 51(3): 515–530. https://doi.org/10.1037/0022-3514.51.3.515.

Sechrist, Gretchen B. and Charles Stangor. 2001. "Perceived Consensus Influences Intergroup Behavior and Stereotype Accessibility." *Journal of Personality and Social Psychology* 80(4): 645–654.

Sechrist, Gretchen B. and Charles Stangor. 2007. "When are Intergroup Attitudes Based on Perceived Consensus Information? The Role of Group Familiarity." *Social Influence* 2(3): 211–235.

Seeman, Don. 2010. *One People, One Blood: Ethiopian-Israelis and the Return to Judaism.* New Brunswick, NJ: Rutgers University Press.

Seligman, Adam B. and Robert P. Weller. 2012. *Rethinking Pluralism: Ritual, Experience, and Ambiguity.* Oxford University Press.

Shantzis, Steven B. and William Wohlsen Behrens. 1973. "Population Control Mechanisms in a Primitive Agricultural Society." In *Towards Global Equilibrium,* edited by Donella M. Meadows, Donella H. Meadows, Tzonis, and Dennis L. Meadows, 257–288. Cambridge: Wright-Allen Press.

Shariff, Azim F. 2008. "One Species under God? Sorting through the Pieces of Religion and Cooperation." In *The Evolution of Religion: Studies, Theories, and Critiques,* edited by Joseph Bulbulia, Richard Sosis, Russell Genet, Cheryl Genet, Erica Harris, and Karen Wyman, 119–125. Santa Margarita, CA: Collins Foundation Press.

Shariff, Azim F. and Clark, B. 2012. Atheists versus Muslims: Comparing Religious Prejudices. Unpublished raw data.

Shariff, Azim F. and Ara Norenzayan. 2007. "God is Watching You: Priming God Concepts Increases Prosocial Behavior in an Anonymous Economic Game." *Psychological Science* 18: 803–880.

Shariff, Azim F. and Ara Norenzayan. 2011. "Mean Gods Make Good People." *International Journal for the Psychology of Religion* 21: 85–96.

Shariff, Azim F, Benjamin Grant Purzycki and Richard Sosis. 2014. "Religions as Cultural Solutions to Social Living." In *Culture Reexamined: Broadening our Understanding of Social and Evolutionary Influences,* edited by Adam B. Cohen, 217–238. Washington, DC: American Psychological Association.

Shariff, Azim F. and Mijke Rhemtulla. 2012. "Divergent Effects of Heaven and Hell Beliefs on National Crime." *PLOS ONE* 7(6): e39048. https://doi.org/10.1371/journal.pone.0039048

Sharrock, Wes W., John A. Hughes, and Peter J. Martin. 2003. *Understanding Modern Sociology.* Thousand Oaks, CA: Sage.

Shaver, John. 2015. "The Evolution of Stratification in Fijian Ritual Participation." *Religion, Brain and Behavior* 5(2): 101–117.

Shaver, John H. 2017. "Why and How Do Religious Individuals, and Some Religious Groups, Achieve Higher Relative Fertility?" *Religion, Brain and Behavior* 7(4): 324–327. https://doi.org/10.1080/2153599X.2016.1249920

Shaver, John H., Susie DiVietro, Martin Lang, and Richard Sosis. 2018. "Costs Do Not Explain Trust among Secular Groups." *Journal of Cognition and Culture* 18(1–2): 180–204.

Shaver, John H., Gloria Fraser, and Joseph A. Bulbulia. 2016. "Charismatic Signaling: How Religion Stabilizes Cooperation and Entrenches Inequality." In *The Oxford Handbook of Evolutionary Psychology and Religion*, edited by James R. Liddle and Todd K. Shackelford. Oxford: Oxford University Press. https://doi.org/10.1093/oxfordhb/9780199397747.013.17.

Shaver, John H., Eleanor A. Power, Benjamin G. Purzycki, Joseph Watts, Rebecca Sear, Mary K. Shenk, Richard Sosis, and Joseph A. Bulbulia. 2020. "Church Attendance and Alloparenting: An Analysis of Fertility, Social Support and Child Development among English Mothers." *Philosophical Transactions of the Royal Society B: Biological Sciences* 375(1805): 20190428. https://doi.org/10.1098/rstb.2019.0428.

Shaver, John H., Benjamin Grant Purzycki, and Richard Sosis. 2016. "Evolutionary Theory in the Study of Religion." In *The Oxford Handbook of the Study of Religion*, edited by Michael Stausberg and Steven Engler, 124–136. Oxford: Oxford University Press.

Shaver, John H., Chris G. Sibley, Richard Sosis, Deane Galbraith, and Joseph Bulbulia. 2019. "Alloparenting and Religious Fertility: A Test of the Religious Alloparenting Hypothesis." *Evolution and Human Behavior* 40(3): 315–324. https://doi.org/10.1016/j.evolhumbehav.2019.01.004.

Sherman, Paul W. and Jennifer Billing. 1999. "Darwinian Gastronomy: Why We Use Spices." *BioScience* 49: 453–463.

Shermer, Michael. 2008. "The Doping Dilemma." *Scientific American* 298(4): 82–89.

Shih, Fang-Long. 2012. "Generating Power in Taiwan: Nuclear, Political and Religious Power." *Culture and Religion* 13(3): 295–313. https://doi.org/10.1080/14755610.2012.706229

Sibley, Chris G. and Joseph Bulbulia. 2012. "Faith After an Earthquake: A Longitudinal Study of Religion and Perceived Health Before and After the 2011 Christchurch New Zealand Earthquake." *PLOS ONE* 7(12): e49648.

Sierksma, Fokke. 1963. "Sacred Cairns in Pastoral Cultures." *History of Religions* 2(2): 227–241.

Singh, Manvir. 2018. "The Cultural Evolution of Shamanism." *Behavioral and Brain Sciences* 41.

Singh, Manvir, Ted Kaptchuk, and Joseph Henrich. 2021. "Small Gods, Rituals, and Cooperation: The Mentawai Crocodile Spirit Sikaoinan." *Evolution and*

Human Behavior 42(1): 61–72.

Skaanes, Thea. 2015. "Notes on Hadza Cosmology." *Hunter Gatherer Research* 1(2): 247–267. https://doi.org/10.3828/hgr.2015.13.

Skaanes, Thea. 2017a. *Cosmology Matters: Power Objects, Rituals, and Meat-Sharing among the Hadza of Tanzania*. Doctoral dissertation. Aarhus: Aarhus University.

Skaanes, Thea. 2017b. "Sounds in the Night: Ritual Bells, Therianthropes and Eland Relations among the Hadza." In *Human Origins: Contributions from Social Anthropology*, edited by Camilla Power, Morna Finnegan and Hilary Callan, 206–223. New York: Berghahn Books.

Skoggard, Ian, Carol R. Ember, Emily Pitek, Joshua Conrad Jackson, and Christina Carolus. 2020. "Resource Stress Predicts Changes in Religious Belief and Increases in Sharing Behavior." *Human Nature* 31: 249–271. https://doi.org/10.1007/s12110-020-09371-8.

Skyrms, Brian. 2004. *The Stag Hunt and the Evolution of Social Structure*. Cambridge: Cambridge University Press.

Slone, D. Jason. 2004. *Theological Incorrectness: Why Religious People Believe What They Shouldn't*. Oxford: Oxford University Press.

Slone, D. Jason, 2008. "The Attraction of Religion: A Sexual Selectionist Account". In *The Evolution of Religion: Studies, Theories, and Critiques*, edited by Joseph Bulbulia, Richard Sosis, Erica Harris, Russell Genet, Cheryl Genet, and Karen Wyman, 167–187. Santa Margarita CA: Collins Foundation Press.

Smith, Eric Alden, and Bruce Winterhalder. 1992. *Evolutionary Ecology and Human Behavior*. New York: Aldine de Gruyter.

Smith, Eric Alden and Mark Wishnie. 2000. "Conservation and Subsistence in Small-scale Societies." *Annual Review of Anthropology* 29: 493–524.

Smith, Johan W. 1979. "Ritual and the Ethology of Communicating." In *The Spectrum of Ritual: A Biogenetic Structural Analysis*, edited by Eugene G. D'Aquili, Charles D. Laughlin and John McManus, 51–79. New York: Columbia University Press.

Smith, Kristopher M., Tomás Larroucau, Ibrahim A. Mabulla, and Coren L. Apicella. 2018. "Hunter-Gatherers Maintain Assortativity in Cooperation despite High Levels of Residential Change and Mixing." *Current Biology* 28(19): 3152–3157. https://doi.org/10.1016/j.cub.2018.07.064.

Smith, Wilfred Cantwell. 1998. *Believing: An Historical Perspective*. Oxford: Oneworld.

Snarey, John. 1996. "The Natural Environment's Impact upon Religious Ethics: A Cross-cultural Study." *Journal for the Scientific Study of Religion* 35(2): 85–96. https://doi.org/10.2307/1387077.

Soler, Montserrat. 2012. "Costly Signaling, Ritual and Cooperation: Evidence from Candomblé, an Afro-Brazilian Religion." *Evolution and Human Behavior* 33(4): 346–356.

Soler, Montserrat, Frank Batiste, and Lee Cronk. 2014. "In the Eye (and Ears) of the Beholder: Receiver Psychology and Human Signal Design." *Evolutionary Anthropology* 23(4): 136–145. https://doi.org/10.1002/evan.21413.

Solt, Frederick, Philip Habel, and J. Tobin Grant. 2011. "Economic Inequality, Relative Power, and Religiosity." *Social Science Quarterly* 92(2): 447–465. https://doi.org/10.1111/j.1540-6237.2011.00777.x.

Sørensen, Jesper. 2004. "Religion, Evolution, and an Immunology of Cultural Systems." *Evolution and Cognition* 10(1): 61–73.

Sosis, Richard. 2000. "Religion and intragroup cooperation: Preliminary results of a comparative analysis of utopian communities." *Cross-Cultural Research* 34(1): 70–87.

Sosis, Richard. 2003. "Why Aren't We All Hutterites?" *Human Nature* 14(2): 91–127. https://doi.org/10.1007/s12110-003-1000-6.

Sosis, Richard. 2005a. "Does Religion Promote Trust? The Role of Signaling, Reputation, and Punishment." *Interdisciplinary Journal of Research on Religion* 1(7): 1–30.

Sosis, Richard. 2005b. "Ifaluk Atoll: An Ethnographic Account," in *eHRAF World Cultures*, edited by Carol Ember, pp. 1–33. New Haven, CT: HRAF.

Sosis, Richard. 2006. "Religious Behaviors, Badges, and Bans: Signaling Theory and the Evolution of Religion" In *Where God and Science Meet: How Brain and Evolutionary Studies Alter Our Understanding of Religion, Volume 1: Evolution, Genes, and the Religious Brain*, edited by Patrick McNamara, 61–86. Westport, CT: Praeger Publishers.

Sosis, Richard. 2007. "Psalms for Safety: Magico-religious Responses to Threats of Terror." *Current Anthropology*, 48(6): 903–911.

Sosis, Richard. 2009a. "The Adaptationist-Byproduct Debate on the Evolution of Religion: Five Misunderstandings of the Adaptationist Program." *Journal of Cognition and Culture* 9: 315–332.

Sosis, Richard. 2009b. "Why are Synagogue Services so Long? An Evolutionary Examination of Jewish Ritual Signals." In *Judaism in Biological Perspective: Biblical Lore and Judaic Practices*, edited by Rick Golberg. Boulder, CO: Paradigm Publishers.

Sosis, Richard. 2011. "Why Sacred Lands Are Not Indivisible: The Cognitive Foundations of Sacralising Land." *Journal of Terrorism Research* 2(1): 17–44.

Sosis, Richard. 2016. "Religions as Complex Adaptive Systems." In *Mental Religion: The Brain, Cognition, and Culture*, edited by Niki Clements, 219–236. Farmington Hills, MI: Macmillan.

Sosis, Richard. 2017. "The Road Not Taken: Possible Paths for the Cognitive Science of Religion." In *Religion Explained? The Cognitive Science of Religion after 25 years*, edited by Luther Martin and Donald Wiebe, 155–167. London: Bloomsbury Press.

Sosis, Richard. 2019. "The Building Blocks of Religious Systems: Approaching Religion as a Complex Adaptive System." In *Evolution, Development and*

Complexity: Multiscale Models of Complex Adaptive Systems, edited by G. Y. Georgiev, J. M. Smart, C. L. Flores Martinez, and M. Price, pp. 421–449. New York: Springer.

Sosis, Richard. 2020a. "Four Advantages of a Systemic Approach to the Study of Religion." *Archive for the Psychology of Religion* 42(1): 142–157.

Sosis, Richard. 2020b. "The Last Talmudic Demon? The Role of Ritual in Cultural Transmission." *Philosophical Transactions of the Royal Society B* 375(1805): 20190425.

Sosis, Richard. 2022. "The ABC's of Evolutionary Signaling Theory and Religion," in *The Routledge Handbook of Evolutionary Approaches to Religion*, edited by Yair Lior and Justin Lane. Abingdon: Routledge.

Sosis, Richard and Candace Alcorta. 2003. "Signaling, Solidarity, and the Sacred: The Evolution of Religious Behavior." *Evolutionary Anthropology* 12: 264–274.

Sosis, Richard and Candace Alcorta. 2004. "Is Religion Adaptive?" *Behavioral and Brain Sciences* 27: 749–750.

Sosis, Richard and Eric R. Bressler. 2003. "Cooperation and Commune Longevity: A Test of the Costly Signaling Theory of Religion." *Cross-Cultural Research* 37(2): 211–239.

Sosis, Richard and Joseph Bulbulia. 2011. "The Behavioral Ecology of Religion: The Benefits and Costs of One Evolutionary Approach, *Religion* 41(3): 341–362.

Sosis, Richard and W. Penn Handwerker. 2011. "Psalms and Coping with Uncertainty: Religious Israeli Women's Responses to the 2006 Lebanon War." *American Anthropologist* 113(1): 40–55.

Sosis, Richard and Jordan Kiper. 2014a. "Religion is More than Belief: What Evolutionary Theories of Religion Tell Us about Religious Commitment." In *Challenges to Religion and Morality: Disagreements and Evolution*, edited by Michael Bergman and Patrick Kain, 256–276. New York: Oxford University Press.

Sosis, Richard and Jordan Kiper. 2014b. "Why Religion is Better Conceived as a Complex System than a Norm-enforcing Institution." *Behavioral and Brain Sciences* 37: 275–276.

Sosis, Richard and Jordan Kiper. 2018. "Sacred versus Secular Values: Cognitive and Evolutionary Sciences of Religion and Religious Freedom." In *Homo Religiosus? Exploring the Roots of Religion and Religious Freedom in Human Experience*, edited by Timothy Samuel Shah and Jack Friedman, 89–119. Cambridge: Cambridge University Press.

Sosis, Richard, Howard Kress, and James Boster. 2007. "Scars for War: Evaluating Alternative Signaling Explanations for Cross Cultural Variance in Ritual Costs." *Evolution and Human Behavior* 28: 234–247.

Sosis, Richard, Erika J. Phillips, and Candace S. Alcorta. 2012. "Sacrifice and Sacred Values: Evolutionary Perspectives on Religious Terrorism" In *The Oxford Handbook of Evolutionary Perspectives on Violence, Homicide, and War*, edited by Todd K. Shackelford and Viviana A. Weekes-Shackelford, 233–253. New York: Oxford University Press.

Sosis, Richard and Bradley J. Ruffle. 2003 "Religious Ritual and Cooperation: Testing for a Relationship on Israeli Religious and Secular Kibbutzim." *Current Anthropology* 44(5): 713–722.

Sosis, Richard and Bradley J. Ruffle. 2004. "Ideology, Religion, and the Evolution of Cooperation: Field Tests on Israeli Kibbutzim." *Research in Economic Anthropology* 23: 89–117.

Sosis, Richard and John Shaver 2015. "How Rituals Elicit Shared Sacred Values." *Interdisziplinäre Anthropologie* 3: 75–81.

Sperber, Dan. 1985. "Anthropology and Psychology: Towards an Epidemiology of Representations." *Man* 20: 73–89.

Sperber, Dan. 1996. *Explaining Culture: A Naturalistic Approach*. Malden, MA: Blackwell Publishing.

Sperber, Dan. 1997. "Intuitive and Reflective Beliefs." *Mind and Language* 12(1): 67–83.

Sperber, Dan. 2018. "Cutting Culture at the Joints?" *Religion, Brain and Behavior* 8(4): 447–49. https://doi.org/10.1080/2153599X.2017.1323783.

Spiro, Melford E. 1952. "Ghosts, Ifaluk, and Teleological Functionalism." *American Anthropologist, New Series* 54(4): 497–503.

Spiro, Melford E. 1982. *Buddhism and Society: A Great Tradition and Its Burmese Vicissitudes*. Berkeley, CA: University of California Press.

Spiro, Melford E. 1987. *Culture and Human Nature: Theoretical Papers of Melford E. Spiro*. Chicago, IL: University of Chicago Press.

Spiro, Melford E. 1996. *Burmese Supernaturalism*. Abingdon: Routledge.

Stagnaro, Michael N., Duncan Stibbard-Hawkes, and Coren Lee Apicella. 2022. "Religious and Market Based Institutions Help to Promote Cooperation in Hadza Hunter–Gatherers." *Religion, Brain and Behavior*.

Standing Bear, Luther. 1975 [1928]. *My People the Sioux*. Lincoln, NE: University of Nebraska Press.

Stark, Rodney. 2001. "Gods, Rituals, and the Moral Order." *Journal for the Scientific Study of Religion* 40(4): 619–636.

Stark, Rodney and Roger Finke. 2000. *Acts of Faith: Explaining the Human Side of Religion*. Berkeley, CA: University of California Press.

Stausberg, Michael. 2005. "D. Jason Slone, Theological Incorrectness. Why Religious People Believe What They Shouldn't- Oxford: Oxford University Press 2004" *Numen* 52(1): 149–151.

Steadman, Lyle B. and Craig T. Palmer. 2008. *The Supernatural and Natural Selection: Religion and Evolutionary Success*. Boulder: Paradigm Publishers.

Stevenson, Daniel B. 2007. "Pure Land Buddhist Worship and Meditation in China." In *Buddhism in Practice: Abridged Edition*, edited by Donald S. Lopez Jr., 271–292. Princeton, NJ: Princeton University Press.

Stinchcombe, Arthur L. 1968. *Constructing Social Theories*. New York: Harcourt, Brace & World.

Strauss, C. and N. Quinn. 1997. *A Cognitive Theory of Cultural Meaning*. Cambridge: Cambridge University Press.

Swan, Thomas and Jamin Halberstadt. 2019. "The Mickey Mouse Problem: Distinguishing Religious and Fictional Counterintuitive Agents. *PloS ONE* 14(8): e0220886.

Swanson, Guy E. 1960. *The Birth of the Gods: The Origin of Primitive Beliefs*. Ann Arbor, MI: University of Michigan Press.

Tan, Jonathan H. W. and Claudia Vogel, 2008. "Religion and Trust: An Experimental Study." *Journal of Economic Psychology* 29(6): 832–848.

Taylor, Bron, Gretel Van Wieren, and Bernard Zaleha. 2016. "The Greening of Religion Hypothesis (Part Two): Assessing the Data from Lynn White, Jr., to Pope Francis" *Journal for the Study of Religion, Nature and Culture* 10(3): 306–378.

Teehan, John. 2010. *In the Name of God: The Evolutionary Origins of Religious Ethics and Violence*. Malden, MA: Wiley-Blackwell.

Teehan, John and F. LeRon Shults. 2019. "Religion, Empathy, and Cooperation: A Case Study in the Promises and Challenges of Modeling and Simulation." In *Human Simulation: Perspectives, Insights, and Applications*, edited by Saikou Y. Diallo, Wesley J. Wildman, F. LeRon Shults and Andreas Tolk, 157–178. Cham: Springer.

Tetlock, Philip E. 2003. "Thinking the Unthinkable: Sacred Values and Taboo Cognitions." *Trends in Cognitive Sciences* 7: 320–324.

Thornton, Arland, William G. Axinn, and Daniel H. Hill. 1992. "Reciprocal Effects of Religiosity, Cohabitation, and Marriage." *American Journal of Sociology* 98(3): 628–651.

Tian, Allen Ding, Juliana Schroeder, Gerald Häubl, Jane L. Risen, Michael I. Norton, and Francesca Gino. 2018. "Enacting Rituals to Improve Self-Control." *Journal of Personality and Social Psychology* 114(6): 851.

Tillich, Paul. 1957. *Dynamics of Faith*, 1st edition. New York: Perennial.

Tomasello, Michael. 1999. *The Cultural Origins of Human Cognition*. Cambridge, MA: Harvard University Press.

Tonkinson, Robert. 1991. *The Mardu Aborigines: Living the Dream in Australia's Desert*. Fort Worth: Holt, Rinehart, & Winston.

Tooby, John and Irven DeVore. 1987. "The Reconstruction of Hominid Behavioral Evolution through Strategic Modeling." In *The Evolution of Human Behavior: Primate Models*, edited by Warren G. Kinzey, 183–237. New York: SUNY Press.

Trimingham, J. Spencer. 1971. *The Sufi Orders in Islam*. London: Oxford University Press.

Turnbull, Colin M. 1961. *The Forest People*. New York: Simon & Schuster.

Turner, Jonathan H., Armin W. Geertz, Anders Klostergaard Petersen, and Alexandra Maryanski. 2020. "Explaining the Evolution of Religion: A Response to Commentators." *Religion, Brain and Behavior* 10(1): 100–114. https://doi.org/10.1080/2153599X.2018.1513864.

Turner, Jonathan H., Alexandra Maryanski, Anders Klostergaard Petersen, and Armin W. Geertz. 2017. *The Emergence and Evolution of Religion: By Means of Natural Selection*. Routledge.

Turner, Victor. 1969. *The Ritual Process: Structure and Anti-Structure*. New York: Routledge.

Turpin, Hugh. 2018. *Failing God? A Cognitive Anthropological Examination of the Relationship between Catholic Scandals and Irish Secularisation*. Doctoral dissertation. Belfast: Queen's University/Aarhus: Aarhus University.

Tuzin, Donald F. 1976. *The Ilahita Arapesh: Dimensions of Unity*. University of California Press.

Tuzin, Donald F. 1980. *The Voice of the Tambaran: Truth and Illusion in Ilahita Arapesh Religion*. Berkeley, CA: University of California Press.

Tuzin, Donald F. 1997. *The Cassowary's Revenge: The Life and Death of Masculinity in a New Guinea Society*. Chicago, IL: University of Chicago Press.

Tylor, Edward B. 2006 [1873]. *Primitive Culture: Researches into The Development of Mythology, Philosophy, Religion, Language, Art and Custom*. Vol. 1. Minneola, NY: Dover Publications.

Van Vugt, Mark, Robert Hogan, and Robert B. Kaiser. 2008. "Leadership, Followership, and Evolution: Some Lessons from the Past." *American Psychologist* 63: 182–196.

Van Vugt, Mark and Robert Kurzban. 2007. "Cognitive and Social Adaptations for Leadership and Followership: Evolutionary Game Theory and Group Dynamics." In *The Evolution of the Social Mind: Evolutionary Psychology and Social Cognition*, edited by Joseph P. Forgas, William Von Hippel and Martie G. Haselton, 229–244.

Vardy, Tom and Quentin D. Atkinson. 2019. "Property Damage and Exposure to Other People in Distress Differentially Predict Prosocial Behavior after a Natural Disaster." *Psychological science* 30(4): 563–575.

Veblen, Thorstein. 2007 [1899]. *The Theory of the Leisure Class*. New York: Oxford University Press.

Visuri, Ingela. 2020. "Sensory Supernatural Experiences in Autism." *Religion, Brain and Behavior* 10(2): 151–165. https://doi.org/10.1080/2153599X.2018.1548374

Voland, Eckart and Wulf Schiefenhövel. 2009. *The Biological Evolution of Religious Mind and Behavior*. New York: Springer-Verlag.

von Bertalanffy, Ludwig. 1968. *General System Theory: Foundations, Development, Applications*. New York: George Braziller.

von Bertalanffy, Ludwig. 1972. "The History and Status of General Systems

Theory." *The Academy of Management Journal* 15: 407–426.

Vygotsky, Lev. 1994. *The Vygotsky Reader*, edited by Rene Van der Veer and Jaan Valsiner. Malden, MA: Blackwell.

Walker, James R. 1917. *The Sun Dance and Other Ceremonies of the Oglala Division of the Teton Dakota.* New York: Anthropological Papers of the American Museum of Natural History XVI, Part II.

Walker, James R. 1991. *Lakota Belief and Ritual*, edited by Elaine A. Jahner and Raymond J. DeMallie. Lincoln, NE: University of Nebraska Press.

Wallace, Anthony F. C. 1956. "Revitalization Movements." *American Anthropologist* 58(2): 264–281.

Wallace, Anthony F. C. 1966. *Religion: An Anthropological View.* New York: McGraw-Hill.

Wallis, Wilson Dallam. 1996. *Heyoka: Lakota Rites of Reversal.* Kendall Park: Lakota Books.

Ward, Samuel. 2019. *Vodou Economics: Contagious and Reciprocal Exchange with the Spirits in New Orleans.* Doctoral dissertation. Belfast: Queen's University.

Watanabe, Hitoshi. 1972. "The Ainu." In *Hunters and Gatherers Today: A Socioeconomic Study of Eleven Such Cultures in the Twentieth Century*, edited by Marco G. Bicchieri, 448–484. Prospect Heights, IL: Waveland Press.

Watts, Joseph, Simon J. Greenhill, Quentin D. Atkinson, Thomas E. Currie, Joseph Bulbulia, and Russell D. Gray. 2015. "Broad Supernatural Punishment but Not Moralizing High Gods Precede the Evolution of Political Complexity in Austronesia." *Proceedings of the Royal Society of London B: Biological Sciences* 282(1804): 20142556. https://doi.org/10.1098/rspb.2014.2556.

Watts, Joseph, Oliver Sheehan, Quentin D. Atkinson, Joseph A. Bulbulia, and Russell D. Gray. 2017. "Ritual Human Sacrifice Promoted and Sustained the Evolution of Stratified Societies." *Nature* 532(7598): 228–231.

Weber, Max. 1947. *The Theory of Social and Economic Organization.* Oxford: Oxford University Press.

Weeden, Jason, Adam B. Cohen, and Douglas T. Kenrick. 2009. "Religious Attendance as Reproductive Support." *Evolution and Human Behavior* 29: 327–334.

White, Douglas R. 1988. "Rethinking Polygyny: Co-wives, Codes, and Cultural Systems." *Current Anthropology* 29(4): 529–572.

White, Douglas R. and Michael L. Burton. 1988. "Causes of Polygyny—Ecology, Economy, Kinship, and Warfare." *American Anthropologist* 90: 871–887.

White, Leslie. 1952. *The Evolution of Culture.* New York: McGraw Hill.

White, Lynn. 1967. "The Historical Roots of Our Ecologic Crisis" *Science* 155(3767): 1203–1207. https://doi.org/10.1126/science.155.3767.1203.

Whitehouse, Harvey. 1995. *Inside the Cult: Religious Innovation and Transmission in Papua New Guinea.* New York: Oxford University Press.

Whitehouse, Harvey. 2000. *Arguments and Icons: Divergent Modes of Religiosity.* New York: Oxford University Press.

Whitehouse, Harvey. 2004. *Modes of Religiosity: A Cognitive Theory of Religious Transmission*. Walnut Creek, CA: AltaMira Press.

Whitehouse, Harvey, and Jonathan A. Lanman. 2014. "The Ties that Bind Us: Ritual, Fusion, and Identification." *Current Anthropology* 55(6): 674–695.

Whiteley, Peter M. 1998. *Rethinking Hopi Ethnography*. Washington, DC: Smithsonian Institution Press.

Wigger, J. Bradley, Katrina Paxson, and Lacey Ryan. 2013. "What Do Invisible Friends Know? Imaginary Companions, God, and Theory of Mind." *International Journal for the Psychology of Religion* 23(1): 2–14.

Wildman, Wesley J. and Richard Sosis. 2011. "Stability of Groups with Costly Beliefs and Practices." *Journal of Artificial Societies and Social Simulation* 14(3): 6.

Wildman, Wesley J., Joseph Bulbulia, Richard Sosis, and Uffe Schjoedt. 2017. "Models, Simulations, Abstractions, and Insights." *Religion, Brain and Behavior* 7: 175–177.

Wildman, Wesley J., Richard Sosis, and Patrick McNamara. 2011. "Reductionism in the Scientific Study of Religion." *Religion, Brain and Behavior* 1: 169–172.

Wildman, Wesley J., F. LeRon Shults, Siakou Y. Diallo, Ross Gore, and Justin Lane. 2020. "Post-supernatural Cultures: There and Back Again." *Secularism and Nonreligion* 9(6): 1–15.

Willard, Aiyana K., Joseph Henrich, and Ara Norenzayan. 2016. "Memory and Belief in the Transmission of Counterintuitive Content." *Human Nature* 27(3): 221–243.

Willard, Aiyana K., and Rita A. McNamara. 2019. "The Minds of God(s) and Humans: Differences in Mind Perception in Fiji and North America." *Cognitive Science* 43 (1): e12703. https://doi.org/10.1111/cogs.12703.

Willard, Aiyana K. and Ara Norenzayan. 2013. "Cognitive Biases Explain Religious Belief, Paranormal Belief, and Belief in Life's Purpose." *Cognition* 129(2): 379–391. https://doi.org/10.1016/j.cognition.2013.07.016.

Willard, Aiyana K., Adam Baimel, Hugh Turpin, Jonathan Jong, and Harvey Whitehouse. 2020. "Rewarding the Good and Punishing the Bad: The Role of Karma and Afterlife Beliefs in Shaping Moral Norms." *Evolution and Human Behavior* (July). https://doi.org/10.1016/j.evolhumbehav.2020.07.001.

Wilson, David S. 2002. *Darwin's Cathedral: Evolution, Religion, and the Nature of Society*. Chicago, IL: University of Chicago Press.

Wilson, David Sloan, Yasha Hartberg, Ian MacDonald, Jonathan A. Lanman, and Harvey Whitehouse. 2017. "The Nature of Religious Diversity: A Cultural Ecosystem Approach." *Religion, Brain and Behavior* 7(2): 134–153.

Wilson, Edward Osborne. 1978. *On Human Nature*. New York: Bantam Books.

Wilson, Margo and Martin Daly. 1985. "Competitiveness, Risk-taking, and Violence: The Young Male Syndrome." *Ethology and Sociobiology* 6: 59–73.

Wilson, Margaret R. and Erik E. Filsinger. 1986. "Religiosity and Marital Adjustment: Multidimensional Interrelationships." *Journal of Marriage and the Family* 48:

147–151.

Wiltermuth, Scott S. and Chip Heath. 2009. "Synchrony and Cooperation." *Psychological Science* 20: 1–5.

Winkelman, M., 2002. "Shamanism and Cognitive Evolution (with Comments)." *Cambridge Archaeological Journal*, 12(1): 71–101.

Wood, Connor. 2017. "Ritual Well-being: Toward a Social Signaling Model of Religion and Mental Health." *Religion, Brain and Behavior*, 7(3): 223–243.

Wood, Connor and John H. Shaver. 2018. "Religion, Evolution, and the Basis of Institutions: The Institutional Cognition Model of Religion." *Evolutionary Studies in Imaginative Culture* 2(2): 1–20. https://doi.org/10.26613/esic.2.2.89.

Wood, Connor, Catherine Caldwell-Harris, and Anna Stopa. 2018. "The Rhythms of Discontent: Synchrony Impedes Performance and Group Functioning in an Interdependent Coordination Task." *Journal of Cognition and Culture* 18(1–2): 154–179.

Wood, Connor and Richard Sosis. 2019. "Simulating Religions as Adaptive Systems." In *Human Simulation: Perspectives, Insights, and Applications*, edited by Saikou Y. Diallo, Wesley J. Wildman, F. LeRon Shults and Andreas Tolk, 209–232. Cham: Springer International Publishing. https://doi.org/10.1007/978-3-030-17090-5_12.

Woodburn, James. 1982. "Social Dimensions of Death in Four African Hunting and Gathering Societies." In *Death and the Regeneration of Life*, edited by Maurice Bloch and Jonathan Parry, 187–210. Cambridge: Cambridge University Press.

Worsley, Peter. 1957. *The Trumpet Shall Sound*. London: MacGibbon & Kee.

Wright, Robert. 2009. *The Evolution of God*. New York: Little, Brown and Company.

Xygalatas, Dimitris. 2008. "Firewalking and the Brain: The Physiology of High-arousal Rituals." In *The Evolution of Religion: Studies, Theories, and Critiques*, edited by Joseph Bulbulia, Richard Sosis, Russell Genet, Cheryl Genet, Erica Harris and Karen Wyman, 189–195. Santa Margarita, CA: Collins Foundation Press.

Xygalatas, Dimitris, Uffe Schjoedt, Joseph Bulbulia, Ivana Konvalinka, Else-Marie Jegindø, Paul Reddish, Armin W. Geertz, and Andreas Roepstoff. 2013. "Autobiographical Memory in a Fire-walking Ritual." *Journal of Cognition and Culture* 13(1–2): 1–16.

Yeh, D. Justin, Laurel Fogarty, and Anne Kandler. 2019. "Cultural Linkage: The Influence of Package Transmission on Cultural Dynamics." *Proceedings of the Royal Society B* 286(1916): 20191951.

Zahavi, Amotz and Avishag Zahavi. 1997. *The Handicap Principle: A Missing Piece of Darwin's Puzzle*. New York: Oxford University Press.

Zelnik, Melvin and Farida K. Shah. 1983. "First Intercourse among Young Americans." *Family Planning Perspectives* 15: 64–70.

Zou, Xi, Kim-Pong Tam, Michael W. Morris, Sau-Lai Lee, Ivy Yee-man Lau, and

Chi Yue Chiu. 2009. "Culture as Common Sense: Perceived Consensus vs. Personal Beliefs as Mechanisms of Cultural Influence." *Journal of Personality and Social Psychology* 97(4): 579–597.

Index